Things I Did
...and Things
I Think I Did

JEAN NEGULESCO

LINDEN PRESS/SIMON & SCHUSTER

NEW YORK 1984

Filmography: p.
1. Negulesco, Jean.   2. Moving-picture producers and
directors—United States—Biography.   I. Title.
PN1998.A3N336   1984   791.43'0233'0924 [B]   84-17084
ISBN: 0-671-50734-6

To Dusty,
who had the patience to listen time
and again to these stories . . .

AND

to Harry Gilroy,
who criticized and helped

FOREWORD

THIS book is justified by speculation, truth, literary imagination, and dialogue which, if it wasn't said, I wish it would have been said. The drawings are part of my way of telling the stories. Some people posed for me; others I fixed in my mind with a sketch, a caricature, or a photograph. Each drawing is a composition of what a person meant to me.

Things I Did
...and Things
I Think I Did

RUMANIA

İN Rumania—for a king or a peasant—a son means pride and continuity, a daughter is punishment and worry. A son chooses a bride, a daughter waits for a man to take her away. A son will carry your name, but a daughter will take the name of another.

The first daughter was welcomed by my father as a normal mistake of Rumanian performing might. He ignored and tolerated her presence.

The second child, again a daughter, hurt his pride. For six months he moved temporarily out of the nuptial bed into his bachelor studio over the office quarters. He talked to Mother seldom and in no gentle terms.

When the third offering was a repeat, another girl, he held Mother and her family guilty of this humiliation. His hunting trips with the boys in the Carpathian Mountains increased. There was gossip of a torrid romance with a Hungarian chanteuse from Budapest. He became morose, unpleasant, quarrelsome. There were no friendly greetings to his associates or gentle words to his children. "Don't cross his path," his partner cautioned. Servants were fired, friends hated to do business with him. An ultimatum was served to Mother: "A boy! No substitute, or else." During the labor pains he bought expensive fat cigars for well-wishers.

The fourth child—a daughter. Father went berserk. He never left the bars. His friends consoled him: "See a psychoanalyst; use stimulants and acrobatics; change the rhythm of your stroke; drink hot water every hour; diet on hard-boiled eggs and raw garlic." Remedies came from everywhere.

The girls—Georgeta, Aneta, Virginia, Gabriela—grew in beauty, good manners, and kept away from him. Business prospered, and when Mother was again with child his comment to her was a grunt. "So what?"

Soon after, one evening, four little daughters rosy-cheeked and puffing ran up the stairs to his office screaming in high-pitched voices: "A boy, a boy! It's a boy!"

For a long time Father said nothing. Then he sat heavily on his chair and cried.

Three days and three nights, Father, Grandfather, and friends celebrated. "A banker." "The Mayor of the city." "A general." "The Minister of Finance." "Maybe the Prime Minister." The boy's future was planned and toasted.

And that was my triumphant entrance into this wonderful world.

A normal Rumanian family—a proud father, a resigned mother, and eight good children. Extreme right: the author at 12

Then another son was born, George, and two more daughters: Athena and Sabina.

To father, my brother and I were different. "My Johnny, our George"—we were the chosen ones, the sons of the richest man on our street. The others were the "girls"; he never mentioned them by name. "The girls will carry the baskets; the girls will clean the place; the girls should write to Grandma to thank her for the Sunday lunch. Johnny and George will ride with me to the vineyard."

Father was not a big man; he wouldn't stand out in a crowd. In business, if he made a bad deal, his word was a legal contract, no matter how much he lost. He was an honest man. In my mind his honesty was close to ridiculous. His eyes were kind. He was shy and cautious. He couldn't resist a bargain. Many days he would bring home two trucks of watermelons, or six goats, just because they were a bargain. We were eight children and we loved watermelon, but *two* trucks? "And where can I keep six goats?" Mother despaired. A passionate collector, he picked up nails, wires, and pieces of rope he found on the street and would place them methodically in cardboard boxes lined up in his office, carefully marked. One of the boxes was labeled "Pieces of strings too short to be used." He was clever without being conspicuous, and he succeeded where others failed. He had his own way to help people in need—strange, unsuspected, sometimes cruel.

In our town Father owned a hotel. In its courtyard he let a poor tenant build himself a small shack. A one-room beggar's shack, where for a few pennies he would fix anything—a hole in your shoe, a broken dish, a leg to a wobbly table. The "Fixer" everybody called him. He was a good man, humble, always with a kind smile; he worked hard all day and late into the night, didn't drink or smoke or play around, paid his small rent on time, and put aside some money. Father liked him and often he would stop to share an apple or half a melon. We children dropped by his place on our way home from school. He always had a present—a sweet or a toy he made. Or he fixed our bicycle or fixed a torn page. We loved him and listened, glued to his invented stories, which always ended with a wise proverb. His favorite: "A small pebble overturns a big carriage."

One evening we found him crying. He was packing his tools, his few belongings. Father was there. "I need the place. I'm enlarging the stables. Get out by morning."

"But where?" "Your problem. You can fix everything. Fix yourself a home, a bigger shop of your own. You're old enough to have your own place and not get low rent in a beggar's shack."

When Father left, the Fixer sat dejected on his three-legged stool. His head fell sobbing on his chest. For a long time we hated Father for this.

Not far from our house on the same street, an empty lot covered with overgrown weeds and trees and rocks was our "game kingdom." It was a hiding place, and on Sundays the battleground of cops and robbers. The Fixer bought the lot with his meager savings, cleaned it, and started to build a small home with a big studio—his shop. We children helped him. He never spoke to Father again, and Father never mentioned his name.

The First World War caught him still building. I left home; I became a displaced teenager in Moldavia, the unoccupied part of our country. Three years later when I returned, the Fixer's house was finished. The shop was booming; four young men were working for him. He was now a *domnule*—a boss. He received me with tears of joy and showed me around his home. "My palace," he called it with pride.

Later that night I mentioned his name to Father and reminded him how he threw him out on the street. "It was time for him to become a man" was his short comment. Next day my father's partner told me that the lot the Fixer had bought belonged to Father and was sold to him through a third party at a ridiculously low price.

The Fixer was almost a hundred years old when he died.

Memories are like awakening from a dream in faraway places. I remember my childhood life: the first day at school, another marvel, and the first teacher—a giant—and the first time I solved the mystery of a problem in arithmetic; and the first map of my country, so clear and so rich: and the freedom of the holidays, and when the whole world was just the smile a passing girl had for me. I remember those first moments, all woven forever in my carefree past.

In her simplicity and beauty Mother was a saint. Thin and delicate like a leaf, straight and grave, she would spread around an air of joy and riches, and she talked about death as a patient friend. "I wouldn't like to die in the winter. It's cold and everything is frozen. I don't want my children to walk behind my coffin in the snow. And in the summer it's too beautiful. Maybe the autumn." Then just a faint giggle. "Anyway, it isn't time yet."

On Sundays and holidays she went to church, her little black hat brought down on her forehead. She prayed at length in front of all the icons, burned two dozen candles, sat on the high chair with her name on it and listened with reverence to the holy service. At the end, the priest would come to her chair, and old friends would talk about health and good times, and she would tell long stories about her children, but mostly about the son in America, "my boy over the waters."

The girls made good marriages, all arranged by family and friends: Georgeta to the chief of police of our town, Aneta to a wealthy banker in another town. Virginia was a brilliant student in Germany and returned home tired and bored; Gabriela married a distant relative. Sabina, the youngest and most sensitive, married my best friend, Vasile. They all raised honorable families, safe and comfortable. Only Athena, the seventh child, rebelled against the family setup of having the elders find and approve of a husband. She eloped with the first attractive playboy, divorced him a year later, led a free life of affairs and independence, managed for some time a fashion magazine. Yet in her advanced years Athena is alone, unhappy, and still searching for an answer.

In World War I, half of our country was invaded by German troops. I was fourteen, too young to realize the seriousness of war. Prince Carol, the eldest son of King Ferdinand and Queen Marie, was the leader of the National League of Boy Scouts. I was sworn in and with my older sisters, Georgeta and Aneta, joined the hospital branch in Moldavia, the northern part of our country. Some of us Boy Scouts were assigned to the Red Cross trains. We brought

Mother—portrait of a saint

The author, age 7. World War I shall be met with authority and purpose.

wounded soldiers from the front to the hospitals in Iasi, the new capital of Rumania. To us, war was an adventure and we were inspired with excessive patriotism. "To die for the country was the most wonderful dream we could wish for," and we meant it.

Georges Enesco, the Rumanian musical genius who adapted his country's folk tunes into popular rhapsodies, was a violin virtuoso. He played for the troops on the front line and traveled from town to town giving concerts for the benefit of refugees, war widows, and war orphans. The sound of his violin delved into the human soul. I made a silhouette drawing of him playing. With a simple black frame the drawing was exhibited in a bookstore window. I lingered for hours by the store to listen to the bystanders: "Who is it?" "Enesco, of course." "Who did it?" "Yon." (My pseudonym.) "Yon? I never heard of him!"

You will, I thought. And then and there my future was decided: to be a painter, a "famous" painter.

One day the drawing wasn't there anymore. The Maestro himself bought it. "My first fifty lei [Rumanian francs]. From now on I shall avoid forever my patriotic wish to die for my country."

In those days of war, I witnessed the friendly invasion and sloppy parade of the Russian troops—our allies—their vodka exuberance and their nostalgic songs, their conceited brutality. Our country was hurt more by them than by the invading German armies.

When thousands of prisoners of war arrived from the front to be sent to prison camps or army barracks, before they entered the town they were spread over the hills as far as the eye could see. At a set signal, a gunshot, they all dropped their pants, and whether they needed or not, they had to crouch and perform. And stay down until another gunshot ended the ordeal. Thirty thousand white and pink asses covering the hills, a garden of blooming daisies.

The war meant adventure, new places, strangers and freedom. We were in the war and yet we were not. Nor were we with it. What I remember are light shades of simple needs, like hunger and cold, sweets and warm clothes, black markets and quick glimpses of happiness. The war was a picnic. The drama was played for us on a small stage. Even wounded soldiers took on a romantic aspect. So the memories are frivolous, lighthearted nightmares:

In full daylight in the town market an old hag bends down and props herself against a table with both hands to serve a long waiting line of drunken Cossacks, each holding one ruble, payment in full for services rendered, to the howling laughter and lewd remarks of the brother Cossacks. My first encounter with lasciviousness, nudity, and adultery.

The war ended. I was back home from my hospital branch in Moldavia. I had lived through moments of great danger and yet I had very little to say. I wanted to forget. I forgot. My only thought was to paint. A studio, a model—that was all I wanted. Simple. And just as simply I had become a big problem to my father.

I was young, decisive, and quite foolish. I was also ardent, and so fell in love. She was blond, petite, and also had some artistic talent. She had a guardian angel too, a mother. They adopted me. They admired my amateurish work. I was hooked and a mess. When my girl and her *maman* moved to Bucharest I went after them. They had a cozy flat. I rented the one next to them. Warm tea, good bites to eat, languishing glances from my love, and afternoons of wild wrestling were all very satisfying. Not only that, but she showed me how to reproduce in pastel colors the official portraits of King Ferdinand and Queen Marie and sold them to public offices for a good price. So I too forgot my studies at the academy; and a life of kings and queens, love and commercial artistic pursuits, opened before me.

Observing from afar the trend of things, my father came to Bucharest. Did he tell me I was too young to get involved? No. He knew me too well. Certainly he knew me well enough to realize that if he delivered such a pronouncement on the morning he arrived, I would have married the girl in the afternoon. So Father came to call full of smiles and gifts and flowers for the ladies: gallant, grateful for the kindness they were showing to his son, almost enamored of the whole— Shall I say setup? He was a charmer. He delighted the old lady with risqué stories of his youth. Somehow he made these stories sound personal. The old lady blushed. To my loved one he was courteous, gave her fatherly advice on how to handle my youthful conceit. He had two enamored females on his side when he left us late that night.

Next day he took me off to lunch at Capsha—the best restaurant in Bucharest, the Maxim's of the Balkans. I remember the menu like it happened yesterday: gray caviar with frozen *tzuika* (prune brandy), sirloin tips braised over rice pilaf, chilled strawberries in heavy cream, vintage wines, and Turkish coffee—a meal with a purpose.

He was clever. He was skillful. Oh, I wish I could find the perfect word to tell you how wisely he hid his purpose. He made me believe the kind of life I chose for myself was the only life a young talented man should have: "She is right for you—lovable, productive, even the same age." "Only two years older, Father." "So much the better. With age a woman gets wiser. Remember the old Rumanian proverb 'The old chicken makes good soup'?"

I remembered. I laughed and felt good. And yet he said something over the brandy, something that changed the leisure of my pleasant setup: ". . . a possibility you might be interested in a remarkable chance to pursue your passion in the arts."

He had a friend, a ship captain who owed him a favor, and some money. He was sailing the next day from Constantsa on the Black Sea for Naples, with three-day stops in Istanbul and Greece, a voyage he would repeat only one year later. He had given father a ticket—my passage to Naples. I could go on to Rome, Florence, Venice, the great trail of art all the way to Paris. I could paint some on the way: the golden light of the Bosporus, the miracle of the Acropolis, the Bay of Naples, the sunlight of Italy. My uncle Costea would meet me in Paris. Some more money would await me. He could not give it to me now, but he would be able to get it to Paris before I arrived there. That is if I wanted to go to Paris. Did I? Paris, the dream of every painter: everything—museums, exhibitions, the Gardens of Versailles— "And the twisted little streets at night," Father interrupted. "Yes, but the museums—" "The museums too, but the little streets, and the French girls, their eyes and their mouths, and the way they dress or undress like no other girl does anywhere. The air of Paris. The freedom and the nonchalance. After one year, come back and show a different exhibition—and get married and go back together, if you still want to."

I was convinced. I was drunk. I was light. I was free. I was on my way.

My father did not go back with me to the ladies, to their nest. Instead, I bounced in so cheerily. I yanked out my bags and began to pack, spouting out the story of the wonderful opportunity my father had arranged for me. No daggers stabbed him to the heart. He wasn't there. Nor did he hear the recriminations. It was into my ears that the doubts and questions were poured. Why did I have to leave so abruptly? Why not the next sailing? When we all might have known one another better? When there might have been developments? To be blunt, why did I have to leave alone? With each word the ladies were arguing my father's case. I came to see the cozy nest as a web. My girl and her mother were trying to keep me from Athens and Rome and Paris, to destroy the wonderful opportunity that my good, kind father had opened for me.

I finished packing, dodged the final kiss that might have been my undoing, and went down to the express train that carried me away to the ship on the Black Sea.

As the lines were cast off, my father was probably watching from a port cafe, smoking a black cigar and sipping an amber brandy. Alone? I hope not.

PARIS

For how many years had I thought about the moment when I would approach Paris? How often had I imagined the rows of Paris buildings with their special roofs and black chimneys, all combining in a gray color, soft and friendly; the first sight of the Eiffel Tower; the smell of Paris. I had read and listened to stories about it. So, in advance I took pleasure in anticipating what was coming. I felt the pleasure in my bones—and waiting, I fell asleep.

Alone in the train compartment, the cleaning woman bombarded me with an avalanche of shouts which had no resemblance whatsoever to the French language—at least not the French I had carefully learned in school. Uncle Costea had a room for me in Rue de Rivoli. I took a taxi. The streets seemed narrow and dark, and the pissoirs gave the smell of Paris a difference.

The taxi driver was in a bad humor. He didn't understand me, and I didn't understand him. So far a draw. At the hotel he was ahead. He got out of me more than his meter showed. Was I going to argue with an unhappy French taxi driver?

Nenea Costea was out. A brief note said that he would pick me up for lunch. The room, a cubicle, was clean, furnished only just. A small balcony was not meant to be ventured on. I opened my bags and went for a walk in the streets around the hotel.

People were in a hurry, shouting, arguing over what they were buying, what they were selling, pushing me aside, feeling with their hands the meat and fruit and vegetables. And all were carrying long thin crispy loaves of bread, unwrapped, and over all the same smell.

Back at the hotel, Nenea Costea was waiting for me. God, I was glad to see someone who spoke my language and my kind of French. He took me to a small bistro. Small it was. We were sitting on each other's laps, but the food was great, and the Frenchmen—quiet this time—were eating as if they were in church praying—with reverence and passion. It seemed to me that Nenea Costea paid a lot for the meal. I didn't know then that the rarity of small restaurants made them sought after and expensive.

We walked for a while before he questioned me. "Happy to be away?" "Away, yes, but happy? It's not what I expected." I was quiet; he waited. "The gray of the houses is nothing but dirt. The people, the smell—it isn't Venice or Rome or Florence. They were full of light and people laughing, and every corner a masterpiece." I stopped talking, unhappy at trying to explain.

"Paris is like that," he said softly.

At the hotel he saw me started on the way to my room. "Now, Johnny, rest awhile, dress for a party, and let us try to find your Paris."

He was wise, Nenea Costea; he was wise and a loner. No one from my family knew much about him. He talked little, and then quietly, and never about himself. He went away for months, sometimes years, and no one ever knew where he went or when he would be back or where he got the money with which to travel and to always bring back valuable gifts. We children loved him. Not for what he was or gave us or the little he told us about his wanderings, but for what we imagined his life must have been. When we were jabbering about nothing, just happy that he was back with us, he listened patiently and with a kind smile. Then his eyes focused somewhere else, and a faraway look came into his face. God, we all wanted to go "there" with him.

It was dark and late when he picked me up. The first time that I traveled by metro we went as far as the Concorde station. When we came out, I had the answer.

The sight of the Place de la Concorde at night, suddenly from the metro, was a shock: a sea of light. In a perfect setup of space and lines. The past and the present joined together with legends and gray stones.

And Nenea Costea talked. He talked and I listened. This was his Paris. And in the early morning I found out that this was my Paris too, the way I dreamed she was.

We crossed the Concorde, up the Rue Royale, and arrived at Maxim's—"the restaurant more famous than its titled clients."

For years I had collected reproductions of Sem's caricatures, famous for showing the exclusive "gourmet snobs," the regular customers of the place. From Sem, I almost knew them. The maitre d', Albert, the master of snobs, sits the people according to his code: *les élus et les autres*—the chosen and the others.

"Why the difference?" I asked. "No reason. Same place, same food, same wines, same service. Yet they all want to sit in the big room. Title, fame, splendor—the difference." Nenea Costea knew how to order. The wine must have been special. I felt light and bubbling.

One story he told me that night about Maxim's remains
with me as clear as if it happened yesterday. New Year's Eve
of 1900—the beginning of a New Century:

"There was madness everywhere—the streets, the stores,
the restaurants, in every home. A storm descended over em-
battled Paris like a bad omen. It added to the mad excitement. All Paris seemed to be here at Maxim's. The orchestra
was blasting a fast polka. The ladies picked up their skirts—
higher, higher, so they could follow their crazy partners. Suddenly all lights went out: midnight, *a new century*. The noise,

the screams, the greetings '*Long live the twentieth century!*' It was a nightmare—glorious, never to be forgotten."

He stopped and lit a cigarette.

"La Belle Otero—the Spanish gypsy, the rage of Paris—jumped on a table, her heels like gunshots tapping a wild rhythm. The music grew faster. Her hair loosened, sweating, her strong hands countertiming like fireworks the heels. Otero was wild. She was vulgar. She was glorious. Her bosom was covered with rows of diamonds given her by generous lovers. She felt uncomfortable with this valuable junk. She tore off the diamonds, the bracelets, and threw them into the crowd. That night Maxim's with its rules and its exclusive crowd changed to a place of common mad lunatics, because a Spanish gypsy wanted to be alive."

We left Maxim's long past midnight. At this hour Montmartre was at its height. So two places crowned our evening: The Black Cat, where we were teased and insulted as a policy of the place, and The Hell—ominous, the tables covered by blood-red paint, with candles mounted on skulls. The big chandelier was braced by skeleton bones, and each light was set in a different size of skull.

It was daylight as we started walking toward my hotel. "Tomorrow I'll be on my way. I should have gone days ago. I wanted to see you." He stopped to light another cigarette.

As we arrived at the entrance of my hotel: "Thank you, Nenea Costea, for helping me find Paris."

"You would have found it by yourself anyway. Maybe slower. Maybe better. But you would have found her. Don't set a limit to your dreams."

We went into each other's arms. And afterward I watched him walking away, a moving shadow in the early-morning light. So much living lay behind him. Then he turned a corner.

We never saw Nenea Costea again.

L'ACADÉMIE JULIAN

"Don't set a limit to your dreams," Nenea Costea had said. From my window I looked happily at the sea of homes, thinking of the infinite number of lives in my new Paris I had to win over—to understand them, so they could understand me, to love them, so they could love me.

The fun of Paris and the freedom were the wiles of a temptress. I knew I had to give up some freedom and go back to school. L'Académie Julian was where I first signed. You paid a small fee; you came to class and worked. Nobody paid any attention to you whether you were good or bad. It was up to you to make a mark or be ignored forever. There was only one time when you were a person of importance: the first day. You had to buy everybody a drink. The whole class, the secretary, the manager, and the porter went around the corner. "A boire—To drink!" they shouted. They all paid attention to me. They asked me questions and listened to anything I said.

A Greek sculptor leaned close. "*Mon vieux*, remember this day. It is the only day they'll pay attention to you. Today you are somebody. Only today." He was right. The next day I didn't exist.

We worked at the Académie Julian in the morning. In the afternoon, if we had cash, we could practice nude sketches at La Grande Chaumière or L'Académie Collarossi—a twenty-minute pose, or a ten- or five-minute pose. There, from all nations, men and women worked frantically, many amateurs, some talented, some who could only use a pencil and paper to add numbers, ones who paid the fee to give them the right to see a nude woman. The concierge would watch this kind of intruder, and if the scribbling made no appeal to the concierge's artistic sense, the Peeping Tom would be asked politely to leave, or be given the bum's rush.

One day there were maybe sixty of us in the class. It was a special session. The model was redheaded and a ballet dancer. We paid extra for redheads.

Suddenly, as she changed a pose, she covered her breast and screamed, *"Un homme, la haut*—A man, up there!"* A workman was fixing the skylight window and was looking down. There were forty men in the class close to her, but they were painters; "he" was a man.

Every Saturday at Julian, Le Maître Pierre Laurens would arrive to see our weekly efforts. Like his father, Jean Paul Laurens, he dressed in the classic corduroy coat and pants with a big knitted shawl thrown carefully just so around his shoulder and neck. *Les vieux*—the old ones told me that he also gave exactly the same performance as his father in judging your drawings—a sadistic ham. First he would look at the model from your angle, then take a longer look at your drawing. Next he would have an even longer look at you. Nothing was said, maybe a grunt. By that time, you *knew* you were wrong. Then he would snatch the pencil out of your hand and make some hard, heavy geometrical lines around the drawing to show your failures of proportion, your lack of values. The drawing you had slaved a whole week on was ready for the junk pile.

I hated him every Saturday. And every Monday I'd start again with new hopes. I would set myself hard tasks. I would choose the most difficult place from which to draw the nude—from the floor at the model's feet—to impress him. One of my great handicaps as a painter was my ability to know the easy way to accomplish something, a facility for quickness. By the end of a year I felt I had mastered all the media: pencil, sepia, charcoal, wash, ink. But still the Master was not impressed. Finally, my drawing was chosen by the director of the academy as the best of the week and hung on the wall of the atelier.

That Saturday I stood in front of my easel with only a big white paper on it. "And your work?" asked the Master. Proudly I showed Monsieur Laurens the framed drawing on the wall. He looked at the drawing and longer at me. And

good God, he spoke: "Negulesco, you have lost all interest in the adventure Art offers. You use the easy superficial manner to cover a surface. I shall save you. Starting Monday, you will draw with your left hand and the hardest pencil. Better yet, hard pen and ink. You may rediscover the miracle one can get out of pencil and paper!"

He continued his class. No word of praise. I was mad.

On Monday I worked with my left hand and hard pen and ink. I sweated and swore with every stroke. After a month I began to take a fierce joy in the struggle. *I was never bored.*

Pierre Laurens saved me from the most destructive enemies: *ability* combined with *boredom.*

CHOU-CHOU AND THE YELLOW CUP PERIOD

HER name was Yvonne, but she looked like what "Chou-Chou" suggests: petite, *rondelette*, mischievous, a gay teaser, with an impertinent sidelong glance.

Place de l'Opéra, the hour when the fashion houses close. She was walking with two girlfriends, laughing. The friends left. I came close. "Mademoiselle, have I met you before?" "No." "But I must have." "No." "You don't remember?" "No." (Three noes, a bad beginning.) "Funny, mademoiselle, I don't remember either."

She laughed. I read somewhere that if a Parisienne laughs she is willing to listen further. "May I offer you a drink?" "Yes." She loved to laugh and her laugh was genuine.

She opened the conversation. "What do you do when not accosting ladies you never met?" "I am a painter, trying to be." "An artist?" For a moment, doubt on that lively face. "An artist should not spend money in boulevard cafes." Did

I have a studio? Yes. Could we have a little bite there?

Well . . . there happened not to be any food there. What did I do for supper? Washed dishes in a restaurant late in the evening and got fed or paid as I pleased. All this while her side-look mixed mischief, puzzlement, concern. "I have a little money," she said. And she bought quickly, prudently, the ingredients of our supper. In the studio she began to slice onions in a pan with butter. "Always start with the onions." My first lesson in French cooking. "Brown the meat. Get the big pot boiling. In go the meat, potatoes, carrots, celery, beans, and more onions. We are done." She sat on my couch and told me something with her eyes. "The stew will take an hour." I sat beside her. . . .

The stew was good too, although I remember that we had to add seasoning. Once or twice.

Chou-Chou's love was, among the others, one of the only real loves in Paris. (Each time then one was blessed with "the only real love.") She laughed and starved with me; she slaved through a time of need and bad luck, a devoted fan and a supreme admirer of every trifling sketch or colored dabble I created. Through her I knew and loved the Latin Quarter— the Pantheon, the Luxembourg Gardens, Bal Bullier, but mostly Boul' Miche—Boulevard St. Michel—the swinging promenade of the Latin Quarter, crowded with youth of all nations, each race with its color, each color with its mentality. The incredible crowd of Boul' Miche filled the cafe terraces four rows deep at little round tables.

Thursday night was *dance* night. In Montmartre, Moulin Rouge was in full blast every night—the first forbidden sight in Paris for every tourist. And then Moulin de la Galette, where every stranger was an intruder, and should you make a pass at the wrong girl there was trouble with Jules her pimp. Jules fought with his feet, and many noses and backs were broken with his heel. But in Montparnasse, Bal Bullier was the dancehall of students and midinettes.

By ten o'clock at night the Boul' Miche cafes and terraces were half empty. Chou-Chou met me in front of the blue blazing lights of the Bullier. Inside, the students and their tipsy dates were in full swing; Thursday we were out for all the joy and fun we could get for one louis. We danced and sang all night, and in the gray light of the morning we reached my studio in Rue de Seine.

But for four weeks, no Bal Bullier, no Chou-Chou, no country on Sunday, no Concert Colonne, no restaurants.

I fell in love . . . in a junk shop in Rue Jacob I fell in love with a yellow cup. But not just a yellow cup with white inside and a yellow-and-white plate. This was special. It was delicate, with a smooth lemon-yellow color that time and long exposure in the window had helped to transform into an unbelievable transparency. The price was four francs—four weeks of privations, four weeks of late dishwashing, four weeks of passing twice a day the junk shop to see my cup. It was still there.

Finally it was mine. It was there on my mantelpiece among my very few other treasures. Never did a ray of sun bring so much light into the studio. The yellow cup became my talisman. I painted it in every painting I worked on. A nude? The yellow cup was a companion nearby. A portrait? The lady was drinking tea from the yellow cup. A still life? I painted a mirror in the background so there were two yellow cups. A street of Paris? The store window in the foreground exhibited the yellow cup. It was my yellow cup period.

Chou-Chou went to spend her summer vacation in Brittany. I was all right. I began to enjoy the routine of dishwashing. More economies, and another wish was achieved: I bought secondhand four volumes of Romain Rolland's *Jean-Christophe*. I felt rich, content.

One night I was reading until four o'clock. I still remember crystal-clear this passage from the book:

"Jean-Christophe was lying on the grass. It was a day of early spring. The earth was warm and moist with the fragrance of new plants. Drowsy, his eyes contemplated the miracle of life . . . an ant climbed slowly the perpendicular surface of a blade of grass. Sleep stopped him from watching the ant, and he dreamed . . ."

A whole lifetime. Romain Rolland made me enter into the dream life: hopes, achievements, disappointments, the web of ambitious people, the sacrifices of few, the forgiveness of others. Then Jean Christophe awakened. The ant had climbed only a fraction of an inch up the grass, while this dreamed lifetime flowed by. Utter perfection in Rolland's tale-spinning left me keyed up, stimulated, trembling. I got out of bed and made tea in my yellow cup. I felt closed in. I opened the window and stood by the ledge and watched the moonlit street. My heart was pounding. I had to do something. I held out my precious yellow cup in space with my two hands and slowly let it go. It was given the freedom to fall. I watched it smash into moon-burst powder. The end of a dream. The end of my yellow cup period. I slept.

Bread crusts, even chunks from discarded dry chunks of bread tossed into your wastepaper basket could sometimes be a meal. After my yellow cup period, good times were not on my side. I had one of my poorest spells: no help from Father, no work, no money, no Chou-Chou. My furniture, table and chairs, lost legs one by one to the hungry stove.

CONSTANTIN BRANCUSI

CONSTANTIN Brancusi was a beautiful sage, with the face of a god framed by a gray beard yellowed by tobacco, small sparkling blue eyes. His talk was colorful. You were in the presence of a shrewd Rumanian peasant. His studio in the Impasse Ronsin opened directly onto an unpaved courtyard facing a cluster of studios. An old battered door protected him from the outside. Brancusi came from the same province in Rumania I came from—he from Tirgu-Jiu in the north, I from Craiova in the center. It was the best calling card I could present.

When I entered his studio it was far from what I expected. In Brancusi's world, I was in the presence of the unknown—a world apart, hard to admire or judge. I wanted to ask questions, I wanted to know. He understood and let you alone, until the language of his simplicity became a soft cushion for your comfort. He invited me for lunch and served his famous steak cooked on a stove of his own design, with sour cabbage and cucumbers and champagne.

He talked of coming to Paris at the age of twenty-eight after art schools in Bucharest and Munich, traveling much of the way on foot. In an empty studio, he built his own furniture, and there he worked—a Rumanian peasant living in the sophisticated glory of Paris.

In his studio all around were beginnings of plaster sculptures—some discarded, some put aside for later labor—plaster casts and wood blocks, carved and uncarved, and boulders of marble, one holding a small vase with a wilted bouquet. The white walls were covered with an uneven parade of his sculpture tools, black, rusty forms. Many days followed, hours of listening, questioning, and remembering with Brancusi and some of his friends. Modigliani, Erik Satie, Tristan Tzara, and Man Ray were among his friends I met.

One afternoon, he, Tzara, and Man Ray were carving a walking stick out of a twisted heavy branch, the kind that in his childhood Brancusi used to carve, just as his ancestors had done before him—walking sticks and shepherd pipes. Rain began to fall and the little courtyard at the back of the studio became a lake of mud. These three masters rolled up their trousers and, singing bawdy songs, played in the mud like dirty kids. Later I said, "Nene Constantin, I can't understand grownups like you playing in the mud like children." He smiled and, leaning with his back against the warm stove, said "Iancule [a pet name for Jean], the day you're no more a child, you're already dead. Never forget that!" I've never forgotten.

Another day on the streets of Paris, out of a heap of trash he picked up a discarded tin washbasin, rusted and full of holes. With a stick he created a rhythm of his own, a beat merging in a perfect marriage with the noise of the city. "My life was nothing but miracles. Like a song you like and want to hear often, so shall be my sculptures. To be seen again and again with the same joy as the first time your young heart opened to love and beauty."

When Brancusi first got to Paris, he had to wash dishes in

Restaurant Chartier in Boul' Miche—the same place where I went to work. He sculpted a bust of the *patron* and when it was completed trundled it in a wheelbarrow to one of the official salons. It was accepted and exhibited.

The great Auguste Rodin, who dominated the world of art of that period, noticed Brancusi's work and invited him to join his studio in Meudon near Paris. For any young artist this offer meant a sure way to success and fortune, but not to Brancusi. In his peasant wisdom he answered the Master with a Rumanian proverb: "In the shadow of the big oak tree the grass fades away." It was fine praise for the great Rodin, but also a firm statement of Brancusi's own belief.

One day I was showing him some of my well-behaved academic drawings. "And if you drew a full face with only one eye, would they put you in jail?"

I thought the old man was nuts. Later, when the real meaning was clear to me, I understood my first lesson in freedom. He was a prophet but with the heart of a child—enraged at unfairness, grateful for one word of love or appreciation.

"To be mad and capable of hate is borrowing time away from your life."

About his sculptures: "My work should not inspire respect. It should be loved. Fame is the worst sin man has created."

No polishing machine or any other mechanical instrument was ever used for the smooth surface of his works. He insisted that the polish should be made with his own hands, as the material becomes a living form through the passing of the sculptor's soul into the sculpted stone: "A sculpture must be lovely to touch. Happy to live with. A blind person should be able to touch and love it."

His imagination led him to bring from the country a stump in the shape of a big elongated head. Rain and time had produced an extraordinary form unnoticed by passers-by but not to the piercing eyes of the Rumanian peasant. He placed it with mock reverence on a sculptured block. A hoop from a discarded barrel, rusted and bent, was planted with ceremony on top of the stump: "The *King of Kings*." After such a private triumph: "Look until you will see. . . . Simplicity is not the purpose of art. . . . The work is not difficult. What is really difficult is to achieve the state of mind—the step to do it."

Constantin Brancusi was a simple man, and yet often it was hard to start a proper quiet conversation with him. His voice was sarcastic and his eyes ironic and contradictory no matter what you said. A born worker, he did everything by himself, for himself: "Manual work brings you closer to God."

In his teens, while working in a tavern as a servant, he built a violin out of an orange crate, on a dare from a customer. The guitar and the golf clubs hanging on the walls of his studio in Paris were made by him, and once when he broke his leg he made the plaster cast and refused to see any doctor. He saw the world with the candid instincts of a child but with the experience of his peasant ancestors: "I hope my sculptures will print just a few small steps on the sands of eternity."

In 1909, a thirteen-year-old Russian girl, Tanosa Gassevskaia, committed suicide out of childish hopeless love. Moved by this tragic story, Brancusi set on her grave in the Montparnasse Cemetery the first cut-in-stone sculpture of *The Kiss*. (Later he was making many variations of this work.)

The Kiss is that rare masterpiece situated on the dangerous tightrope position between two opposite styles—the most primitive art and the most modernistic art. Reminiscent of primitive idols and inspired by Rumanian folklore sculptures, *The Kiss* assumes the miracle of a love beyond death.

There is a reason why he insisted that his sculptures be seen together in the surrounding in which he created them. Every piece of stone, wood, or metal was transformed day by day— a dent here, a cut there; leave it alone for a while; pick it up again to change; let it go again for a few days until the answer came. Patience, and finish it with joy and knowledge till each piece became an integral part of the Brancusi world.

When Brancusi attacked a new work he felt he needed a thousand years to discover the forms that hide in only one block of marble or wood. "You should create like God, decide like a king, work like a slave."

One dream he never achieved was to make a version of his sculpture *Leda*—one of enormous proportions, placed in a shaded park or small square, just on the ground, where it would turn slowly. Children could climb and ride on it and drop water or sand on its head—"just to make them happy."

Another dream that went unfulfilled was the project proposed by the Maharajah Olcar of Indore to design a Temple of Contemplation, which was to contain five sculptures of the *Bird in Space* purchased by the Maharajah—white, gray, black marble, and two in bronze—placed around a pool of water and lit by shafts of sunlight. The temple was never constructed because of civil turmoil and the death of the Maharajah.

What an irony that in 1926 the U.S. Customs decreed that the *Bird* was not a duty-free object of art but a taxable piece of metal, like machinery. Brancusi had to sue the United States to finally win, when three judges decided that the *Bird* was art.

His vision explores the depth of the very existence of his models. The *Maiastra—Bird in Flight*—with all twenty-nine variations, does not represent or suggest any kind of flight. But it is a form created by Brancusi to give to those who see it the fundamental essence of flight. He achieved this relation with the universe by continual and savage work. "In the year 2000 Brancusi's sculptures will embellish the squares of every capital of the world," wrote Paul Morand in 1926.

Eugene Ionesco recounts his last visit to Brancusi before he died. His wife and daughter were with him, and Brancusi held the hand of the little girl like a lover on his wedding day: "I'm so old now, I can only stretch my arm and touch God."

All his life Brancusi touched God, in each of his creations.

To me, I'll always remember him with his ridiculous little white hat, doing a couple of steps of the Rumanian hora, and with sparkling eyes: "Art is youth without age and life without death."

AMEDEO MODIGLIANI, MODI

MODIGLIANI was Jewish and beautiful. His bright black eyes had genuine irony, the melancholic sarcasm of a tubercular Venetian. At moments, because of drugs, his eyes took on a faraway, fixed gaze. His speech was voluble and fluent and accompanied by dramatic Italian gestures, and there was style in his performance.

I met him first one evening when I knocked at Brancusi's door. Before it opened, I heard loud chanting marked by strokes on some tin can. Brancusi had his usual wicked smile when he let me in. "Who?" I asked. "The Crusader of Livorno." Constantin pointed over his shoulder. With his back to us, the stranger was standing on one of Brancusi's higher blocks and with full voice was reciting in Italian a kind of passionate oration, a sermon I didn't understand or make any sense of. His furious banging on a water can didn't help make the sense any clearer. Dressed in brown velvet corduroy, a bright red scarf around his neck, a big felt hat pushed back on his head, he suggested in his worn clothes the poverty of the traditional bohemian painter, yet he had distinction. For a moment he stopped his showy rhetoric to take several thirsty swallows from a bottle carried in his pocket. "Modi, this is another Rumanian," Constantin shouted.

He didn't hear or give any acknowledgment but asked abruptly, "Do you like Laudi?" "Who?" "*Laudi*. I worship him. Laudi and Dante. It's in my blood." (It took me two days to find out that Laudi was Gabriele d'Annunzio, the famous Italian writer adored by women, lover of Eleonora Duse, and fiery partisan of Italy's participation in World War I.)

That night at Chez Mère Louise, where I had arranged to meet Chou-Chou, he drank his dinner. Because I paid for his Pernods, he gave me a drawing, a drawing he made of Chou-Chou on the white paper table cover. Just returned from Brittany, she was shining with health and suntan and full of silly chatter. I remember little of his talk that night. I have wanted to forget that night. "We must tie life and art together. I want to live intensely, every moment, no matter how short."

I considered this old-fashioned nonsense. But Chou-Chou was completely under the spell of the beautiful Crusader of Livorno. (Was she feeling fat from the food in Brittany and loving the drawing Modigliani made of her with a long swan-like neck?) And Modi was drunk. When he left, he simply said to Chou-Chou, *"Tu viens*—Coming?" Chou-Chou, mesmerized, got up and followed him. I watched them. How could she? She was "my" girl. In my studio that night, I burned Modi's drawing of Chou-Chou. That is my story and the end of my life with Chou-Chou. I missed her. Not for long, though. Soon another "only real love" took her place.

Amedeo Modigliani was born 1884 in Livorno on the Tuscany coast, northwest of Rome. The fourth child of an old well-to-do Jewish family, he was only fourteen years old when typhoid fever struck him, followed by lung complications—tuberculosis. His body never recovered the damage. When at the age of twenty-two in 1906 he arrived in Paris, it wasn't easy to forget him: a young Italian archangel, black flaming eyes, delicate nervous hands. His presence was commanding. He dressed and looked like a conservative dandy. But soon he adopted the bohemian uniform. Still he was a prince. A slave of Venus, his fights in Montmartre were his claim to male glory. Bragging, inviting, daring, whenever a lovely female admired his looks. He did everything furiously. He worked furiously. He drank with passion. He lived with the violent desire of self-destruction. Cafe life, hashish (the taste of infinity), absinthe, cocaine, opium, women, and alcohol were his fire of life, his constant companions.

During his bad times—and they were crowding his working days—he had only one buyer, Father Leon, an old collector who thought—rightly so—that among all the young artists he was buying one would be famous, to help him retire in comfort; but he lost his sight and had to sell his collection for almost nothing. "I have only one buyer; he is blind," Modi commented ironically.

In 1909 he decided to move from Montmartre to Montparnasse. Before he left his studio in Rue Lepic, he lit a big fire on its terrace and burned every drawing, hundreds of them, his work of the last three years. "These *babioles* [baubles] of my youth don't deserve better" was his goodbye to Montmartre.

In Montparnasse he met Brancusi. The friendship of the Rumanian and his sculptures—the ultimate search for the perfect form in itself—gave Modi the freedom he needed. He was impressed and inspired by Brancusi's *Maiastra—Bird in Flight*. In his drawings and paintings, the line was of prime importance—pure, without hesitations, sensuous and majestic. His portraits became elongated like saints in Byzantine icons. He gave these portraits an elegance he possessed himself. In simplicity and melancholic lines, the necks were developed like undulating columns on which reposed a long face. Often the eyes were spots of green or blue or violet—the immediate inspiration of the holes in Negro masks. In spite of these simplifications, his portraits have a haunting life of their own and an astonishing likeness.

He was a Jew and proud of it. He spoke beautiful French, rolling his r's like music; it pleased him. His laughter was short but not offending. He loved Picasso when they met; but then he found out that Picasso thought of him as a *rapin famélique*—a starving young amateur. Modi found Picasso's clothes of a Parisian worker phony, and Picasso despised the beautiful young Italian for his excessive drinking and his open use of drugs. Modi took the beautiful model and mistress Fernande away from Picasso.

"Yes, he is different. Of course he has ability. He is a draftsman, even a very effective draftsman. But painter? No, he is not a painter," Pablo concluded.

His friendship with Utrillo was unique. They were together for days and nights. They were searching for each other's company, following each other when their legs were able to, hanging on each other's arms. The *patrons* and the waiters of bars in Montparnasse feared the couple's fights.

"Utrillo is the grrrreatest painter of today; nobody drrrrinks like him." "No, Modi, you're better. You're the greatest."

"Don't copy me, you arrrre the grrrrreatest, Utrillo." "You are, Modi, and if you repeat once more . . ." "You arrrre . . ." He couldn't finish. Utrillo hit Modi. Modi hit the table. The noisy fight made a path of destruction around the bar, tables and chairs were overturned, bottles and glasses broken. They were thrown out into the gutter, where they continued fighting, but in slow motion. Finally exhausted, they fell asleep. In the cold morning they awakened shivering. They were naked, all their possessions stolen, their clothes removed by night prowlers.

Modi was one of the first pure hippies. A table, a chair, a trunk serving as a divan for sleep—that was all his comfort—with paintings and drawings everywhere. He was hungry, he was drunk, he was rich with a few francs, he had grandeur and generosity, he was noble and primitive all at once. He was like his nudes, sophisticated and vulgar.

In 1918, at the end of World War I, Modi had his first one-man show of paintings at Berthe Weill's Gallery, Rue Victor Massé. It was a resounding scandal. The police seized five nudes as indecent and insisted on the removal of the nude in the window or the show would be closed. One painting was sold, only to be returned by the baffled collector two days later, asking for the return of his investment—250 francs. (Forty years later the same painting was sold for one million dollars.) *Le peintre maudit*—the cursed painter, he was called by those who saw his first exhibition in Paris.

The cops liked Modigliani. They liked him for no particular reason. They smiled and apologized when they arrested him; they smiled when they brought him their own coffee in the cool morning in his cell. The cops of Paris, like no other place in the world, were different, enforcing the law but understanding the guilty. Especially in Montparnasse. They would listen to the artists' complaints with a kind, bored expression. They helped us carry the trunk when we changed studios. If we were boisterous, insulting, or even fighting, they separated us kindly but firmly. And when the moment of danger passed, they left us, shaking their heads wearily. "*Vas, mon vieux, c'est pas gentil ce que tu fais*—Go, my friend, it isn't nice what you're doing."

Modi thought, and often said so, that Soutine was a genius, one of the greatest painters alive. They loved and painted and drank together. One night when the absinthe and drugs had gone beyond their usual level of consumption limit, Modigliani and Soutine lay down in the middle of the streetcar rails singing and shouting, "A *bas les pompiers.* V*ive la folie*—Down with the conventionals. Long live madness." And in answer to the curses of the streetcar conductor: *"Détour! Détour complet. Tu n'oseras pas tuer des génies*—Go back! Turn around! You wouldn't dare kill geniuses." With mounting laughter and loud encouragement from us to the troublemakers, three phlegmatic but amused policemen carried the culprits inside the cafe. Traffic went back to normal, Modi and Soutine back to drinking, and the cops back to their slow walk, with looks of gentle scolding. The wonderful understanding Parisian cops—*flics.*

Modi tried to join the French army at the beginning of the war in 1914. Rejected, he went back to his friends—drugs, alcohol, poetry—reciting d'Annunzio, and Dante's *Divine Comedy*. Finally he found his Beatrice—an English writer, a poetess, Beatrice Hastings. A wild passionate affair followed. She was his model. She also represented security and socially was better than his usual company.

It was the beginning of a productive period of important portraits—Jean Cocteau, Moïse Kisling, Paul Guillaume, Jacques Lipchitz—a rich collection in which he tried to escape the Cézanne influence and create a personal style—the architectural line of the Italian Renaissance, the elegance and the sensibility of the Florentine masters. His nudes gained the sensuous line of Botticelli.

In his portraits, the details of the face are treated with full liberty—asymmetry and elongation. He uses every imaginary aid to express the metaphysical side of the model as much as the external lines—but never a caricature. "In my portraits I shall try to expose the metaphysical structure of life," he wrote to his friend Giglia. In each of these portraits Modi was able to bring out the joy and the pain of his models, and also his own.

Though this was an important productive period in the life of Modi, it was also a period of excess and destruction. Soon he was to meet the Polish poet Leopold Zborowski—his agent, protector, admirer, and lifelong friend, whose total devotion was responsible in part for the quality of his work and later for his meteoric success. It was during this time that he created the *Cariatide*, a sculptural drawing of a woman's body used as a supporting column, by far the most exciting accomplishments among his drawings. The *Cariatide* is the closest passage from drawing to sculpture. Brancusi was impressed and helped him to start cutting directly in stone. Modi's few sculptures—crude, barbaric, deliberately affected by and based on African masks—are rare, superb, and savagely poetic. He was proud of them. However, when friends, dealers, and critics were invited to see his latest work, they were silent and embarrassed. "They say you paint. Why don't you go back to it?" was one parting comment.

Jeanne Hebuterne, the other woman in his life, was quiet and gentle. From a normal French Catholic family, she talked in a low voice with a smile of understanding. She was there when he wanted her; his abuse and his inexplicable tyranny were met with calm devotion. She gave him a child—a child he had no time to know and who grew up without meeting him. He depended more and more on liquor and drugs. . . .

Modi died at the age of thirty-six, on January 25, 1920, in the Charity Hospital. That day, those who were his friends and companions—in work, drinks, and drugs—received a *pneumatique* from Moïse Kisling asking each of them to be at the funeral of Modi. "Let him have the funeral of a prince," his brother Emanuele Modigliani, a deputy in Italian government, wired Kisling. An endless crowd, seemingly all Paris, stepped in line with friends, critics, and models. They followed the hearse to the cemetery. The cops who had arrested him regularly in bars stood at attention and saluted the flower-covered coffin. *"Tu nous manqueras, mon vieux*—You shall be missed, my friend," you almost heard them say.

Jeanne Hebuterne, pregnant with his second child, jumped from their fifth-floor studio only hours after she heard of his death.

Modi was an impossible friend, a selfish lover, a cruel father, but had he been ten times worse we should still love him, admire him, revere him for the gift he gave us with but one of his drawings.

BECASSINE

THERE is a time when a man, with the arrogance of youth and with trust in his own importance wants to say something significant; not just to paint but to compose in a new way: the gray period, the still-life period, the blue, the green, the yellow period. So I had the pains of the nightclub period: a crowded dance floor in a smoky bluish haze. In the foreground was a young, naive girl with her fat madame and an equally fat rich slob; fat hands full of expensive rings; lust in his sidelong glances at the delicious morsel.

I had made many studies of the lecher and the madame. You meet them in every cafe, but not the girl—clean, untouched by time and city. A friend told me about a new girl at the Pascal, a new club in the Boul' Miche. She was from Brittany, and everyone called her Becassine (a character from French children's books as popular as Peanuts in America). Naive, pink-cheeked, round. I went to see her. She answered my dreams. She also understood my problem. Yes, she will be happy to pose, but in the afternoons. She slept all morning until late. A call girl's life was a busy one, and she was unusually busy every night. I promised her a drawing of herself. I am sure that in her wise peasant way she understood that a fee was not to be considered.

So every afternoon she climbed the five flights of stairs to my studio. I worked until the light left us. Then I offered her tea and sometimes a croissant with marmalade. The first day as she left I thanked her and kissed her hand. She burst out laughing. Then she apologized. The second day when I kissed her hand she thanked me. The third day she blushed.

Ten days later the studies were complete in pencil and oil. I presented her with the drawing of her head, framed. She liked it. She was honestly moved. Nobody had ever painted her. When after the tea (without croissant) I thanked her, saying goodbye with the usual hand-kissing, she pulled her hand away so hard and so unexpectedly that it knocked off my charmer pose. She sat down on the sofa.

"Anything wrong, Miss Becassine?" "Oh, plenty!" "Because I couldn't pay?" "No. I don't want it. I don't need it." "Then?"

"Am I dirty? Repulsive? The bed is there. I am used to being in bed the first time I am alone with a man. And I do my job. What's wrong with me?"

I was dumbfounded. For the first time a Rumanian ran out of words. "Miss Becassine, you see . . . I'm not in love with you."

She looked at me as if I were crazy. She picked up her portrait, blew her nose, said *"Oh, merde!"* and banged the door as she left. Women's ways are many. And puzzling.

I finished the big painting of my nightclub period. I called it *The Bargain.* I presented it to the Salon des Indépendants. It was refused. The big canvas was split into a few small ones. I had spent all my money on the frame, the varnish, the colors of my rejected masterpiece.

As months passed, things went from bad to worse. The rent was not paid for three months. The tea was light from being used over and over for weeks. There was no coal or furniture to be broken for fire and no jobs to be had anywhere. And it was Christmas Eve. To keep warm I went to bed fully dressed and with my overcoat on. Only an illusion of warmth. I fell asleep shivering in the early hours of Christmas morning.

Midday: an insistent knock. I did not want to answer. I was sure the concierge, Madame Genty, was there demanding the three months' rent. "Jean, Jeanot": a strange feminine voice. I still did not want to open the door. Madame Genty could be using her granddaughter's voice. Then under the door slid the receipt for my three months' rent. On it—*paid!* Signed: *"Merci, Mme. Genty."*

I opened the door. There stood Becassine with two baskets full of breads, chicken, ham sausages, butter, oil, cakes, wines. Behind her a man with a sack of coal and firewood. Santa

Claus! "Jean, I am alone, away from my family. Will you share Christmas with me? Please."

The paid rent, the goodies, the gift of a silver wristwatch—and the beautiful girl—nothing in my life looked so miraculous. In no time, with the fire roaring, the studio was warm, and rich, and singing. I went behind the curtain, shaved, changed. Becassine spread the feast and opened the bottles. And the whole Christmas Day, in the luxury of the warmth of my studio, we ate and drank and made up for the days of posing and not touching.

In the evening hours we abandoned ourselves to lovers' fantasies. Becassine performed a gymnastic maneuver at an angle of acrobatic finesse that might be described as a flying scissors. I swore I heard a c-r-a-c-k. A sharp pain shot through my coupling fixture. I sank back. Becassine too conceded we had enough.

Next morning my painful Christmas present looked like an uncompleted L. Quickly I made a drawing of its shape. (I may have exaggerated a little its size.) I pawned the wristwatch and went to see a specialist who has seen everything that could be seen in the City of *Amour*. He looked with delight on my injured lover's lance. "Congratulations, mon ami. A great possession. *La fouilleuse!*" (A bottle cleaner with a bent-up brush.) "Fix it," I implored. He looked as if I were attacking the flag of France. "Don't touch it. You'll explore corners you've never reached before."

I hated my bad luck; and no news from Becassine. It was a sad awakening from the memory, still bright, of her Christmas visit.

Four years passed. I was shopping in Trois Quartiers when somebody screamed behind me, *"Jeanot, mon cher Jeanot!"*

There stood Becassine—fat, beautifully and expensively dressed, a string of diamonds and plenty of rings. She took me in her fat, strong arms and quickly told me of her fortune: A South American fell in love with her, married her, and took her to live on a big ranch in Brazil. She had two kids, a young husband she adored and who adored her, and another child on the way.

Over a *fine à l'eau* she bubbled with happiness. She met her husband the second day of Christmas. My portrait of her, in a big important gold frame, dominated her marble fireplace, the pride of the house, an object of precious comments from her friends. Nostalgically, she talked about our Christmas feast. For the second time she blushed.

I didn't mention *la fouilleuse* or my bent tribulations. It remained just a gentle Christmas story.

JULES PASCIN

HEMINGWAY, in his book A *Moveable Feast*, called Jules Pascin "a lovely painter." He was so much more than just a lovely painter. Few artists have given us paintings of the woman's body like Pascin. Not the body of a healthy, muscled American girl swimmer. No, a perverse body of soft curves—too much sleep during the day, and nights of pleasure; half covered, a petticoat too high, a skirt slipping low; no time to take off the light shoes, the pink stockings hang over them, all messed up. Soft colors covered his canvases; luminous tones marked the gracious lines of his half-dressed girls, sad and sleepy, an orgy of softness.

Jules Pascin was born Julius Pincas in Wildin, a small village in Bulgaria near the delta of the Danube. His father was Jewish of Spanish origin, his mother Italian. He spent his childhood in Rumania and became an accomplished draftsman in his teens. At sixteen he fell in love with a woman twice his age. She maintained the best call house in Bucharest, and his initiation in the art of love was accomplished during the many drawings he made of the fattish perverted girls working in the lusty bordello. This harem touch was to prevail in all his work. He preferred the streets to the museums—and a woman's body to anything else. Pascin was the "Wandering Jew" in search of his place in Western civilization—only to

lose his rare stability and finish in confusion and total disorder.

Two years later his wanderings brought him to Munich.
His drawings and caricatures—sarcastic comments on German morals—were published by *Simplicissimus*. He was successful and rich. In Berlin he admired and worked with
George Grosz, the brilliant painter. Then Paris. The great
war exploded, and Pascin ignored it. He spent it in America:
Harlem in New York, New Orleans in Louisiana, Carolina,
Havana, Charleston. These were his studios—the streets, the
bordellos, the crowded cafes, the cheap nightclubs. His favorite models were dark girls—sensuous, lost, whistling for clients
ready for pleasure and hospitality.

He was a surgeon of his sensual world. His sketches were
statements bursting with a colorful disorder, a world caught
unexpectedly, the vicious truth. With one line, a touch of
color, he tried to catch the moment, the smell, the sound,
interpreted with his own special distortion. His drawings yell
at you: "You too should have time to see it."

At the end of the war he returned to Paris, and in 1920 he
married Hermine David, his constant companion of his self-
imposed exile. Pascin was bored. He had become an American
citizen, but now in his work he didn't find any satisfaction or
happiness or refuge. He despised regular work, and for a time
he broke all connection with his friends, country, and family.
He returned to Rumania only once, for the funeral of his
mother, then he wandered to Tunisia, Spain, and Portugal.
Against all conventions, in his black boredom, he would have
exchanged his fame, his prodigal talent, his riches, for the
simple joy of the fishermen or even the sleepy beggars of
Portugal. "To do nothing" was his desperate wish.

He was an *élégant*, sinuous in his walk, dressed always in
black, correct in white shirt with stiff collar, pointed shoes,
never missing his black bowler hat or summer straw. Seemingly he was timid, yet I witnessed scenes when this civilized,
gentle man could become a savage, provoking fights, illogical,
a deliberate offender. Most of the time, even when drunk, he
was worth listening to. He loved money. When he had it, he
gave it away carelessly until it was all gone. Then every Friday
the door of his studio was closed. With his favorite models,
he would paint for the whole day, drunk with the color and

the soft lines and the luminosity of a woman's body. The completed canvas would go that night to Bernheim-Jeune, his dealer; and that night he had as much as ten thousand francs. He was ready for his party. His Saturday-night parties were famous all over Montmartre and Montparnasse. His friends came, his good friends and also people he had met that day or the day before and liked. His models, brazen young girls, perverted black mulattoes with generous lips and velvet skins, unashamed lesbians, old degenerate hags, pimps and harlots, famous artists and the lesser known, a world of promiscuous shadows—they were all there.

Pascin received all of them as a king, but a sovereign who was almost ridiculously considerate and grateful that they had come. The food was hung by strings from the beams and from the staircase going up to a loft—hams, cold chickens, cheese, sausages, exotic fruits. On the only table, a forest of bottles of wine, Pernod, and bread. Guests moved around with knife and fork in hand, feasting whenever they felt like it. For that night, in his big studio at Boulevard de Clichy, Number 36, Pascin was the boyar—the boyar of the Rumanian plains.

When I met him, one Saturday night in 1924, I thought he did not acknowledge me as one of his guests. He just repeated my name, Negulescu, the Rumanian way, and turned his back. I was hungry and thirsty, and at my age I was not sensitive about my social status, not when such a feast was so close for the taking. But later in the night he came and talked to me. First a few words in Rumanian and then in French.

He had a way of quietly talking—almost in slow motion— never finishing his sentences, convinced that the listener knew the ending. He talked, as a Rumanian, about Bucharest: the rich and the fat at the famous Cafe Capsha, the corrupt, easy girls strolling by day and night in the Calea Victoria, the ghostly whistles from the straw piles rolling before the wind on the Baragan, the Black Sea desert.

But most emotionally he remembered the people of his native place, the delta of the Danube. The quiet and bearded fishermen, the Lipoveni. It was then that I learned about their origin. They had been Russians living near the Caucasus—a strange, mostly tall race with pagan roots and curious immoral religious habits: On the marriage of a son, the bride's first baby was with the son's father. "Imagine," Pascin said, "the fun of the pioneer work for a father with seven sons."

Peter the Great, Pascin went on, a religious and cruel czar, sent his wild Cossacks to exterminate the Lipoveni in their home province. The remnants migrated toward the Black Sea and settled in the Danube delta. Pascin smiled as if he were casting himself in the role of a Lipoveni father: "They never changed their customs."

"In the delta," he said, "the Lipoveni fish the sturgeon and give to the world the best caviar. Only in Portugal I met fishermen like them—barefoot, happy, putting away all duties for the next day, or the day after. . . . To do nothing, just to live like them . . ." His voice trailed off and he went away.

A legendary personage—corrupt, embarrassed, he was loved by friends, adored by women, a Jew and a dandy—and successful. Bernheim-Jeune offered him an exclusive contract—he would buy anything and everything Pascin did.

"Don't hate me too much that I sold out," he confessed to friends when congratulated. He felt useless, empty. He felt trapped. He was not ready to settle for success, fame, or fortune. That was not enough in his world of rundown young girls with pure, naive children's faces. He could expose the way they swaggered, their vices, their meanness, brazenness, and perversity with the last quick line on his canvas. Sleep and alcohol, girls and pleasure, became an unsatisfactory reason to live.

He loved Lucy Krogh, but she never left her husband or her child. "I'll never die in my bed," he often told Lucy. "Death is a labor or art, to be accomplished with reverence and knowledge. I did what I wanted to do. I can't go further."

One warm afternoon he closed the door of his studio to the spring day. He drew a bath. With infinite precision he slashed his wrists in it and waited. The studio was silent and empty. Death was late in coming. Somebody knocked at the door. A model was looking for work. Pascin answered softly that he didn't need her services: "I will not work today." She went away.

The studio was quiet again. He wandered around for the last time, reread a letter, smoked a cigarette.

"In Spain they hanged themselves very low," he confessed one day to his doctor, Tzank. Somewhere he found a heavy cord, a sash from his model's dressing gown. He tied the cord to the knob of his door and slipped a noose around his neck. This time death came swiftly, but not before he dipped a brush in his open wrists and scrawled on the wall unevenly, "Pardon." Not to anybody in particular—to Jeanine? Lucy? friends?—mostly to the softness of the woman's body.

Three days later, worried friends forced open the door. He was resting awkwardly on the floor against the door, motionless.

For the man who always said that death should be approached with awe and reverence, he had made a clumsy mess of it.

The long procession of his funeral disturbed the Paris traffic. It contained almost every nationality from every walk of life.

Side by side, Hermine David the wife and Lucy Krogh the friend walked together without hostility. They were to share fifty-fifty in the estate of Jules Pascin. But it was Hermine, the wife, who fainted across his grave.

"Jules Pascin, 45," said the marble stone in the cemetery of St.-Ouen. The man who was never alone by day or night made his messy departure on a soft melancholic evening surrounded by the clutter of a thousand drawings—delicate half-clad girls painted in gentle colors, but as cruel and precise as a gifted surgeon's cut.

Some he never had time to finish.

DADA, DADAISM

"DADAISM." Who started it? Where did it begin? Switzerland? Russia? Berlin? Paris? New York? Was it Tristan Tzara or was it Francis Picabia? Or Max Ernst, Man Ray, Jean Arp, George Grosz, André Breton, Marcel Duchamp, Giorgio di Chirico, Paul Klee, Pablo Picasso, Joan Miró? They all claimed it. They all renounced it. There is as much mystery about this as about the origin of Etruscan art.

Dada—an event or a movement, a happening or non-happening—occurred and developed all over the artistic map between 1916 and 1923—Zurich, New York, Berlin, Hanover, Cologne, Paris. There was Post Dada and Neo Dada; it was the natural result of Expressionism, Cubism, Futurism, and the poetical antecedents of Surrealism. (Many Dada artists called themselves Surrealists after 1924; let's keep the score card straight.)

The total and complete freedom from all social and moral restrictions, the joy and the optimism of new experiences following the Great War, were the revolutionary forces that produced Dadaism. It wasn't intended to destroy the existing forms of literature, music, or visual art, but to create a new form of expression—purely free; a contradiction; a fanatical rebellion against the standard art forms; a dismissal of the banality of everyday happenings; a spiritual anarchy; no limits; no walls; no obligations; no rules; sometimes insane; and always at the service of the ridiculous. Destructive as it seemed, it still had a decided influence on the art of the period. Dada was not just a way of life but a state of mind, against everything and all things.

To name just a few: the flamboyant shocking impact of new sounds in music like Erik Satie's *Socrate*; the primitive purity of Brancusi's sculptures, ultimate perfection of form; the eroticism of an already full-blown Cubism; the protest of Man Ray's photography; the fashion design of Paul Poiret clothes; the radical innovations of Frank Lloyd Wright's architecture; the Isadora Duncan school opposing fiercely the very successful Diaghilev Ballet; and so many more. All were astonishing, every one connected in purpose in a world of fresh inspiration and unrestricted freedom.

Monsieur Dada was Tristan Tzara.

Monsieur Dada was a sarcastic doubting Thomas, humorous, tricky, never still, always excited, unexpected. His name was Tristan Tzara, a talented and elegant poet. Tzara was Rumanian, a small man, dynamic, never without his monocle or his expensive cane, a master at stirring up a sudden brawl, shouting, sobbing, screaming, and mixing Rumanian, French, and German. He took off from Bucharest, and together with

another Rumanian—an elegant architect, Marcel Janco—
settled in Zurich, where Tzara originated the Dada movement
and formulated the philosophy of Dadaism. Together they
produced hideous abstract masks cut out of cardboard and
painted in colored plaster, shocking and primitive. When seen
on the stage or worn, the effect was irresistible, with a definite
touch of madness.

In Paris, Tzara was awaited as the "Anti-Messiah," the
Prophet of Dadaism. I was present at two of their meetings.
A weight lifter, Ion Terzieff, got two tickets. (He wanted to
start a Dada trend in weight lifting, I suppose.)

To the music of Satie, Milhaud, Poulenc, and Auric, Tristan Tzara read his manifesto and his poetry. He was noisy,
screamed his verses, tapped tables, and produced wild sounds
out of metal plates and beer mugs, a bedlam of roars and continual joy. He defined Dadaism as the joy of a child finding
in his repetitive scream of "Da-Da . . . Da-Da" the novelty
of new adventure, the anticipation of the "Beginning." He
concluded with: "To be against this manifesto is to be a
Dadaist."

A few months later Terzieff took me to the best meeting
the Dadaists had in Paris. I was surprised when my friend
brought two paper bags full of rotten vegetables and overripe
fruits he had picked up that morning in the Halles. "Help
Dada to instant fame and success." (One way to put it.) The
show was advertised days in advance. A concert hall, Salle
Gaveau, was the place, and the Dadaists promised the audience that they would shave their heads on the stage in front
of the public. They never did. Things got out of control.

They appeared on the stage amid boos, shouting, and
whistling, each wearing a different costume, a different mask,
one more ridiculous and unbecoming than the next, and on
their heads they wore high stovepipe hats made out of car-
tons and colored paper, and each was holding a sign with his
name. Tzara's hat and sign were the tallest. How else? All
talked at the same time, reciting, arguing, reading individual
manifestos. These manifestos were chanted like psalms. The
whole was a mockery of any organized ensemble or any form
of entertainment.

The audience was accompanying this phony, indecent exhibition with catcalls and continual booing. But when the artistic talent on the stage began to perform Tzara's musical composition *The Symphony of the Vaseline*, all restraint was cast aside. Eggs, tomatoes, rotten fruits, and spoiled steaks rained over the performers. They stood the fierce and smelly attack bravely, even with delight. I was amazed at my enjoyment of this brawl, also at my accuracy.

It was ridiculous. It had no style. But the public had a good time being a part of the whole performance, active appreciators of this pandemonium. The police arrived, and with their arrival Dada accomplished its aim: Dada was famous and the talk of Paris.

Around this time Man Ray contributed something new to the art of photography. His assistant by mistake opened the door to Man Ray's darkroom. Objects placed directly on sensitive paper left strange impressions of light and shadow. Man Ray improved and varied the technique of the mistake and a new photographic art was born—"Rayograma." ("A line, a face, an egg, a cloud, are just the beginning of an adventure," he said.) A photograph called *Le Violon d'Ingres* became popular and lasted through ages—the nude back of his mistress and favorite model, Kiki of Montparnasse, painted to resemble a violin.

Paul Klee's paintings of this period disclosed new forms, each with a different and totally new identity in color, basic lines, and technique. "I let a line take a walk" was Klee's explanation of his work, based on definite styles and in the shadow of child art.

Le Groupe des Six—the French composers Darius Milhaud, Francis Poulenc, Arthur Honegger, Germaine Tailleferre, Georges Auric, and Louis Durey—assembled by Cocteau and somewhat under the musical influence of Erik Satie, were closely linked by friendship and to a lesser degree by their interest in Dada. Satie and the Six never had identical esthetic outlooks and artistic aims, yet each of them produced masterpieces of modern music, all, if not influenced, at least touched by the unusual attitude of Dada.

From Dadaism we inherited in our time its eccentric mutations: Pop Art, Op Art, and the grotesque and insulting Punk Art.

In 1925, November 25, in the Galerie Pierre, 13 Rue Bona-parte, an exhibition of paintings opened for only eleven days to show the latest work of nine Surrealist painters—all not admitting, but all touched by Dada: Arp, Chirico, Ernst, Klee, Masson, Miró, Picasso, Man Ray, and Pierre Roy. It was homage to a renounced art liberation.

About the same time, new methods and ideas in the seventh art—the *cinema*—exploded and affirmed it as the most excit-ing dream of freedom and magic that we've ever been blessed with.

MÈRE ROSALIE

Paris, the Paris of 1920, when inspiration shone on so many artists, needed a Mère Rosalie. How many memo-ries focus around her as the artists' innkeeper? Who knows how much of their inspiration came from her bean soup?

Two doors from Boulevard Montparnasse and right across the street from Kiki's Jockey Club, in the quiet street of Rue Campagne-Première, was an insignificant bistro. Over the door in faded letters was the name Mère Rosalie.

Insignificant, yes, but Mère Rosalie's bistro was the meet-ing place of artists of all nations. Hungry people ate well and argued and sang and fought for new ideas and new religions, sane or mad, but alive.

Her full name was Rosalia Tobia, a Neapolitan. When young, she was a beautiful model. Her claim to glory was posing for Maître Adolphe Bouguereau, a celebrated painter of the late nineteenth century, as Venus. Now old and irri-table, she treated her clients as a mother with wild children.

The place was small, crowded with tables and hobbling benches. The walls were covered with paintings of all schools and sizes.

A sign proclaimed: *"Aujourd'hui on fait du crédit. Demain on paye*—Today we give credit. Tomorrow you pay."

So the old customers, the habituals, took advantage of this and departed with the satisfied farewell *"Mère Rosalie, on payera demain*—Ma Rosalie, I'll pay tomorrow." Kindly she would push them out: *"Madonna mia, che banditos*—Mother of God, what bandits." But they all paid their bills. When the muse smiled at them with a commission or an unexpected sale, they paid every cent. And if the hungry times persisted for long periods, they would bring some of their good work and she would wipe clean the slate.

Mère Rosalie was a lady. She was what everyone imagined the perfect mother should look like. She was the matriarch and we were her children. Her Italian heart was open to us and grieved at any trouble or bad fate of her children.

Proud and majestic on the doorstep of her tiny kitchen, her lovely face surrounded by silver braids, sometimes wearing a formal hat, always smiling cordially, she received every day *les Montparnos*, her children.

She had of course favorites, *"les préférés."* She wouldn't accept any pay for their food, and when they left she would bestow a noisy Italian smack on their cheek as proof of her favor.

But if strangers came in, if she felt they were just prowlers, curious tourists, or rich snobs wanting to watch the bohemians in the raw, then the Mother Hen would scream at her queendom being invaded and dust 'em out noisily and by force if necessary. *"Va étrangers, y'a d'autres bistros à Paris*—Out strangers, there are other bistros in Paris."

Luigi, her son—tall, fiery, turned-up mustache, black flaming eyes—would move between the tables with dignity carrying plates of steaming spaghetti and big bowls of bean soup with chunks of peasant bread. Over the roaring noise of contented diners, of songs and art quarrels, Luigi shouted at Mère Rosalie the addition of the bills.

"Armand, twelve cents of soup, no wine, but two breads."

"Giorgio, one spaghetti, drinks water, brought his own bread."

"Ivan Petrovich, soup and spaghetti; brought his drink. To-day he'll pay."

And Mère Rosalie would add the bills and shout back, "Luigi, bambino, give an extra serving to Yvonne. She's expecting."

"No more spaghetti for Peppi, he'll break the bench."

Among her "favorites," Modigliani was the chosen special one. The Montparnos talked for days about the first time Modi met Mère Rosalie. One evening he burst into her restaurant, drunk and shouting: "I'm Modi. Amedeo Modigliani. I want to eat. Now give me food." The customers stopped eating and looked up at the handsome intruder.

Mère Rosalie came out from the kitchen. "Can you pay?"

"I despise money."

"Then get out. I don't feed beggars."

"I'm an artist. I don't have time for food. Look." Modi took a piece of heavy chalk from his pocket and made a drawing of her on the wall. It was good and it was flattering. The crowd applauded. Modi took off his hat and said with an exaggerated bow, "Madame, now you are the Goddess of Love."

Mère Rosalie turned to her son. "Luigi, give him soup and bread. No wine." And side-glancing at the flattering drawing on the wall, she smiled. "He's no beggar. He paid for it."

And Modi joined the "habituals" and went to the top of the list of her "favorites." "*Caro* Medeo, anything you want. And no more paintings. You paid enough."

Beautiful as an archangel, with too many Pernods and standing on his bench in the smoky, noisy room, his fists clenched, Modi was shouting in Italian verses of Dante's *Inferno* mixed with swear words and curses of the streets.

"*C'est qu'il est beau, mon Medeo*—How beautiful is my Medeo," Mère Rosalie whispered.

"How noisy is your Medeo," Matisse mumbled into his distinguished beard.

Pascin, between two of his perverse young Negresses, was talking to Tsuguharu Foujita about the ways of love in New Orleans.

And Kees van Dongen argued with Utrillo, who was watching the wild Soutine gulping his dinner in silence, absent from reality.

His eyes rolling, searching, judging, Maurice Vlaminck still gave attention to his plate, but there was on his face the enigmatic look of a star who wondered if he wanted such success.

One ate well at Mère Rosalie's. One was happy in her place with hope and no worries. Mère Rosalie gave you credit. Mère Rosalie gave you the security of tomorrow's meal. And one was loved in her small bistro.

Years later, in 1926, I had my first Paris one-man show at Galerie Campagne-Première, next to her restaurant. I had my lunch there every day. The place was quiet. Mère Rosalie had lost most of her "children." Fame and fortune had called on many of them. And, with their increased value, the paintings and drawings that had covered the walls had gone to add to famous collections around the world. Some of her children returned to their countries or to a convenient marriage. Others were claimed by drugs and hospitals. And yet others, one day, just never came back.

One day Utrillo came to see Mère Rosalie. He was drunk, smashed. It was early afternoon. Rosalie fed him spaghetti, and plenty of it. He refused to go back home. He wanted to paint. "Now." And with that he fell asleep on the table.

Mère Rosalie went to the paint shop around the corner and bought colors, brushes, oil, turpentine, even a palette. So when Utrillo came to, he prepared to paint. Only Rosalie had forgotten to buy canvas. The only place to paint was the wall. So he painted the wall: *La Place du Tertre*. A year later a rich Swede bought the wall for a fortune.

Mère Rosalie was tired and lonely. And the few old favorites remaining in the quarter seldom came to eat at her place. The new clients paid cash; they didn't need Rosalie's credit. Her "world" had changed.

I asked her to visit me at Cagnes-sur-Mer, where I had a home then. "Just to cook me some of your wonderful spaghetti."

She smiled. Gently she put her arms around me. "I may . . . I will, *caro* Giovanni."

In 1927, in Nice, I was married to Winifred Ayers, a beautiful American from Chicago—a redhead, a divorcée, and rich. And Mère Rosalie came to visit us. She wanted to work for us as our cook. But her famous soup and the steaming spaghetti didn't taste the same. Maybe I wasn't a starving painter anymore. Or maybe I needed the noise and the joy and the people of her little bistro.

But her stories, the stories of her Montparnos, were still precious nostalgia, good to listen to, even if repeated again and often.

"*Eh, caro mio*, how the world has changed—lights and metal on the terraces, and bored people waiting for something to happen. My tired eyes are waiting for my children. They left me, so many gone. Only strangers come, by car, to look at my place, like my little bistro was a circus. Asking the same questions: 'Where did Modigliani sit—which one was his bench?' And Utrillo? And Soutine? I tell you, *caro— Basta! J'en avais marre*—I had enough.'"

To the dismay of my wife, she would sit down at the table and tell me the same story for the nth time.

"My beautiful Medeo died in the charity hospital. *Povero* Medeo! So young, and just as richness kissed him. . . . And *Haricot Rouge* [Red Bean, Jeanne Hebuterne] *la poverina, pregnante*, waiting for him at home. And when they told her that her Medeo was dead, she threw herself from the fifth floor. *Madonna mia*, and she and her baby died on the pavement . . . *la poverina*."

She wiped her eyes with her long apron. Then she started to laugh. It was a shock to my wife, but I knew what was coming.

"Weeks after his death, a bearded foreign gentleman came to see me. 'Mère Rosalie, do you have any drawings by Modigliani?' 'Drawings by my Medeo? Of course I have. Maybe a hundred. Maybe two hundred. Down in the cellar.' 'I will give you a thousand francs for every one of them. Now.' I thought he was crazy. But then he opened his briefcase full of beautiful bank notes. *Madonna mia*. I lighted a candle and I stumbled down the cellar stairs. Behind old trunks I opened the box where I kept Medeo's drawings. Nothing, just some white confetti. The dirty rats, they ate everything." And she laughed and we joined her. Then, tired, she got up and went to the kitchen shaking her head. "Even the rats liked my beautiful Medeo."

One day she was gone. She didn't wait for her wages. She

came to us because she had promised. She just wanted to cook once more her bean soup and her spaghetti for one of her children.

KALEIDOSCOPE
AND CONFETTI

O F my student life in Paris, two motifs are crystal clear—hunger and ecstasy. Those were the lean years. They were inventive years, trying to hold body and soul together against the shortage of necessities and the missing of comforts, but mostly we had to be inventive. Not how to live—that was easy once you got used to it—but how to enjoy to the full the everyday surroundings.

How do you see a great ballet—a shattering experience—for free? (Befriend a sculptor, Greek, whose mistress, French, has a brother, French, who prints programs for the ballet and is on the free list.)

How could you be one of the lucky ones present at the opening of a long-awaited play? (Apply for a commission painting posters and end up hired to shout "Bravo" at the ripe moment.)

How do you read the celebrated new book without buying it? (Stand in front of the book stalls along Place de l'Odéon painting the square with the bookstore in foreground, attracting tourists, tourists buying books. The owner is pleased, and you are free to read the celebrated book at lunchtime.)

We managed. So life itself was never boring in Paris.

The lean years—the after-the-First-World-War period—were truly rich because of an infinite crowd of different and

Jean Cocteau—le monstre sacré

fascinating people and of pendulumlike events that still cross and recross my memory—a kaleidoscope of gifts:

Tango, Ballets Russes, the leaps of Nijinsky, the fame and unjust death of Modigliani, the excitement of Pascin, Sartre, Gide, Proust, Valéry, Cocteau (*le monstre sacré*), Josephine Baker, Coty the perfumer, Poiret the genius of fashion, Gandhi, Freud, Voronov, the metaphysical dummies of Giorgio di Chirico, psychoanalysis, psychogenesis and relativity, the songs of Damia, the Negro masks, Cubism and Surrealism, Brancusi, Dada, Mistinguett and Chevalier, the fight of Carpentier and Dempsey, Valentino and Boeuf sur le Toit, Kiki the Queen of Montparnasse and Foujita, and the flics of Paris, Soutine and Pirandello, Ubu Roi, Raymond Radiguet, and Max Jacob.

No, time was never boring in Paris, be it bad time or white-collar time.

Jean Cocteau decided to create for him and his friends their own "Bistro" in Paris, a refuge for artists, a meeting place for relaxation and cultural atmosphere. A young man, Louis Moise, found in the Madeleine district two empty stores at 28 Rue Boissy d'Anglais. The bistro was baptized by Cocteau Le Boeuf sur le Toit—The Bull on the Roof, the title of a Brazilian song popular at that time. The bar was spacious, with Surrealistic paintings by Picabia. Over a mahogany bar was a clutter of incongruous objects—glasses and bottles against mirrors, hanging Japanese balloons of shocking colors. There were comfortable tables, and squeezed in were two pianos back to back blasting music from Chopin to Gershwin.

The opening night was a crushing success, surpassing all expectations. That night Jean Cocteau renamed it Le Mauvais Lieu—The Bad Place, as the original intention of a quiet home for talent was lost totally to a wicked, noisy *boite*.

The owner Moise and the spiritual father Cocteau were surrounded by André Gide, Diaghilev, Picasso and his wife Olga, Mistinguett and Maurice Chevalier, Satie and René Clair, Paul Poiret and Tzara, Picabia, Radiguet, and Brancusi—all wearing white tie and tails, all drinking champagne till early dawn.

The Boeuf sur le Toit became overnight a power station of frivolity, where the snobs, the rich, princesses and pederasts, the ready and the easy, mingled in an artistic sewer with some of the giants of the time and with curious tourists looking lost and wondering.

On the right wall, Picabia hung an empty canvas on which he painted realistically the orb of an eye. Because at one time in his youth his own eye was treated with a medicine called cacodylate acid, he named the painting *L'Oeil Cacodylate—The Cacodylate Eye* (from the Greek *kakodes*—bad scent). He asked the bar's regulars to scribble something or just sign

LE BŒUF SUR LE TOIT
PAR DUFY

it. Within a few nights famous names surrounded *The Caco-dylate Eye.* I translate some of the scribbles:

"To write something is good. Not to is better!"   —Bran-cusi.

"I borrow from myself."   —Marie Laurencin.

"Everybody with his creed."   —René Clair.

"It's difficult to be a painter."   —Picasso.

"I've accomplished nothing. So, I sign."   —No signature.

"Isadora [Duncan] loves Picabia."   —Radiguet.

"I still hope to awake."   —Jean Hugo.

"I find myself very."   —Tristan Tzara.

"I love the salad."   —François Poulenc.

"I have nothing to say!"   —Georges Auric.

"My name is Dada since 1892."   —Darius Milhaud.

"Long live Agaga."   —Jean Cocteau.

The *L'Oeil Cacodylate* canvas covered with signatures and scribbles was the gossip novelty of the formal Salon d'Automne in 1921 and later accepted officially by an honorable museum of France.

The night I was finally able to see the famous bistro—invited of course—a national surprise waited for me. In a corner surrounded by his officers and dubious ladies covered with fake pearls, was my *king*, His Majesty King *Ferdinand of Rumania*, enjoying a night of freedom from his numerous children and a busy beautiful Queen. *"Le tout Paris"* seemed to be there, with sexual insolence, crowding, dancing, shouting, talking, and not listening. Most of the noisy action was around the bar, named in defiance The Nothing Doing Bar. Jean Cocteau in tuxedo and red tie, his dialogue as brilliant as fireworks, dominated his friends and admirers. Of course he was perched on the highest stool. Around him were Radiguet drunk, Satie in melon and velvet jacket with Tristan Tzara solemn and monocled, René Clair anxious and angelic, all listening to Cocteau's innuendos, proud of his sins and weaknesses. That night he was justifying Landru's crimes with an elegant, cunning approach.

"The ordinary *lover* when dismissed burns his memories of *her*—a lock of hair, her love letters, a glove she forgot late one afternoon, a few dried flowers. *Landru* was simpler: He burned the lady."

Radiguet fell off his chair laughing. Satie was not amused. René Clair and Tzara applauded noisily. Cocteau, elusive and unimpressed, holding his beautiful nervous hands as in a prayer, joined King Ferdinand's party and a pretty corseted officer from His Majesty's honor guard.

A refuge for artists? Not tonight.

Jean Hugo, a talented painter and a regular customer of Boeuf sur le Toit, called the place "The Crossroads of Destiny, The Cradle of Love, The Source of Incongruity, The Navel of Paris." It was considered a national institution from 1922 to 1927.

I loved the people of Paris, the gifts they gave me, the sights of an unusual rich time, the tragic or the savage or the gentle life—restless, uneasy, and productive.

Art was a whimsical imagination. Fame and pleasure and richness remained, as always, a wild temptation for young and old, for talented and phony, for kings and poor.

Women tattooed roses on their legs. Poiret dressed them. Painters and lovers undressed them. Landru burned them. This was the *jazz* time, with African influence.

Picasso could be ferocious or have the touch of an angel. A painting by Modigliani sold for 300 francs when he was alive, 6,000 francs after his death, 400,000 two years later. Léger painted machine cylinders, robots, functional and polished engines. The past and the present were joined together by mysterious whisperings.

I was among the selected ones. I was young and I was poor. I wasn't bored, and I drank because it was good to feel without obligations or ambition, but just to be alive, to love Paris, to be in Paris, to live in Paris, and maybe to be destroyed by her.

But, then, a postscript. All these marvels, this merriness and madness, went into the knapsack on the back of a young painter and were there when an aspiring moviemaker had to show his bag of tricks before the dream merchants of Hollywood and get the chance to entertain millions of people when pictures of the real and the imaginary worlds became a reality.

Paris lived with me after I went away.

J.N.: Sun worshiper.

THE RIVIERA

IN my memories, the Riviera is a world apart, a golden light that changed everything. Men growing young again, a glow of beauty in the women, and hopes and health and dreams were constant luminous companions.

Every winter from all corners of the world the Riviera attracted untold richness, the beauty and the luxurious power of the selected few. And they felt even more at home than when home, because the Riviera was also St. Petersburg and London and Berlin and New York and Bucharest. The fashionable, restricted life of elegance, flourished during the winter season in this magic place of light and imagination.

And then about this time it became fashionable to be on the Riviera in the summer. The greens of the Riviera in the summer sun blast with tropical fragrance, with the oranges

and lemons dots of crazy colors, the villas white and orange
and pink. The exclusive elegance changed to a different god—
the worship of *sun*. Excesses without limits: shorter and
shorter dresses; nudity past the navel; the skin a mahogany
parchment: sweating; extreme diets; loose morals and easy
conquests; *dancing* and *boites* at night.

But during the day everybody was roasting. The "whites"
wanted to lose their shame. Dark was the key to youth, health,
and sex. Burn your skin, sweat, suffer, but burn it. Be a part
of the Riviera crowd. Don't move. Don't turn. Cover yourself
with oil. Stay rigid, stiff, until the sun is gone. And it hurts.
But how well you'll look tonight in a white shirt.

Cannes was where the English aristocrats with their exclusive clubs, the dukes and the lords, the royalties and retired
presidents of small forgotten countries congregated, but especially Cannes was Le Prince de Gaule.

Nice was the Carnival, confetti and flowers, youth and
sunny dust; and long walks by the sea on the Promenade des
Anglais, the Casino accessible to smaller losers. There was

Cagnes-sur-Mer, 1923—my haven by the sea

rivalry between the two famous hotels—Negresco and Ruhl—and old, hopeless, overpainted ladies tried for their daily quota on the wheel. There were pimps and summer girls and Russians of all kinds.

Cagnes-sur-Mer was my haven by the sea. In a fisherman's cottage, for twenty francs fifty centimes a month I had two rooms—one to paint in, one for sleep—and three meals a day.

Cagnes—le vieux Cagnes—rose up a rock mountain surrounded by hundred-year-old olive trees, twisted, tormented, but still producing fruit in abundance, crowned by Château Grimaldi, and populated by a few dozen painters of all nations. In the corner of the Place Grimaldi was the house of Renoir.

I listened to stories in the village bistro from the older painters. In his last years, an invalid from advanced arthritis, crippled and bent, Renoir still kept his youthful inspiration. Infuriated by his sickness, he insisted on working every day.

Every morning he was carried in a stretcher-armchair to his small studio, which had glass openings in the four walls. The studio was hermetically closed; he couldn't stand a draft of fresh air. His models, nude, stretched out in the garden. The brush tied to his wrist by a metal strap, his eyes young and enchanted, he painted life seen through the windowpanes. Young nude bodies with generous buttocks, small heads, full breasts, healthy and pink skin, with inviting lips.

In 1923, because painters couldn't live from their work and dreams and because I owned a tuxedo, I applied and was engaged as a professional dancer at the Negresco. When people asked me if I was related to the Hotel Negresco—Negulesco—I defended myself with mystery: a relative one doesn't want to remember, a dark secret. As a gigolo-dancer I had a good time. I was paid fifty francs a night plus tips. A fortune, when one remembers that my rent and meals were only 20.50 francs a month.

(Around the same year, 1923, my illustrious confrère, the brilliant film director Billy Wilder, was enjoying the same hobby, a gigolo-dancer in one of the famous hotels in Berlin.)

Mostly we were supposed to dance with the young ladies of rich American families. But when the tango was played, we found that a mother was better business—with a possibility of larger tips from Father. You see, even if you have never

J.N.: *Dark secrets*

done the tango before, it is easy to follow. A professional partner can guide a mature lady into putting on for five minutes real elegance of movement. With the violins emotionally crying the insinuating South American tango, we fixed our double-breasted tuxedos, shot our cuffs twice with purposeful flicks: *"For the mothers, charge!"* An engaging smile, a bow, and an invitation, but the prize had not yet been won. Mother refused.

The daughters insisted. Still Mother showed no enthusiasm. But then Father, her matrimonial psychiatrist, would say something like this: "Go on, Marian. Think of the look on the faces of Pat and Violet and Liz when you get back to the Wednesday bridge game and you tell them of the night you danced the tango on the Riviera with a romantic stranger."

Of course, we danced with bodies distant and a polite smile. But after a turn or two, there was a twist and Mother was sent away, brought back in slow tempo, and held hard before attacking a new, more dangerous step. She was maneuvered to put on a good show while I remained just a little remote. (The maitre d' was watching.) When I brought my fair partner safely to the table, the daughters were applauding in some astonishment, Mother was embarrassingly grateful, and Dad was relieved. (This will take care of Mom for months!) Magnanimously, he would pass me under the table as much as a ten-dollar tip.

The rules of the professionals were very strict: no dates with the clients; same pleasant smile for every victim, as if you enjoyed the dance; left hand high, respectful distance, no insinuating undulations as you glided by; no enthusiastic cooperation with an ardent lady, no matter how obvious the approach, just a dignified acquiescence. And no drinks on your table until 11 P.M. You might accept an invitation to join the table of your partner—two-minute limit on parking and maybe a soft drink.

These two minutes were used hopefully to charm an extra tip. If no invitation ended the ordeal, a reserved bow, the same smile used for the esthetic light wrestling, and a return to join the other professionals at our reserved table, where most of the time was spent massaging poor, tortured crushed feet.

At one time, tips were seldom and meager. We complained to our maitre d'. "You boys have no imagination. If I only

could have your youth." He sighed. Then confidentially and fatherly: "You know the key to your locker, with the large metal knocker? Keep it in your pocket when you dance. The result should be rewarding." (Rewarding? It was an understatement. Especially during tango.)

"No dates with the clients" was a severely enforced rule. The hotel did not consent to any romantic complications between the professionals and the female clients. It was good pay. It could amount with tips to a hundred francs a night. But I was always mindful that for each dancer's job there were many eager amateurs on the side waiting to take the place of one who deviated from propriety.

We were five professionals—two Russians of dubious nobility, one Argentinian, one American, quiet and overwashed, and I, the Rumanian. We knew very little of each other's life, past or present. There was no desire or any curiosity to change this anonymity. Our credo—a job well done—to please the clients and produce no frowns from the maitre d'. After this last was accomplished every night, each professional went his way. To a wife? Mistress? Kids? A dream? Why not?

J.N.: Killer

A photograph of me at this period shows an impetuous and contented young man of offending self-confidence: the elegance of the day badly translated, pointed shoes and flashing tie, with matching pocket handkerchief. A classic pose of nonchalance, one hand in my coat pocket and the other holding a cigarette: a killer!

But one day I wavered from my well-enforced rule and dated a young American. I broke the sacred *rule*. So I lost my job.

When later, in 1960, I returned to the Riviera to film *Certain Smile*, the studio booked our suites at the Negresco while we were working in Villefranche. I reminded the manager of the hotel that in 1923 I was engaged by them as a gigolo-dancer. He smiled, with that superior Gallic smile, and with a twinkle in his eye replied, "It is pleasant to see, monsieur, that you have not changed. Twentieth Century–Fox is paying for your rooms. Thirty-seven years later you are still a gigolo."

THE MOST BEAUTIFUL MAN IN THE WORLD AND JUAN-LES-PINS

Rodolpho Alfonzo Rafaelo Pierre Filibert Guglielmi di Valentina d'Antonguolla

I N 1925, at Nice-St.-Augustine, Rex Ingram built and developed an excellent studio.

The Hollywood stars in all their glory replaced the omnipotence of all the other maharajahs.

The ex-kings, English lords, and the grand dukes took to playing fast and ferocious tennis with the champions of that time, Suzanne Lenglen and Jean Borotra.

The sports cars, mostly silver and white, were competing in elegance and carrying the goddesses of the sun. Their owners were bragging of the speed of their cars—unheard of: 100 kilometers per hour.

One sports car had long, smooth lines, a marvel of special design: a gray color that only the fashion peerage achieved in their clothes and ties; fine red leather upholstery and shimmering silver fittings. It belonged to Rudolph Valentino.

Wearing a leather coat with a matching beret—always in the company of a chauffeur in a gray uniform and, in the backseat, his secretary—he would drive his car with love and Latin passion. His publicity claimed him to be "the most beautiful man in the world," the hero of every woman's dream. The story was spread worldwide that the female Riviera crowd were hanging like sacrificial victims from the sides of his car, wanting to be carried away and destroyed by his iron charger, just to be near him, with him.

The Valentino legend was being made not by such publicity but by the camera. As the Arab prince in his film *The Sheik*, Valentino stripped to the waist and, galloping on his white charger across the sands of the golden desert against the sunset, set the flapper hearts palpitating all over the world.

In life, his features were common, beautiful but not uncommonly so. He was well built but no tall god, somewhat on the short side. One night on the floor of a *dancing* that was in vogue I came close to him. I was just a little taller than he was. I am 5 feet 9½. One of my small claims to fame.

That year I got married, and my young brother died in Nice. I made a portrait of Richard Le Gallienne. Isadora Duncan posed for a portrait and sketches while dancing on the beach. We moved to Juan-les-Pins, a small sleepy village between Cagnes and Cannes near the Bay of Antibes.

Juan-les-Pins had the only beach on the coast with sand. Very small but enough to make everybody feel that this place was his own discovery, a place to keep secret. The life in this village was different from the other places. Lights went out at 11 P.M. A small, badly equipped cinema was showing silent films three times a week. A local musician played the piano, suiting the music to the mood of the scenes. That is, if he didn't have that night more than his usual quota of Pernod. Then a fast march accompanied the tender love scene and sentimental music came during the cowboy-Indian chases.

On the beach, because it was so small and sheltered by the numerous pine trees, the bathing costumes grew briefer with

the heat, and one was so crowded that to turn meant to encounter almost every inch of his neighbor's anatomy. Of
course, I would choose to squeeze myself close to a beautiful
young bronzed female, and after a whole afternoon of twists
and pleasant bumps, I regretfully parted with satisfied thanks:
"If it's a boy, promise to call him Jean?"

In Juan-les-Pins, one mostly heard English spoken with an
American accent. But there was the unusual sight every noon
of a famous English politician in a one-piece striped bathing
suit facing the gentle Mediterranean waves—never taking off
his monocle. Perhaps he was pondering the famous history of
the bay, the Golfe Juan. It was here that in 1815 Napoleon,
the exiled emperor, landed on his return from Elba.

The famous pine trees, which gave the name to the town,
were spaced symmetrically. God was the best art director, even
in the golden age of Metro-Goldwyn-Mayer. Their silhouettes
stood proudly against the dark blue and green water, broken
by small white waves and agile white boats gliding under the
cobalt blue of the skies.

Three days in a row I painted them. The day I finished my
canvas, as I was packing the box and stool, a stocky man in
white sailor trousers and striped jersey stopped to look at the
painting. Annoyed, I hurried packing and turned away. He
remained there smiling: "May I see it, please?" "Why?" I
answered gruffly. He, still smiling: "I may like it." "You want
to buy it?" "Not yet . . . but I like paintings." I was still
annoyed. "Do you paint?" "A little."

That was different. I liked to impress a confrère. He looked
long and never lost his smile. Then said quietly, "Thank you."

As he turned to go, he stopped: "Would you like to see my
paintings?"

"I'm sorry. I can't," I answered quickly. "I'm busy preparing for my exhibition in New York—a big one."

Still smiling as he went away, he wished me "Good luck."

A few days later in a restaurant in Cannes, Rex Ingram
introduced me to him. "Jean, I want you to meet Picasso."

People who owned homes and gardens in this paradise very
seldom enjoyed them as much as travelers who rented them
for the season.

René Clair, the brilliant French film director, owned one of the most attractive villas on the Riviera overlooking the sea. He spent his summers there, but then Hollywood lured him away. With a fabulous contract, he had little time to spend in the South of France. One summer though, with a picture location in England, before he returned to Hollywood he took a week's vacation in his villa. A young French couple, Louis and Simone, were living there the year round, taking care of the house and garden.

This summer the Provence was more beautiful than ever. The variety of flowers, the colors and the scent, the lighting and the sky, were competing with the flight and song of the birds. So René Clair never enjoyed his place so much. It was a sad awakening when he realized that he had to return to Hollywood and finish his job. The day before he was to go, he went around the garden, followed by the young couple, telling them what he wanted them to do in his absence: a small wall here; plant some roses there; an extra step on this walk; replant this and fix that.

Louis the gardener was making notes. "Oui, Monsieur Clair. Oui, monsieur, it shall be done . . . as soon as possible." Only, with all this obedience, there was an ironic smile, a smug smile that couldn't be missed.

Finally, René Clair stopped. "What the hell are you smiling about? There is nothing funny in what I want you to do."

Louis looked at René, scratching his head. "You see, monsieur, I cannot help thinking. You go around and give me orders to do things for you. Like we are working for you. We are *not*. You, Monsieur Clair, are working for us. We live in this paradise all the year round, and you work for us to eat what we want, when we want. Then we get paid for living a rich life. And that is why I am smiling."

When he told me this story, René Clair commented, "He was right, the S.O.B. I finished the job I was doing, then I broke the contract. They were not too happy with my pictures anyway. And I came to live in my place on the Riviera, where I lived with Louis and Simone happily ever after. Why should they have all the fun in the paradise I had created for myself?"

MY BROTHER GEORGE

My brother George was a good boy. Not a shade of the selfish, egotistical adventurer I was and still am. He was a good boy. He listened to my father's ambitious plans. He enrolled in Paris to study economic and political science. Rumanian high schools did not prepare their youth to stand and compete against the complicated, brilliant French education. Ambitious and wanting to prove his quality to the family and to himself, he studied day and night. It was too late when I finally brought him to the Riviera.

It was past midnight when the hospital in Nice called me, to be with him for his last hour. He was asleep and almost gone. I waited. I made a few sketches of him and waited some more. He opened his eyes and I leaned to hear him.

"Iancule . . . I can't . . . I shouldn't die. . . . Somebody has to be back . . . to be the head . . ." It was his last worry.

That simple. I closed his eyes and ran out into the cold night. By the sea I sat on the pier and let myself sob. He did what my ambitious father wanted—and paid for it.

How long was it before I felt somebody close to me? A night girl was holding my shoulder. "*Ça va mon p'tit. Pas si mal que ça*—It's all right, my little one. It's not that bad." I told her my hate, the wrongs, the sacrifices. "Why didn't he listen to me?" She drew my shaking head against her bosom. "*Mon p'tit . . . mon p'tit.*"

Her silk blouse felt good and cool. Her overpowering cheap perfume brought back so clearly another time, another place, so many years ago. . . . I was four or maybe five. I could see that past moment. I could hear it. I could smell it.

Our bedroom—my brother's and mine—was close to my

parents' room. The door between was always open. I couldn't sleep at night. I was listening eagerly, trying to grasp all their news, though it was always the same. My family was an honest family, a rich family. Our house was a big house. At least it seemed that way to me, with gardens, courtyard, and a vacant lot behind. Next to us was an enormous empty building, a series of barracks, where our children's war games were held daily, phantoms of our fantasies. But this play stopped the day the barracks became a storage place for a factory making soap and candles.

In front of our home there stood a rich, splendid building. It was the house of a "bad woman," "a kept woman." A very rich man, whom I had never seen, kept her. From the talk of my parents, I gathered he was so rich that he could never spend his income of one day even if he wanted to. He lived somewhere out of town.

I couldn't understand why this lady could be so bad and the shame of the neighborhood. Her house was better than ours. Her servants better-dressed than ours. They had style. The horses of her carriage were livelier than ours. The woman herself dressed better than any lady I had seen. My mother was beautiful, but it seemed to me that this woman was more beautiful than my mother, or my sisters, who were all beauties. So this injustice made the "bad woman" more fascinating every time Mother had something new against her.

One night, Mother got us up from our sleep. She was crying. She hurried us into the courtyard. The stored candles and wax and soap in the old barracks were burning beyond control. Sirens, noise, shouts in the street. The sky was on fire. Angry flames exploded behind our house. The neighborhood was in danger and our home was the closest. Father, my sisters, and the servants were carrying furniture, rugs, paintings, silver, and clothes into the courtyard. My brother was crying and I— my spirit of curiosity led me into the street to watch. Everything around me—the black silhouettes of running people, the shouts of policemen and firemen, the crackling of the burning barracks, the pushing around—was all part of my hysterical nightmare.

I was cold and beside myself. I wanted to be back in our courtyard. I cried for my mother. The noise was louder than my screams, and I was swept away with the panic-stricken horde. I ran toward the iron gates of the "bad woman." She was watching from the balcony, surrounded by her staff. I started to scream and tried to open the heavy gates. A servant took me to her. I couldn't stop crying. I was ashamed of it. She took me in her arms and tried to calm my sobs. Her voice was soft, her skin softer, the velvet robe was smooth. The warmth of her body, her silky delicate arms, and her perfume! (I decided that this was going to be one of the hobbies of my life.) My hysteria miraculously disappeared. The noise and the danger faded away.

How long did heaven last? I was torn from her arms by my crying mother and hustled away in a hurry toward our home. "My poor child in the arms of that woman!"

"But she was nice . . . and smelled so good—"

Whap! My cheek was hot from the slap. Home, I got a good beating. Miserable in my bed, I cried myself to sleep. The only time I hated my wonderful mother.

I was brought back from my memories to Nice as the tide was slapping my shoes. It was early morning. The night girl was gone. And so was my wallet.

The cemetery of Nice is vast and anonymous. A white slab of marble is the sign of my brother: "Born 1902, died 1926." A poor carved statement to replace the justification of dreams, and devotion and ambition. My brother George was a good boy.

ISADORA DUNCAN

THE *last dance of Isadora.* Saint-Paul-de-Vence is situated on the road from Grasse to Var among orange trees and jasmine, like a long balcony, the two extremities being the village cemetery and the Place de la Colombe d'Or. Here in the Auberge de la Colombe I met Isadora Duncan. It was 1926; she was in her late forties. I have seen many pictures of her in her youth. Her brother, Raymond Duncan, had his studio and classes almost across the street from my studio in Rue de Seine in Paris. I passed the front of his studio every day; the place had a strange fascination. I always stopped and looked at the display in his windows—art books, paintings, photos, and colorful cloth woven by him and his pupils.

Isadora's photographs as a young girl were unbelievably beautiful: a slender body, a gracious long neck, slim and smiling. Her innocent looks hide the ferocious tenacity of a dedicated artiste. Her dance she called "The Renaissance of Classical Ancient Tragedy."

Twenty years later the divine Isadora was a fat slob. She was fat. She was foolish. Often she was embarrassing, sometimes diabolical, devilish, but never stupid. She had no sense of the ridiculous or any sense of values, never realizing the embarrassing situations that were her own doing. Her unconventional behavior and complete disregard for morality were as natural as life itself. Maybe she wanted to be like that. Maybe she wanted to offend, to shock the bourgeois crowd.

I was young. I was healthy. I was happy. She hated marriages. She was excessively nice to young men and bitchy to wives. This strong barefooted woman, half naked, with a tip-tilted nose and firm chin, talked a lot—about unimportant nonsense. With girlish giggles, hopping around with quivering squeaks, she talked on and on: rubbish—but often projecting profound greatness and power.

Isadora never saw what she didn't want to see. In my studio in Cagnes she posed for some drawings. She would change the pose to a grandiose gesture of a silent movie siren. And stretching her fat, shapelessly naked legs: "Sweetest, have you ever seen more beautiful legs in your life?"

She would always address men in terms of fulsome endearment: "You sweetest, loveliest, dearest painter, best . . ."

And forgetting her size, she would run on the beach in an orange bathing suit and a flowery Dutch cap.

Yet I adored her. She was the most fascinating raconteur, with a vivid imagination, inventing visual examples to make a point, a combination of rarely used words if she wanted to

tell you something, or to defend her theories or to attack what
was considered the art of dance, the ballet. Of course she was
passionately against classical ballet, the Diaghilev import to
Western Europe.

"It lacks an aim, the very spirit of the dance. It's acrobatic.
It's epileptic movements. It is deformity on pointed toes. One
remembers only the Nijinsky leap. Yet a panther jumps farther
and is more graceful. Turns, twists, and leaps—it is tasteless
and against all rules of harmony and all inspirations."

Despite her looks, she projected ecstasy and animation in
her speech. When she danced or talked about what she wanted
to present as a gift to those who were watching, then her smile
had a quality that I found only on the mask of *l'inconnue de
la Seine*—the unknown girl drowned in the Seine—the smile
of clear calm and ecstasy of peace.

It was in Nice-St.-Augustine that I saw the last dance of
Isadora. Her studio was an empty public garage that she had
rented for that occasion. The walls were covered in gray-blue
curtains draped from ceiling to floor, the same color of curtains that she had employed as the background for her dance
since she was a child of seven. This was, however, disputed by
her lover Gordon Craig in their first meeting: "You are marvelous, but why have you stolen my ideas, 'my' blue curtains?"

The people invited that night were Jean Cocteau, Richard
Le Gallienne, Marie Laurencin, Picasso, Marguerite Jamois,
Rex Ingram, Walter Shaw (a friend of Cocteau), my fiancée
Winifred, and I. On a platform a few steps higher than the
floor, all of us were seated on enormous, comfortable cushions
of the same color as the draperies.

Some twenty tall church candlesticks with heavy unlighted
candles were spaced around the walls and front (furnished by
Rex Ingram, courtesy of Metro-Goldwyn-Mayer).

The décor was majestic in its simplicity. It was in complete
darkness. A Bach sonata on a record player weighed heavily on
us. It was Isadora's way to embarrass us into silence with
heavy, almost funereal music. By the last note we were emotionally moved—quiet, relaxed.

Then on the waves of a new record Isadora appeared suddenly between two curtains holding a single lighted candle,
draped in a simple white classical toga, barefooted, hair free,
not moving, still. It looked as if she listened only to the music,

all alone, far away from us: music, the very essence of living; music, a longing to fly, untroubled, motionless. It was not even the beginning of a dance. She was there but not with us. She was there not to dance but to listen, to be still. She was like a stopped frame in a film, stopped in motion, not moving, just projecting. She moved. Or did she move? How long before she was in front of the first candlestick giving light? Her bare feet did not move; there was no moving of her toga; she was ahead of the music. You felt that in her motionless attitude—completely oblivious of her surroundings—she was trying to convey the very essence of music, and dance.

It's more than half a century since I saw this last dance, and I still cannot remember exactly or explain. It was never the same excitement that she expressed with each light she gave. The toga listened to her language and arranged its lines in perfect rhythm. The light in her face was never the same, her free hair seemed another light around her face. Was she following the music? Was the music following her? As my memories run—in and out of focus—the only possible comparison to Isadora's dance is the film in slow motion of a seagull's flight: stillness, line, rhythm.

And then the music ended and Isadora was gone.

To have been a part of this miracle . . . We couldn't talk, or move. How could one relate this experience to dance or theater or poetry or music? Our silence was the tribute.

The music started again, a Chopin mazurka. Isadora in a loose pink gauze half-tunic, her fat legs bare, with a white flower in her red hair, leaped barefooted around the bare stage—the *Primavera* of Botticelli. Only what was once perfection, slender sculpture in magical simplicity, was now a distorted, overdone exhibition of puffs and grunts, jerks and jumps. Her oversized breasts were hanging and dangling out of her loose costume, which soon became sweating rags.

We were quiet—not shocked, not embarrassed. Her grotesque nudity was unnoticed. We looked at and followed every leap and languorous swaying not as a dance but as a plastic tragedy. (It came to me suddenly what Duse told Isadora: "There is a moment in the life of a woman when she doesn't dress, she covers.") To my relief, the Chopin mazurka ended, and Isadora with a wild last leap froze unsteadily, her flabby arms stretched toward us.

All of a sudden she was gone. We continued looking at the bare stage, afraid to look at each other. It seemed a long, sinful silence. Then the voice of Jean Cocteau: *"Elle nous a donné la réponse. Isadora a tué la laideur*—She gave us the answer. Isadora killed ugliness."

Later that night some of us—Isadora, Cocteau, Rex Ingram, Walter Shaw, Winifred, and I—piled in the big sedan of Rex and drove to Marseilles to Chez Basso for a midnight bouillabaisse. The port was full of sailors, and so was the restaurant—young sailors. Cocteau and Walter were in heaven. We didn't finish ordering before Walter brought to the table a handsome blushing young sailor. An animated quarrel started between Isadora and Jean Cocteau as to who would get the tempting morsel.

Jean was ahead in points in the argument when Isadora started to moan like a child: "Sweetest Cocteau, you had the one last night. Let me have this one." And turning to us: "Make him realize how unfair he is."

In happy chorus we gave our pacifying verdict: "She is right. It's her turn." To which, sulkily, he agreed. "She can have him. But this is the last time."

Strange that two giants became two envious animals contending in bad temper over an embarrassing intimate problem.

During dinner and into the early morning the theory of and justification for homosexuality were declaimed and placed in

The divine Isadora twenty years later

proper perspective—according to them, and to the time, 1926.

Three days later, Isadora arrived by taxi from Marseilles at our place in Juan-les-Pins: "Just to nibble on a few grapes and champagne." She had kept the taxi for three days and owed 18,000 francs, more than the taxi was worth. In the garden, while she was picking grapes, we took some pictures. Stretched on the ground "Mother [Isadora] Earth" held an enormous pumpkin on her bosom. Fade out.

Her death in 1927 was a tragically perfect ending. A soaring long loose scarf caught in the speeding wheel of an open car ended the "Renaissance of Classical Ancient Tragedy."

Jean Cocteau concluded so rightly: "Isadora's end is perfect—a kind of horror that leaves one calm."

ON TO HOLLYWOOD

PARIS was the City of Freedom in the twenties. By the thirties, Hollywood had become the World Capital of Dreams.

My life was twice saved by the cinema. This happened before I had even thought that one day the cinema would give me a chance—and a rich living.

One afternoon in Bucharest, I was with three friends in the Cafe Capsha. Grigore Petrino, one of the richest playboys in our town of Craiova, owned a magnificent Mercedes sports sedan that had a special body and a supercharged motor. We were all four intending to return that evening to Craiova. We planned to drive home together. I left them to pick up my suitcase from the house of my brother-in-law. On my way, I passed the local film theater. A new picture was announced: Dolores Del Rio in *What Price Glory*. I reserved a seat and turned back to tell my friends that I was not joining them. They kidded me about my dubious explanation for staying overnight in the city.

That night a train hit their car. They were carrying an extra tank of gasoline. The car ·exploded. All three were burned to ashes. A tragedy. Yet, for me, a film saved my life.

Years later in Paris another sign of destiny: a bad-luck period. I was sick and broke. The doctor at the city hospital, after analysis and X rays, concluded that I had a touch of tuberculosis in my left lung. Prescription: "Go south. Live in the sun. Eat well and rest."

Desperate, I sent to the Salon d'Automne a painting of a nude. Rex Ingram, famous M-G-M director, saw it there and bought it. Dear God, *three thousand francs*. Again the cinema saved me.

I paid my debts, bought new clothes, oil colors, canvases, pens and paper in abundance, and a tuxedo for crazy luxury. Still rich, I traveled south to sun and health. I lived almost nude in the sun, swam and ate, and achieved a complete recovery. Then, Negresco and my marriage.

Even if Dolores Del Rio and Rex Ingram had not in turn been the agents of fate's kindly intervention to save my life, two years later, in America, film had become an affair of the heart. Alone in the flickering darkness of the cinema theaters in New York and Washington, D.C., I laughed, suffered, and shared the lives of my heroes. I reverently held the hand of Mary Pickford's innocence. I performed and accomplished in precise mastery the skips, jumps, and leaps of Douglas Fairbanks. I held communion with the light and heavy acting of the Gishes and the Barrymores, the delicious smile of Laura La Plante, the nice naughtiness of the Bow named Clara. I held my breath all through the close-ups of Marlene Dietrich and Greta Garbo and decided that beauty had achieved its limit—but, say it again, Garbo. It did not matter, come to think of it, that there was always a man or two in each picture with these goddesses. They were mere stock figures standing in for *me*, the fervent lover in Row 23.

For over a year we lived in Greenwich Village at 3 Washington Square North. I painted furiously New York's skyscrapers; we built a shack in the Catskill Mountains; I bought my first car, a Maxwell. My English improved but the accent remained. Lindbergh crossed the ocean, and my marriage collapsed. Winifred left home for Europe, and I moved to Washington.

Flattered by friends from the Rumanian Legation, I opened a school to teach children and people who had never painted before what I knew about *art*. My teaching theory was an ancient one: "Talent is the result of work."

"But I cannot draw a straight line" was the usual confession of my prospective pupil. "Great, you are perfect for my school," I answered. I was helped by a clever publicity gimmick: "*No pay* for the first three months; but pay for them if you wish to continue." I did not lose a pupil.

An exhibition of my work gained me the sponsorship and the friendship of Duncan Phillips, a king among rare art collectors. A portrait of the Chilean Ambassadress, Doña Herminia Arrate di Davila, almost convinced me and the critics that all my fight for understanding the unusual in Paris was not in vain.

When the legal time period for marital separation ended, I filed for divorce, closed the school, and left in my car to cross America—to see and paint the country of Indians and cowboys, and to go to Hollywood.

True, the magnetism of Hollywood also meant money. In the depression years, Hollywood still had money. To me, Hollywood was bread and butter and wine, not to mention dreams and promises of ecstasy. Those the studio publicity and my imagination furnished in abundance.

The Western Association Museums invited one foreign and one American painter each year to exhibit their work in the West Coast museums. That year I was the chosen foreigner and Rockwell Kent the American.

I went to Hollywood as a Royal Rumanian Painter. Queen Marie of Rumania had posed for me.

Unattached, foreign accent, good dancer (remember the Hotel Negresco), and most important, no competition for the rich jobs of the film people I met—all these attributes, which I employed with a dash of calculation, made me an instant social success and a most desirable "single man" for Hollywood parties.

I met stars and romanced hopeful starlets. Tired executives and busy producers asked me to escort their wives and mistresses to openings and glamorous parties. They lived to regret it. I became the woman's confidant and often her revenge. Everybody was misunderstood. Everyone was lonely.

Greta Garbo posed for me, and other signs of favor came from the film crowd. I got a few commissions to paint children. "The Portrait of a Child" is the most unfair and unappreciated side of portrait painting. Though the child doesn't care how he looks, I had to please the mother, father, grandmother, grandfather, aunts, sisters—all great *critics*. The hardest to please was the nurse: "Why, *my* child does not look like that!" One day, exasperated, I made the unforgivable remark, "All children when born look like cross-eyed constipated lobsters." From that period, I have a great collection of unaccepted portraits.

"What, four hundred dollars for two small portraits of my little children?" a famous Hollywood director complained. He was paid $7,500 weekly, before taxes.

I was tired, I was bored. Painting in Hollywood was not amusing. And again, for the third time, the cinema came to my rescue. Elie Faure, the great French critic, philosopher, and historian of the arts, was a passionate fan of the cinema. On his way to deliver lectures in San Francisco and Japan, he came to Hollywood.

Because of my fluent French and my experience of Paris art life, I was asked by the ladies of the Hollywood Art League to be Monsieur Faure's companion and interpreter. Monsieur Faure was a little Frenchman with white hair, pointed Vandyke, hard collar, and black suit.

The Welcome to Hollywood lunch was a total disaster. On the huge terrace of the Bel Air Estate of the President's Art League, Monsieur Faure was introduced to American cuisine: a generous cup of grapefruit slices covered in rich gooey mayonnaise with a cherry on top, cold cuts and potato salad, and rich chocolate mousse. And vin rosé. The little Frenchman almost had a fit. "*Mais, ils sont des barbares*—But they are barbarians."

That night I took him to a drive-in for Southern fried chicken with french fries, and a bottle of California wine. He was delighted.

"When I come to Hollywood I want to meet stars, see the making of a picture, talk to professionals."

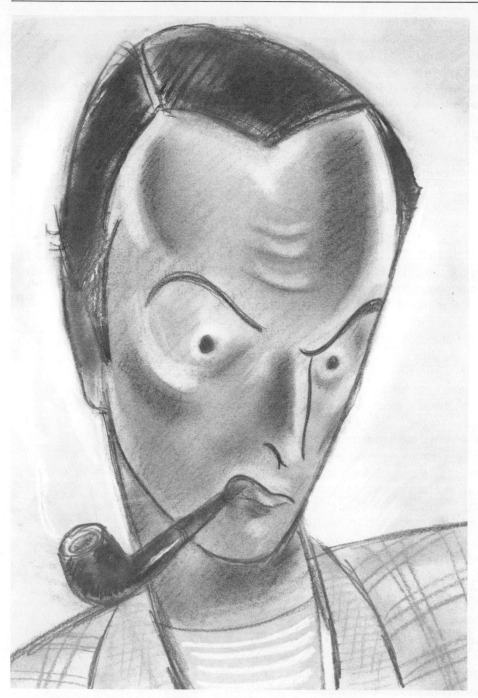

J.N. by J.N.

My friend Laura La Plante got us two tickets for the opening of Chaplin's *City Lights*. Faure met many of the cinema people I knew, had supper with Laura and her friends, visited studios, sets, and talked with producers, directors, and cameramen—the pros.

The old man was like a child—happy, content. Every night we saw a new film—a gift and a luxury. And afterwards he talked for hours about the cinema, the enchantment of film.

Somewhere on Sunset Boulevard one night, he asked a direct question: "And you, Jean, what do you do? In the cinema?"

"I am a painter," I said.

"A painter?" He looked long at me and then changed the subject of conversation. I was hurt. I had read the many great articles he had written about painters, especially Soutine. He had discovered and made famous many artists. So this dismissing of my work, my career, was baffling and rude for a Frenchman.

In front of his hotel, he gave a surprising explanation: "Ordinarily, I would ask to see your work—as a critic and as a friend. I do not wish to do that. I do not want to know how considerable your talent may be. Genius? Possibly. But I say to you *now*, after this time here in Hollywood, stop painting. Quit it. This is a great new art, the *cinema*, where all forms of art are assembled—the art of our time. Put your brushes aside. You may want to pick them up some time, but for now, you have your foot in the door of the magic place. Go through the door and use all your creative powers to work your way into the making of the movies—right here, where the vast apparatus of creation exists. I like you, and I hope you will remember an old man's dream."

I wanted to hear this, and to hear this from a man I respected. Oh, yes, I had been ready for a long time to change my dream.

My friends, the big executives and stars, when they learned of my new determination tried to discourage me. "Why would you give up a successful career you know something about and start to fight this fucking racket. To wait and get kicked and have to 'yes' and kiss asses for a lousy check every Friday? Is that what you want?"

My friends did not know, but that was exactly what I

wanted—to fight and wait and get kicked around. Not for a
Friday check, but for a dream, a dream I shared with an old
Frenchman who had made his mark in the arts and who com-
manded my love and respect. And who had put this dream
into words as he walked with me one night in 1931 down Sunset Boulevard.

THIS IS THE TIME

Iᴛ is one thing to say, "I quit painting," but a Pegasus of
another color to declare, "I'm going to make films."
My first qualification for filmmaking was that I loved
films—hungrily, with no reserve, passionately—and I loved
filmmaking, not only for the enjoyment of the finished product, but in all its phases, from the conception of an idea to
the film in the theaters.

I had to wait for something, something in which they
needed me. They needed my talent. They needed what I
could offer.

First I earned the luxury to wait. My painting exhibitions
with the Western Association Museums were profitable. I
pocketed a nice tidy sum and set out to keep that door open
into Hollywood film society.

Lady Mountbatten was the guest of William Randolph
Hearst and Marion Davies. Marion's nephew, Charlie Lederer,
a writer of note and one of the great humorists of the industry,
arranged for me to make a portrait of Lady M. at Marion
Davies' house in Santa Monica. And so overnight I became
a member of this exclusive crowd, the Hearst crowd. The sessions went smoothly; I made two drawings and a few detailed
sketches.

During the posing, Lady M. expressed with gentle humor how amazed she was to see all over the beach house great paintings by Franz Hals, Velasquez, Goya, El Greco, and other giants piled on the floor against the walls, while the places of honor were covered with bigger-than-life standing portraits of Marion in each of her past films. "And with live orchid plants growing at the base of every portrait. It is a little too much, no?"

An understatement, to say the least.

The second day I was asked to stay for dinner. After my drawing session, Charlie lent me a pair of shorts and I joined the beautiful crowd around the giant marble swimming pool with a "Venetian" bridge across it. (Venetian? Cross my heart and hope to die!) Finally Mr. Hearst in a one-piece black bathing suit appeared and asked in his high-pitched voice, "Would anyone care to join me for a swim in the sea?"

Nobody would leave the comfort, the drinks, the flirtations. Enthusiastically I offered my company. I felt excited to bathe with the *great man*. I was a good swimmer. I dived in and started to swim away. The great man, encouraged by my boldness, entered the waves with self-assurance. Great man he was, but swimmer he wasn't. A little playful Santa Monica wave caught him off balance, twisted and turned him around. He came up a coughing, a spitting mess of arms and hair and legs and sand. I helped him out and we returned to the luxury of the swimming pool. My awe of the great man was definitely shaken. A small Santa Monica wave focused the values in their rightful place.

The dinner was *regal*. As I remember, there was a serving person behind each chair. Plates were changed with the correct speed. Glasses were filled regularly and often. I was seated at the end of the table across from Charlie Lederer but close to people I didn't know. I was self-conscious about my poor English. The few attempts I made met with questioning looks and impatient shoulders raised. ("I have to talk. I have to tell them a story. I have to impress this exclusive gathering. I have to be a success.") These and other decisions crossed my already hazy mind. And I kept on drinking.

Lady Mountbatten was kind enough to shout a few French questions, but my answers passed unnoticed by the noisy crowd. We were in the middle of the dinner when Mr. Hearst appeared through a small door in the wall carrying his special bottle of wine. For a few moments the gathering was quieter. When the great man saw me, he raised his glass. "Ah, my Rumanian friend, who saved me from drowning this afternoon." The whole table turned to me. ("This is my chance. Don't lose it.") I plunged in. (By then my English was still wobbly.)

"It is not difficult. You feel with no force in the water. No legs. You are afraid. Last Sunday at Catalina Island I am in a boat with friends. Six o'clock next morning, everybody is asleep. But I am all up. The ocean is big. Quiet like a mirror. So I jump in. When I came up from the ocean, I was vis-à-vis in front of a beautiful black wet seal."

Only I didn't know at that time how to say "seal." I imagined it must be similar to the French *phoque*. So my speech went like this: "I was vis-à-vis in front of a beautiful black wet *phoque*." I don't know how I pronounced the word *phoque*, but apparently, adding my Rumanian accent to the French word, *phoque* sounded like "fuck." There was an embarrassing "ah!" from the ladies.

Charlie shouted, "What did you see when you came up from your dive, Johnny?" This gave me courage. My story was good and appreciated.

"The most beautiful black wet fuck!" I shouted back.

Everybody started to talk fast at the same time. Lady M. was busy explaining to the puzzled Mr. Hearst my story. And people ignored me. Only after dinner Charlie explained the mistake I had made. "You were good, Johnny. Once in a while they need a little explosion." I was embarrassed and ashamed and left unnoticed soon after dinner.

Lady M. went back to England the next day, and I never had a chance to give her the drawings and thank her for the gracious help she gave to a baffled young Rumanian.

My social life had a definite setback. The story about "Negulesco's *phoque*" went the rounds with various degrees of ridicule and laughter.

This is the time. If the social ladder was not the way to climb to a place in the film studios, there was another way. And that was more to my liking anyhow. I would demonstrate to the movie community how an artist would make a film. I had the arrogance and courage of youth—also a little money that I dared to risk. No time to wait.

I went to work. I wrote a script. Why not? A story is a story. The way you tell it, that's it. Tell it differently. I called it *Three and a Day*, a day in the life of three people. Let's see, a painter (naturally), a ballet dancer (of course), and a young farmer (for good measure). So? What happens? Well, so much could happen. A whole life in one single day.

My cast was readily found: Mischa Auer, the artist. He was gaunt and hungry. The girl, Katya Sergava, the dancer, was beautiful and Russian. The farmer, John Rox, was a well-built athlete. I convinced a talented Yugoslav cameraman, Paul Ivano, to photograph the masterpiece. I bought film—fourteen reels.

The first day of shooting went something like this:

"So, where do we start?" Paul asked.

"Well, a long shot of the room."

"Good. From where?"

"Anywhere. It has to be long and high."

"O.K." So Paul fixed his camera high on a parallel. The girl Katya comes into the studio dancing happily around and stops by the windowsill.

"Now, Paul, I want the same thing close. We put the camera here."

"You can't."

"Why not?"

"It's the wrong angle. In the long shot she moves from right to left. If you put the camera here, in the close shot she moves from left to right."

"Paul," I said quietly, "in the long shot she comes from the door to the window. In the close shot she walks from the door to the window."

"Not if you put the camera here."

"Paul, you make no sense. This is Hollywood's old-fashioned idea."

Paul gave up. "O.K. It's your money."

"Paul, I want Katya to move more to the left, her face against the sun. It's beautiful."

Paul spoke again. "You can't."

"And why not *this* time?"

"You can't shoot directly into the sun."

"Who says so?"

"The lenses won't take it."

"Then change lenses."

"You'll have light spots and moving circles and jittering crosses."

"Look, Paul, you see her against the sun. O.K.? She is against the sun. O.K.? I want her photographed against the sun. O.K.?"

A long look from Paul—defiance, sorrow, hopelessness— his problem.

I added quietly, "You see, Paul, you have lived and listened too long to rules and Hollywood regulations. The cinema is free. Don't pay any attention to what has been done before. Why can't we find our own way? (I didn't realize that then and there I was expounding and defining today's religion of the new generation of filmmakers.)

"Will you do it my way, Paul?"

And Paul shot the film the way I wanted. And the actors acted the way I wanted them to act. And fourteen rolls of printed film filled my studio. I engaged an out-of-work cutter, Joe.

"This is different, Joe. It may show Hollywood how to make pictures. Good luck."

And on this note of complete accomplishment I left that night for a three-day holiday on a boat with friends.

Back on Monday, suntanned and full of anticipation, I found a note next to the fourteen reels. And no Joe.

"Jean: You said it right, buddy. It is different. Nothing matches. Sorry. Joe   P.S. A friend's advice: Burn the fucking mess."

I tried to cut it myself. And with every mistake, with every shot that didn't match, I bled and it hurt. Not my pride, but my pocket. All my savings were gone.

A year later the negative was disposed of, for nonpayment of storage.

A lesson never to be forgotten: Listen to the *pros*. They want the project to be good and *you* get the credit.

PARAMOUNT

Someone did listen—at Paramount. Something good resulted from my disaster. Mischa Auer, the actor in *Three and a Day*, took me to a party given by director Frank Tuttle, who was doing a musical for Paramount Pictures.

Frank, who had heard the gory details of my solo venture from Mischa Auer, asked me, "Would you be interested to sketch the opening of *Tonight We Sing?*" (Interested? Grateful and jumping with joy.)

He explained: "The opening is Paris. Show Paris differently—no usual stock shots, no Eiffel Tower, no Arc de Triomphe. The opening song is 'Madame Has Lost Her Dress.' Promising?"

I started working. First shot: enormous close-up of a Paris cop blowing his whistle. The whistle started the opening song. With every musical phrase, the angle was farther away—a medium shot, a long shot, a very long shot—the streets of Paris. Every new shot—one leaning to the right, next leaning left. Musically the image danced on the screen.

And all my memories of Paris crowded the screen: the dirty-postcard vendor, the midinette with her hatbox, croissants and brioches, the outdoor cafes, waiters counting plates in rhythm with the music, the rug vendor, busy painters, fried potatoes with sharp sea salt, cheeses, fruits, vegetables, lovely legs and delicious smiles—all moving, all images dancing in time with the music.

Frank Tuttle was delighted with my sketches. He took me to meet Benjamin Glazer, the producer. I was engaged on the spot. Seventy-five dollars a week! (Every week? Oh, yes, every week.) I was part of a project in a big studio. Every morning I was early on the set, stumbling over electric cables, asking questions which made no sense. But I was on the floor with *stars* and writers, director, cameraman, and operators, the sound man, the boom man, the prop man, the grips, the extras. I went to lunch with them. I listened to their wonderful talk. *I was one of them.*

Frank Tuttle showed the cameraman (Victor Miller) my sketches. He liked them and said, "If at any time you want to suggest a new angle for the camera, don't hesitate." (That was all I needed.) They rehearsed the next shot: a long shot. Then medium shots, over the shoulder, individual close-ups— twelve setups, one day's shooting.

Timidly I suggested to Victor that this scene cried for a one-shot treatment. "How?" Victor asked impatiently.

"If we put the camera on the boom. Close shot on the door. Lilly Damita walks in. The boom with the camera moves back with her. We discover the elegant entrance hall. The maid picks up her fur. Butler in the background. Lilly gives orders. Camera follows her up the stairway. She meets secretary and exchanges short dialogue. Camera follows her to bedroom door. All in one shot. Harder to light, but—"

Victor smiled. "Let's give it a try."

Next evening the rushes were different, exciting.

A few days later I was called to see the general production manager. "My name is Sam Jaffe. I was in New York last week. I saw all the rushes I missed from all companies. Frank Tuttle's rushes are different. He takes chances. They told me you're responsible for camera angles. Is this good?"

"For a musical, yes. One accepts more freedom, more chances." We became friends. And I got a seven-year contract as an assistant to Barney Glazer. Starting with $75 a week and going up to $350 a week. (Could I spend that much money every week? I did, and more.)

So from then on I could go along every day having a part in making movies. My contributions were complicated by my erratic English with shades of French and Rumanian. Roland Young, the Englishman who played an important part in the picture, giggled politely under his thin mustache at one of my stories.

"Roland, are you making fun of my English?"

"My dear Jean, I am not. But you are."

In those days I saw another career that was in jeopardy because of this fiendish problem of language. The young romantic actor in the film was a good-looking Cockney Englishman, formerly a circus performer who worked on stilts. He was cast in his first film. His name, Cary Grant. After two weeks of shooting, the front office decided to replace him. His Cockney accent was too obvious, and the public would laugh. But thanks to the producer, Barney Glazer, who argued with the front office that girls around the world would forget his accent and sigh longingly at his romantic looks, Cary was kept in the film. The rest is history. And incidentally, he lost his accent very quickly.

TECHNICAL ADVISER ON RAPE

Tonight *We Sing* was a solid success—artistic and box-office. It started a new trend in musicals. The cockeyed angle of camera setups and cutting in time with the music were copied, but very much overdone.

The management seemed to feel that I had special talents, out of the ordinary. At least that was what I concluded when I was given my next assignment. The problem was *Sanctuary* from the book by William Faulkner. It was released under the title *The Story of Temple Drake*, with the sexiest star in films then, Miriam Hopkins. She was beautiful. All men were in love with her.

The problem was how to design a rape scene so that it would pass the censors. On the daily call sheet I saw my name:

"J.N. technical adviser on the rape scene." (Had they discovered my past at the Negresco?)

I made drawings and I supervised the shooting of the rape. Electricians, grips, and the rest of the crew were watching with exaggerated interest. The set was dark: a broken barn; cobs of dried corn covered the floor. I was showing Miriam the positions she should take for the rape scene. A big tough electrician mumbled behind me, loud enough for everybody to hear, "This better be good. Rape with a foreign touch."

The crew laughed. I smiled, embarrassed. Miriam, the beautiful Southern lady, didn't help.

"Jean, are my legs opened at the right angle? Shouldn't my dress be up higher? Do I scream? And are my eyes opened in terror of what I see? Or do I close my eyes and let things happen? Jean, do I enjoy it?"

With that, the laughter exploded all around. I must have blushed. But then, still embarrassed, I joined in the laughter. Miriam felt bad about her teasing questions. She put her arms around me and kissed me fiercely on the mouth. The boys yelled, applauded, and Miriam and I were friends. The scene was shot with all the pictorial cuts as close to my drawings as the censors would let me get away with.

Miriam

Sanctuary gave me the much needed boost in picture-making. Miriam and I became friends for life.

One Sunday afternoon Miriam sent a friend of hers, Ben Wasson, over with a writer she wanted me to meet. "Jean, this is Bill." That was all Ben said, and he left us. Bill was a quiet man, private and taciturn—in fact, so quiet he did not say one word. He just sipped his bourbon contentedly and continually. Thank God the telephone rang often, so I didn't have to make too much effort to entertain him. He picked up a book from the bookcase and was at peace in a corner. I offered to show him the little garden outside my house and his eyes lighted as he saw the Ping-Pong table. Finally a language we both spoke.

For three hours we played Ping-Pong and started the second bottle of bourbon. We raided the icebox, and Bill started to talk. Soft-spoken, he talked about his place in the South, his brakeless OX-5 airplane in which he barnstormed around country cotton gins, about hunting game, farming, riding on the hills and in the woods. Everything he said was interesting and profoundly exciting. I was spellbound, and suddenly I realized that the "Bill" with whom I had spent these hours was William Faulkner.

We spoke about *Sanctuary*. I showed him the drawings of the rape scene. He was like a child at the miracle of the cinema seeing the characters he had created brought to life.

A few more days at the studio, a few more long sessions of Ping-Pong, a few bottles of bourbon sipped in gentlemanly fashion, and Bill went back to his place, Oxford, Mississippi. I sent him a bound copy of the script, and I received this note, which I cherish:

Dear Jean:

   The folio of *Temple Drake* arrived. I am pleased and proud, not only to have it as bibliography, but that its format was planned by one who knows what a book should look like physically: that there is a balance to a book just as there is to a fugue. I won't mention the trouble and time it must have taken to get the material together, because the volume as it stands and regardless of who owns it, is worth it. To me of course its greatest value is the concrete evidence of the venturing of anything as private and nebulous (and perhaps even esoteric) as a writer's created

characters into a dimension which he did
not anticipate and cannot himself
reproduce.

We will take up the table tennis
when I come out again. About
all I do here for pleasure is
ride a horse, though there
will be bird shooting soon,
and the manager of the
river bottom place
claims to have a black
bear hid out for us.

Bill

Oxford, Miss.
7 Oct. 1934

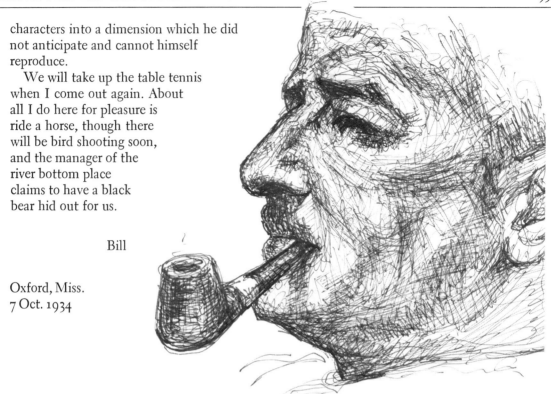

Bill and I kept in touch through the years. Bill Faulkner
was proud to be a writer. Yet, like F. Scott Fitzgerald and
Aldous Huxley, Bill was not a success in Hollywood. He could
work only for director Howard Hawks. They liked to be together. Howard liked the way Bill talked—economically—the
way he was thinking. They liked to talk about flying.

"Howard Hawks is a great director," someone would tell
Faulkner.

"He's just an old broken-down flier," Bill would drawl out.

In 1947 at Warner we signed William Faulkner to write
some added dialogue for a picture I was making, *Deep Valley*.
We never used any of his lines. They were good lines, maybe
too good. But they didn't belong to our story.

In 1949, in Stockholm, Bill Faulkner accepted the Nobel
Prize in Literature.

I'm proud to have known Bill Faulkner.

HEMINGWAY'S CAPORETTO
AND MINE

SOMETIMES the most memorable scenes of a picture are the
work of the director of the second unit. People outside
the film industry often seem to believe that the second unit
is something like the second team in sports. There is no second team in the making of a movie. Everyone involved is first
string.

The director is working with the stars, getting the desired
dramatic or comic performance out of them. But when the
setting of their action has to be, say, the sinking of a ship,
the burning of a building, a great crowd running or fighting,
or a vast cattle drive, the second unit takes on the job. And
its director has to use all kinds of ingenuity and artistic and
managerial skill to produce the desired effect, as in *Ben-Hur*,
Titanic, and *Red River*. So often the whole distinction of a
picture may be in the hands of that little group of real movie
professionals, the second unit.

At last I got my chance to direct the second unit in Hemingway's *Farewell to Arms*, starring Helen Hayes and Gary
Cooper. The scene was the retreat at Caporetto. I decided
this was going to be *monumental*, not just soldiers and refugees marching and running through rain and mud. I would
create *the symbol of a retreat*, a catastrophe that would keep
on growing so that it could not be stopped.

The rain will loosen one small pebble on the peak of a
mountain. It rolls, dislocating other stones, bigger and bigger,
faster and faster, breaking trees, fences, cabins—an *avalanche*.
And I will intercut these shots with the soldiers marching, the
peasants, the children, the carriages, horses, carts, the horri-
fied mob.

Symbols were at a premium in those times. I made sketches, and it looked good on paper. The special-effects department created an avalanche in miniature, and using slow-motion cameras they obtained extraordinary results. I reread the book and studied the chapter on the·retreat in every detail. I found the Negulesco touch! When the army evacuated the townspeople of Caporetto in trucks, they also evacuated the girls from the whorehouse. I could see the shot. In one of the army trucks crowded with old women, frightened children, and sick people there would be six whores, overpainted, in garish clothes, cheap furs, and black stockings—a definite and colorful contrast with the townsfolk, a gaudy sight.

I called the production office. Ralph, the unit manager on our picture, was a kind man. Only he was convinced that every director is half crazy, and if the director is a foreigner, then "Just don't argue—humor him."

"Ralph, for tonight's shooting I want six whores in a truck."

There was a long silence. "Ralph, did you hear me?"

"Yes, I heard you. You'll have 'em."

We were shooting at the Paramount ranch, all night, with 500 extras, wind and rain effects, four cameras, three assistants—the *works*. I felt important and I was dressed accordingly: camel coat, turtleneck sweater, velvet hat, leather boots, and a cane to lean on.

I was met by Ralph. "We have a problem. You may help me."

"I will, Ralph, but first where are my whores?"

"That *is* the problem, Johnny." I followed him to an open truck. A big crane was lifting a horse into the truck in which two other horses were already standing indifferently. "See, Johnny, we can put in a truck no more than three horses, not six."

"I didn't say horses. I said whores. *Whores*. W-h-o-r-e-s. Bad women, women of the streets."

That night was the only time I ever saw Ralph laugh. With the well-known efficiency of the studio, six girls were picked out from among the extras and dressed and made up to look like the whores I wanted. I got the shot I imagined. They got a good extra bonus. But I also decided I should pay more attention to my English.

I worked for two weeks every night, happily, artistically.

Every shot, I thought, was a gem. When the picture was finished, Frank Borzage, the director, went to Metro-Goldwyn-Mayer to do another film. So he was not on hand to decide what use to make of my work. A few days later I saw what Otto Lowering, the cutter, did to my "Retreat at Caporetto." It was butchered, cut to pieces, reduced to a few uninteresting dull shots.

I complained to the producer, Barney Glazer. "All the money we spent. My two weeks of shooting. The great exciting shots I had. There is nothing left. Almost nothing."

Reluctantly, but trying to humor me, Barney Glazer ordered a new print of the film I shot and let me cut it my own way. What I didn't realize then was that I was overstepping somebody else's job.

One afternoon Otto Lowering asked me to come in the big projection room. The film was ready and the projection room was filled with our crew, some actors, and some people from the production department. Before the showing of the film, Otto made a speech:

"In our jobs there comes a time when we are forced to invent and improve. Sometimes we have to borrow film from other pictures to polish and refine the film we have. What you are going to see is what I think is an improvement on material already shot. I hope you'll like it."

The lights went out. An empty screen. Over the sound system boomed the loud voice of Kate Smith: "When the moon comes over the mountain." On the word "mountain" there came on the screen my first shot of the mountain peak as the pebble started the avalanche. Now the song was mixed with thunder and earthquake noise. When the avalanche became menacing, there was a first shot of Cooper walking through rain and mud. He looked back:

Clara Bow ran to the gate of a white fence calling happily, "Bye, lover."

Cooper kept walking.

Second shot of Clara Bow closer: "Bye, lover."

Cooper looked back, turned away, walked.

The avalanche was now impressive.

Jack Oakie, a comedian, was in jail holding on to the bars: "Let me out of here. I'm innocent."

The avalanche was still coming, impressive, still bigger.

Cooper helped a crying child to climb into a truck.

There was a shot of Sylvia Sidney in tears, frantic: "Your honor, I want my baibee, give me back my baibee."

The avalanche and Kate Smith's song were now louder, more menacing.

Big close-up of Cooper wiping the rain from his face.

Then a quick-cut montage of avalanche, Jack Oakie in jail, Cooper marching, Clara Bow, Sylvia Sidney, faster and faster cuts, closer and closer. Over those mad swirling shots a male chorus intoned majestically, "Happy days are here again." Then silence.

An enormous close-up of Charles Laughton looking straight into the camera and giving a long and loud raspberry.

The lights went up. Everyone was in hysterics with laughter. Loud applause. Nobody looked at me. I got up and went out in tears.

When I told Barney Glazer about the humiliating experience I had that afternoon and my decision to quit the business—"It's too hard to take"—he let me ramble for a while.

"You should have laughed louder, applauded wilder, and thanked Otto for showing you how good your film is. You should have congratulated him on his rich imagination. You have to have a sense of humor about yourself if you want to survive in this racket." Barney Glazer's advice stuck with me.

My experience as Barney Glazer's assistant was connected with the making of films from the conception of an idea to the finished job of the final print.

A glorified messenger connecting the producer with all other departments—director, writer, cutter, production manager, music, publicity—I worked with all of them, offering my ideas (for which Barney took credit, of course).

Barney decided after looking at the finished picture of the Hemingway story that an important scene with Cooper and Helen Hayes should be retaken. Frank Borzage having gone off on his new assignment to M-G-M, Barney talked to me about the scene. He felt the scene did not have enough emotional impact.

"Do you think you could direct the scene?" Barney asked me.

"Of course I can," I answered quickly.

"All right. Here is the new scene we will shoot."

I was so excited, that when I first read the scene it made no sense. But at home, quietly, I read it and studied and read it again and again. Then I got frightened. How do I start this scene? Where do I put the camera? This was not just pictorial shots. This was a scene with *stars*. I couldn't sleep.

Next day I asked the cameraman to have lunch with me and I confessed my fears.

"This is the first time I direct stars. What if somebody asks me a question and I don't know the answer?"

"Johnny, do you smoke?"

"Not often."

"Do you smoke a pipe?"

"No."

"Buy one and smoke it. And when somebody asks you a question you'll be busy lighting your pipe, cleaning it, filling it with new tobacco, puffing in and out and spitting. Be so busy that by the time you're through they have their own answer. They are pros. You pick up the angle and I'll help to break it."

It worked. Saved by a pipe.

THE HIGH AND MIGHTY VON

I felt that I was ready to direct a full-length film—with or without a pipe. From the front office Barney Glazer secured for me a story I liked, *The Man Who Broke His Heart*—a poetical story about Christ on a fishermen's wharf. I was looking for a new face, a new young actor to play Jesus. This search led me into close contact with the great director Josef von Sternberg.

My admiration for him had no bounds. It was the way he

photographed his films that impressed me most, and the mood he created in some of his work suited *The Man Who Broke His Heart.*

Von Sternberg was considered a genius in the motion picture industry in the late 1930s. His credits answered for his fame. He discovered and made a superstar of Marlene Dietrich. Somebody suggested that I should look at his rushes of *Catherine the Great* with Dietrich and a young newcomer, John Lodge.

But before I looked at the daily rushes I read his script. I was flabbergasted. The dialogue in his script had no punctuation, no stops, no capitals.

I read an interview that he had given: "Actors are puppets in the hands of a director. Actors don't know when and where to pause. What intonation and meaning to give to a line. What and why they say what they say . . . I *will tell them.*"

At 8 A.M. I went to the theater projection room to see Joe von Sternberg's rushes. There, laboratory people and the sound and camera departments were checking all rushes of all companies for technical errors, an everyday job.

Von Sternberg's rushes consisted of only one scene: Marlene Dietrich, Catherine, walking from the courtyard of the palace to the entrance hall. Dressed in a riding habit of black velvet, with boots, hat with appropriate veil, a whip, she was out of breath. As the camera panned with her to the ornate marble staircase, we discover Alexei—John Lodge. "Your Imperial Majesty," he pleaded.

Josef von Sternberg

Catherine stopped on the third step without turning. "Tonight," she whispered. Then slowly she turned and looked at her lover, brought the whip in front of her face, moved it to the right, to the left. And she repeated, "Tonight. I will see you tonight." She turned and ran up the steps.

Simple scene, beautifully photographed. But, my God! It was shot and printed forty-eight times. I couldn't see any difference between the takes. "Your Imperial Majesty" . . . "Tonight." . . . Whip right, whip left. . . . "I will see you tonight." Exactly the same thing. Were there any small nuances? Nothing.

After the twentieth take, the boys gave up.

That night I had dinner with a writer, Mercedes d'Acosta, a friend of Marlene Dietrich's. During the evening's conver-

Marlene

sation I told her how baffled I was to see the same scene—same lighting, same gestures—forty-eight times. Next morning my desk was covered with messages: "Come immediately to Stage 4." "Mr. von Sternberg called. See him immediately." "As soon as you come in come to Stage 4." I rushed to Stage 4 and there was my erstwhile idol. He wore a big white camel coat with matching belt tied around, a white cap of the same material. He was leaning on his cane.

"You saw my yesterday's rushes?"

"Yes, Mr. von Sternberg."

"Who gave you permission to see *my* rushes?"

"Nobody. I just saw them with the technical crew."

"Why?"

"I'm looking for a new face for my picture *The Man Who Broke His Heart*. And John Lodge—"

"I'm not interested in your stupid problem. What did you see in my rushes?"

"Oh, I liked them all right, but—"

"But what?"

"I was puzzled by the repetition of the same scene forty-eight times."

"And you didn't see any difference?"

"Frankly, no, sir."

A small silence. He looked at me with disdain. "Because you, despicable jerk, don't know anything about film. You and the whole studio. The whole industry. I piss on all of you, clumsy ignorants. And if I ever hear that you, obnoxious shrimp, see my rushes without my permission, or talk about my rushes, I'll break your neck and have you thrown out of every studio. Now get out, you moronic joke."

I looked at him, at this high and mighty bombastic and insulting braggart, leaning on his cane. I suddenly had the wonderful impulse to push his cane with my foot and punch him with my left.

Instead, I turned from him and left the stage.

With *Catherine the Great* over budget and over schedule, Joe von Sternberg's career went on the skids.

The picture was a total loss for the studio, in spite of the remarkable sets and the superb photography.

Von Sternberg lost his contract with Paramount, and other studios were reluctant to employ him: too risky, too expensive. I was burning for revenge. If only one day I could humiliate him like he humiliated me.

Ten years later, Joe von Sternberg was almost forgotten. I was in luck. Nominated for an Oscar with *Johnny Belinda*, I was riding high. At a Screen Directors Guild dinner, six directors were seated together: Lewis Milestone, Willy Wyler, Billy Wilder, Henry Hathaway, John Huston, and I. The food was good. I went for seconds. When I came back Joe von Sternberg was sitting in my place. "Joe, that's Jean's place," said Wyler. Joe looked at me, jumped up embarrassed, and apologized. "I'm sorry. I didn't know." "That's all right, Joe," I said, pushing him back into the chair. "Stay where you are. I'll draw an extra chair."

He stayed and was happy to be with his fellow directors. And I was satisfied and finally revenged.

THE MASTER

ERNST Lubitsch was unique among moviemakers. At the start of a Lubitsch picture, the first image that came on the screen was his name. His *name* was the *star*. It meant to the theater patrons that they could lose themselves in a story told with fascination, humor, taste, and flights of inspiration—"The Lubitsch Touch."

His pictures were a new academy for me, just as they were

Ernst Lubitsch—the master who taught Hollywood the continental touch

for the established directors in Hollywood from the time he came there in 1923. His pictures taught that human passions could be played upon without tearing up the bedsheets or getting out the axe, that many a previously untouchable situation could be presented in a way that was unmistakably risqué yet still tasteful. He lent sophistication to the movies—hardly surprising, considering what he himself was like.

One day my quite inflated confidence made me honestly believe that I could give the best and most amusing dinner of the year in my modest home in Brentwood. My guests were the West Coast chapter of the Algonquin Round Table: Dorothy Parker, Robert Benchley, Irwin Cobb, Donald Ogden Stewart, Deems Taylor, Anita Loos.

Morry, my Japanese cook, outdid himself—the best he knew from his old world. The wines were chosen carefully. The selection of records balanced so as not to interfere with the sparkling conversation.

Yet somehow things went wrong. Not one new brilliant remark was uttered. There were no colorful insults to remember, no compliments to the chef, no growing laughter. A gloom, an indigestible, self-conscious silence, spread over the coffee and brandy.

Then Ernst Lubitsch arrived. He had had a business meeting and could not make dinner. He looked around at all the solemn faces with his piercing black shoe-button eyes and said, "In September of last year I was in Vienna." He sat back and waited. A conviction spread among his listeners that something wonderful was in store for all of us. By the time he had finished a small but perfectly told droll story, the party was a success. Everyone put in a bid in turn to tell a story as well done as the master's.

That was the Lubitsch touch.

All his lively qualities found expression in his love for women. Any man who loved women as much as he did had, of course, women complications. Like a sailor, he had an official mistress in every port.

One evening, arriving from Universal, where I was doing a second-unit job, I found numerous messages by my telephone: "Call Mr. Lubitsch the moment you come in . . . urgent . . . very, very important."

"Ernst, what's wrong?"

"My mistress from New York arrives. And my Viennese mistress here means murder. You have to come to dinner, make love to the New York mistress."

"What time?"

"Eight-thirty."

"I'll be there at eight."

The prospect of a new adventure at that time was music to my ego. In women, Ernst and I had the same taste. The New York mistress and I hit it off like a charm. Ernst must have given me a great buildup.

At our dinner at the Beverly Wilshire Hotel, I was so immersed in doing my duty that Lubitsch and his Hollywood girlfriend faded into the background. His New York girl's legs and my own were like German pretzels under the table.

Suddenly I felt a kick under the table from the direction of Lubitsch. Surprised, I looked at him. He leaned over and whispered, "Not so much!"

My love for him was surpassed only by my admiration for his genius. He could make a more erotic suggestion with a shot of a bedroom doorknob closing than today's generation can do with two nudes twisted around each other.

He showed us in one picture of his how to economically show the transition of time. A young man (Henry Fonda), happy that he is to have a date with his girl, bursts into his small bathroom to shave. We look in the mirror—a young, happy, smooth face. His hand opens the door to the medicine cabinet. We see his shaving brush, straight razor, toothbrush, and one lonely bottle of castor oil. Like a miracle, the cabinet fills with all kinds of medicines in boxes and bottles of different colors—an electric razor, sleeping pills, vitamins, tranquilizers, an abundance of hopeful help. The hand closes the door. In the mirror we see the same face, but old, tired, wrinkled.

Fifty years told in a few seconds.

He represented for his American-born friends that very special quality that is flippantly called "the foreign approach." It was a rich quality, a humble one, making fun of himself, bringing you up to his level of merriment, sharing with you— and only you—his joke, his laugh, his happiness.

His kindness to me, a young director with no assignment, was generous and soothing. "Why don't 'they' see at Para-

mount the potential you have? You could already outdirect
many of the directors there!"

So when one day I read in the *Hollywood Reporter* that
Lubitsch had been made the head of Paramount, I hurried to
the studio. His office in the directors' building was two doors
from mine. I rushed in, waited my turn among the crowd of
well-wishers, and put my arms around him.

"Congratulations, Mr. President. A pity that now just to
love you is not enough, I have to respect you."

A wink from him was "all" that I needed to know. I waited.
And waited.

Three months later my option came up for renewal. The
legal department dropped me automatically. Ernst never had
time to even consider my case. He too found out about his
own dismissal from the studio barber while receiving his
morning shave.

A story was told in the papers after Lubitsch's funeral.
Willy Wyler and Billy Wilder were walking together in
silence toward their parked cars. Finally Willy said, "Pity. No
more Lubitsch."

"Worse," Billy said. "No more Lubitsch pictures."

WILD BILL

IN 1936 Paramount was ready for bankruptcy. Something
was fundamentally wrong. So the New York people sent a
young genius, a business expert, to make changes and avoid
disaster. Armed with unlimited official power, he arrived at
the studio and presented his credentials to Barney Balaban,
at that time the head of the studio.

Top: *The Giants of 1918. From the left:*
Al Jolson, Mary Pickford, Ronald Colman,
Gloria Swanson, Douglas Fairbanks,
Joseph M. Schenck, Charles Chaplin,
Samuel Goldwyn, Eddie Cantor

Bottom: *Paramount 1934. Among the*
crowd: Cary Grant, Maurice Chevalier,
Randolph Scott, Wesley Ruggles, Norman
MacLeod, Charles Laughton, Bill Frawley,
Richard Arlen, Josef von Sternberg, W. C.
Fields, Carole Lombard, J.N.

"Why so much money spent every week? Why pictures made that do not bring in even the cost? The contracts, the organization of departments—cut the waste. Change the policy."

Balaban gave him carte blanche. So the young man cut on labor. He combined departments—art, property, and special effects all under one man, and with half the employees. He took advantage of the lay-off clause in all of the studio contracts. Anyone who didn't have a present working assignment was suspended or put on lay-off for the three legal months. Half the employees were dismissed. Studio expenses were cut in half.

At such moments in Hollywood, those dreaded periods of retrenchment, no one's job seemed safe. Yet even a young economic genius comes to discover that there are some persons in every studio who outrank him.

At Paramount, such a man was one director whose pictures always made money: William Wellman—Wild Bill.

From his first picture to his last he never missed bringing in the profit. This gave him a certain standing at headquarters. The young expert must not have acquired this information before leaving the New York office.

When the young man visited the Wellman office, he found Wild Bill, hat over his eyes and his feet on the desk, shooting craps with two famous writers.

After he introduced himself, the young man asked Bill about his assignment.

"Don't you see, sir, that I and my writers are working on the new script?"

"Mr. Wellman, please do not insult my intelligence. You and your writers are shooting craps. So with the power invested in me by the New York office and Mr. Balaban, all three of you are suspended as of today."

The three players never stopped rolling the dice during this momentous declaration. But Bill spoke: "Sir, would you tell Mr. Balaban to shit in his hat. And you, sir, go and fuck a duck. And please close the door gently from outside."

The New York young man, furious, rushed to Balaban's office: "There's a guy in the directors' building. He and his writers were gambling. And when I fired them, he said to tell you to shit in your hat and he said to me to fuck a duck."

"What's his name?"

"Bill Wellman."

Balaban was sad and thoughtful. "Bill Wellman? Well . . ."

After pondering, Balaban quietly said, "I have a hat. Can you find a duck?"

Such are the realities of success in Hollywood.

MY FIRST TEN THOUSAND DOLLARS

IN 1936 I lost my Paramount job. I was unemployed. Like everyone in the same position, I felt that I had been short-changed. The planning of an exciting future stopped abruptly, clumsily. My business manager—a luxury that beginners insist on having in Hollywood—was not on my side. There was not much of a cushion after three years of work and income. There were moments ahead of despair and embarrassment.

My sponsor at Paramount, Sam Jaffe, also lost his job. And this was a much bigger tragedy than mine. Ironically more so, since his brother-in-law, B. P. Schulberg, was that year the new head of Paramount Pictures.

With his sister, Add Schulberg—separated from B.P. because of his infatuation with Sylvia Sidney—Sam created the Schulberg-Jaffe Agency, which eventually ran the careers of Humphrey Bogart, David Niven, Fredric March, Lauren Bacall, Ginger Rogers, Barbara Stanwyck, Lee Cobb, Vittorio Gassman, and other stars.

I became a part of Jaffe's agency. I had to try somehow to get back into the industry. Avidly, I scanned every newspaper, looking for possible ideas for a picture story. A fascinating article about a colorful gambler in South America became after three months of hard writing the inspiration for a screenplay outline. That was how *Rio* was born. I presented my work to my agent Sam Jaffe.

Joe Pasternak, the Hungarian producer of most of Deanna Durbin's films at Universal, had a commitment with Charles Boyer and Danielle Darrieux, the couple of *Mayerling* fame. *Rio* was acquired as a vehicle for these exciting actors. Ten thousand dollars! Good God, I'd never had $10,000 all at once in my life. So when Sam presented me with a $9,000 check (10 percent to the agency), he also had more news for me. "Johnny, I've arranged for you to work at five hundred dollars a week to collaborate with the writer. You're back in business."

"But, Sam, I have nine thousand dollars. I want to do what I want," I said.

"Like what?" he snapped.

"I want to go to Mexico," I said.

"What for?" he said.

"To paint. I've never been in Mexico. I always wanted to work there," I said.

Sam lost his patience. "Johnny, it's hard to get your foot back in the studio. You're in, and you're back to work."

"But Sam, I don't need to work. I have nine thousand dollars."

"So what? This is peanuts compared to what you'll be able to make if you're successful. They want you now."

"If they do, they'll take me when I'll be back in three months from Mexico."

"Don't you believe it. There are a thousand men waiting to get a chance at your place—and good men, too."

"Sure, but I have nine thousand dollars. And they don't."

Irritated, Sam ended the argument. "Let's have lunch. I'll try to put some sense into your stubborn Rumanian head."

"Love to. If you pay. I've not cashed my check yet."

So we had lunch: and Sam talked—convincingly—about the chances you get in Hollywood. You have *one* chance. They have no time to give you another. They're too busy, too tired.

I listened, but I also talked and argued for my side. How many years I had dreamed of going to Mexico to work, and now I could. I wouldn't let the chance go by, perhaps never to return.

Mildred Jaffe

Sam was right and justified in insisting, after so many years as a professional. Hard to fight, and yet . . .

Next morning at the Los Angeles Airport, Sam, his wife Mildred, and I were on our way to Mexico City. He had seen things *my* way.

Thus started three of the best months of my life: a special model on every corner, singing colors, mañana, and siesta. I was drunk with excitement, and my suitcases started to fill with drawings, Aztec statuettes, pre-Columbian heads, scarves, and sandals. Mildred and Sam, like me, were hungry to see everything. We filled ourselves with memories. We laughed together and loved everything together. We were sick together with *turistas*.

One night after a hot peppery dinner our stomachs groaned in despair. At the first pharmacy we found, I described in poor Spanish our misery. The dark, hairy Mexican pharmacist shook his head. Blank. I tried my Rumanian combined with noisy Italian. Blank. Sam tried his English and German.

Blank. We left the pharmacy in hopeless pain. At the door
Sam stopped. "Let me try something."

He turned and explained our problem in Hebrew. Suddenly
the pharmacist and Sam were conversing noisily and in happy
accord. And that is how we got our stomachs relieved. Moses
took precedence over Montezuma.

Another time we were drifting through the canals of Xochi-
milco. Barges full of roses were crisscrossing the waters. Butter-
flies of every size and color filled the air. White clouds against
the deep blue skies confirmed a perfect paradise.

Sam was sprawled on his back on the bottom of the boat, a smile of ecstasy on his face.

"What are you thinking, Sam?" I interrupted his reverie.

"My clients, working for me," Sam said. "And your crazy dream." And Sam went back to his ecstatic contentment.

We returned home to Hollywood three months later. Sam sold another original story for me, and another. And I was rich with 600 drawings I had made in Mexico.

Sam and Mildred too had a crazy dream. A watercolor by Diego Rivera they bought in Mexico started in them a new passion for collecting Impressionists. And the collection eventually became world famous.

All in all, Mexico had a great finale.

THE WARNER BROTHERS WAITING FOR A UNANIMOUS "YES"

THEY talk about climbing the ladder to success. But my impression of a career in Hollywood is that you fall your way upstairs. You wonder all the time what it will be like to get to the top. You should have guessed it. When you get to the top they put you on the shelf.

Quite a stretch of the falling-upward process for me occurred on the notoriously spasmodic moving stairs of the Warner Brothers studio. The man who put the fits and starts into the studio was Jack Leonard Warner. But naturally he got some help from his brother Harry in the New York headquarters. They were great moviemakers. You had to be close to them to know how incredible they were.

Let me start with an introductory paragraph on the Great Man J.L. One day a young stage director was arguing with Jack Warner on the merits of his assignment, a play he had brilliantly directed in New York. They discussed the proposed cast, the allowed budget, and the length of the shooting schedule. The arguments were loud and convincing. Finally Jack walked to the window looking out on the studio's parking lot and asked the young director, "Hey, kid, will you show me your car?"

"That one"—the director pointed at his new car—"the open blue Chevrolet by the exit."

J.L. put his arm around the director's shoulder. "Do you see that big black shiny Cadillac parked just in front of the entrance?—bigger than all the others?" Jack pointed right under the window.

"Yes," mumbled the young man.

"That's mine." Jack turned and walked to his mahogany desk.

"So?"

"So, *I'm* right and *you're* wrong." And the boss closed the argument.

In 1940, Jack Warner came up with a practical idea. The Warner Brothers studio owned a number of unproduced properties—books, original stories, scenarios, proposed remakes of pictures previously made.

"If any writer or short film director can make a film from any of these properties or do a remake of an unsuccessful released picture, and keep the budget at or under four hundred thousand dollars, I will give them a chance to make it."

I always loved and felt there was a great mystery film in Dashiell Hammett's *Maltese Falcon*. I saw the two pictures Warners had already made of the book: one in 1931 with Bebe Daniels and Ricardo Cortez, the other in 1936 with Bette Davis and Warren William, called *Satan Met a Lady*. Both were unsuccessful box-office flops. My explanation about the failures was simple. In both cases they changed the book, tried to lick the story, as Hollywood is often determined to do. So, under the supervision of Gordon Hollingshead, producer of short subjects and my immediate boss, I got the go-ahead from Jack Warner for the remake.

For four hopeful months I worked out, day and night, a shooting script, "the book." But in the meantime, I was sent East to make an Army short, *Women at War*. When weeks later I returned to the studio, Gordon informed me that J. L. Warner had taken the *Maltese Falcon* property away from us: "John Huston will write and direct the film; Henry Blanke will produce it." By this time I was used to Hollywood tactics—shocks and disappointments. Indeed John Huston made a classic masterpiece of *The Maltese Falcon* with Humphrey Bogart, Sydney Greenstreet, Peter Lorre, and Mary Astor, and I was still looking for *the* story and my chance at a feature film.

A year later, in Thelma Todd's Restaurant, Anatole Litvak gave a dinner for John, on the eve of his leaving to join the U.S. Army Signal Corps.

During the evening, after good food and drinks, John came to me. "Johnny, today I found out that you had worked for

months on *The Maltese Falcon* before J.L. gave it to me. I'm
sorry, but no mention was ever made of you or that you had
been assigned to do a job on it."

"Forget it, John. You were working longer at the studio.
Besides he was right giving it to you."

The usual short dramatic pause from John. Then narrowing
his eyes, he said quietly, "I tell you what, kid. Tonight I'll
make you a present. There is a book the studio owns, as good
as the *Falcon* if not better, *A Coffin for Dimitrios*, by Eric
Ambler. You ask for it. Take it to Henry Blanke. Just do the
book page by page."

John went to war, and in 1944 made *The Battle of San
Pietro*, a stark page of American history. He left with me the
knowledge that here was a man loyal to his friends—and with
a present of great price. I read the *Dimitrios* book, loved it,
wrote a long anxious letter to Jack Warner, and I got this
answer:

Dear Jean:

Thanks for your memo on *Coffin for Dimitrios*. It is very premature to start thinking about this story. However, I am going to
keep you in mind for it. I do not say you will direct it, for I do not
want anyone to get the impression that I have made a promise,
as words are easy to forget, but I will keep you in mind for the
future.

J. L.

That year—another Hollywood habit—I changed agents.
Frank Orsatti, a powerful influence in the industry (because
of his close relation to Louis B. Mayer, the M-G-M mogul),
was now guiding my destiny in films. He used the Las Vegas
Mafia approach: He got an appointment with Jack Warner
and slapped on his desk $10,000 in hundred-dollar bills.

"What's this?" J.L. was astonished.

"A bet."

"For what?"

"That if my client Jean Negulesco makes *Coffin for Dimitrios* this year he'll get the Oscar."

"That's crazy, Frank. First, I have not yet assigned him the
property, and second he's in New York working."

"I know. But if you don't, he's not returning to the studio."

"He has a contract."

"Not if he doesn't get the book." Frank pushed the stack of bills toward J.L. "What can you lose? Is it a bet?"

J.L. pushed back the money. "I don't make bets in my studio."

Relieved, Frank pocketed the money. "O.K., but remember, Jack, no *Coffin* and Jean stays home."

On my return from the East there was an official note from Jack Warner on my desk. My next assignment was A *Coffin for Dimitrios.*

Thank you, John Huston! Thank you, Frank Orsatti!

Mask of Dimitrios. *Listening to the pros. From the left: J.N., Peter Lorre, Zachary Scott, Sydney Greenstreet*

With Sydney Greenstreet, Peter Lorre, and Victor Francen—the dependable regulars—the film was made under budget and brought to the limelight a young stage actor, Zachary
Scott, as Dimitrios. It was an artistic and box-office success,
and my first break into feature films.

Four years later in London I met Eric Ambler, the writer
of the book—a frail, soft-spoken man, with white skin and
light complexion, not touched by wind or sun, like a character
from one of his brilliant books. I was grateful that Eric liked
what was done with his child. I was presented with an autographed copy of *A Coffin for Dimitrios*. The inscription read:

London, November 1948

My dear Negulesco:

You may be surprised to hear from one who signs himself
Dimitrios Mackropoulos. My friend, do not worry. I did not die.
I am not a ghost flittering out from the back streets of your mind.
Let me ask you a question.

Do you really think Dimitrios would go in person to deal with
a deadbeat like Peterson? Do you? My dear friend, I have
watched your career with so much friendly interest. At one moment I was alarmed· at the possibilities inherent in your treatment of my earlier career. I confess it. I am sensitive especially
about my notorious reputation. I made confidential inquiries
about you in Italy of a simpleton named Huston. I considered
ruining Warner Brothers. Then, your film *all* was *well*. There was
nothing compromising. It represented a side of my character
which has been described by many of my former business associates as my most lovable, my most sympathetic aspect. I saw the
film in a brothel in Istanbul. I go again to Istanbul next week.
There are plenty of pickings still. Join me there if you have a
mind. Your friend and associate. Baron Dimitrios M. (P.S.) I will
give you an Armenian girl you will really "like"!   D.

At the Warner studios, Harry Kurnitz, humorist and writer,
was among the selected ones to have luncheon in the executive dining room. The chef made great efforts for successful
gourmet dishes. I tried to be seated next to Harry, to savor
his soft mumblings and to be close to the door, as far away
as possible from the boss—the two bosses.

Here is a picture of one of those lunches with the Brothers
Warner, Jack and Harry, in good form, discussing politics,

national and international, the state of the picture market, and last success and last failure. What rumors were coming from New York? How would these affect the home office on the Coast? They were regular chatterboxes. And pointing a finger at us listeners, if we agreed or not: "Don't you think so, Bob . . . Harry . . . Bill . . . Jean?" It was less trouble just to say a noncommittal yes.

Mark Hellinger, one of the better producers at the studio, must have had a hard night. Big dark glasses were hiding his blurry eyes. The food lay there in front of him untouched. A cold, fizzing glass of soda water was his only understanding companion that noontime.

One of Hollywood's tycoons, powerful and very much disliked, had died that week. So his life and work came up for praise and appreciative analysis by Harry Warner: "A man of integrity and vision, a friend in need, generous and helpful, an example to all of us, a great loss to the industry." He turned directly to Mark Hellinger. "You worked for him, Mark. Didn't you find him an inspiring leader?"

We all looked at Mark. He swallowed the last of his soda, got up, and turned to Harry Warner. "He was without doubt the most obnoxious son of a bitch—cruel and moronic, a stupid bastard. Good riddance." And Mark left. (That afternoon Mark Hellinger left Warner and joined Universal studios.)

"What's the matter with him?" Jack found his voice.

"Just too much drinking," Harry commented.

"Like Errol Flynn," Jack said.

"What's wrong with Errol now?"

"He wants us to pay his last year's taxes. And he always waits until the middle of the picture. Last picture was his mortgage."

"Fire him, Jack!" Harry banged the table.

"I told you, he's in the middle of the picture. He refuses to continue. He pretends the worries affect his performance. I guess we'll have to pay."

"It's our own fault." Harry looked around at us. "We made the jerk. He was nothing, an English extra. We put him in *Captain Blood*. We made him. We can break him. We gave him the chance. Spent a fortune on him. Made him a star. We can pick any of you and make a star the same way overnight." Harry looked around and pointed his finger at Robert Buckner—a good writer, producer, and a gentle, good-looking man. "What's your name?"

Bob's attention was on his pea soup. Harry Kurnitz nudged him. "What?" Bob turned a faraway look on Harry Warner.

"Your name—what's your name?" Harry Warner boomed, still pointing his finger.

"Me?"

"Yes, you. What's your name?"

"Bob."

"Bob what?"

"Robert Buckner."

"Like the general?"

"My grandfather."

"Simon Bolivar Buckner, your grandfather? Better and better. We can take you, spend money in publicizing you, make you a star. And if you act like Errol, a son of a bitch, we can break you and send you back where you came from." He banged the table again to make his meaning clear.

"Yes, sir." Bob went back to his pea soup, finished it, and suddenly had to leave. One by one around the executive table the lunchers found that they were busy—an appointment they had forgotten, an important meeting, time to get on the set—and suddenly only Harry Kurnitz and I were left to listen to the Brothers Warner and feebly give them our agreement. (Why had I ordered a complicated gourmet dish—with thyme, yet?) Harry Kurnitz finished his chef's salad and got ready to leave.

"Harry, please don't leave me. I can't take it alone," I whispered pleadingly.

"I have to, Johnny," he whispered back, getting up. "I've run out of loyal yeses."

I was alone. I smiled, resigned. (Oh, God, I thought, the things I had to do for the Brothers Warner!)

Salvador Dali was brought to California by Jack Warner to do a portrait of Jack's wife, Anne. There was a party for Dali at Jack's house, to meet the crème de la crème of Hollywood. I was having a drink at the bar with Salvador Dali. Three beauties were seated together on a small settee—Merle Oberon, Virginia Bruce, and Dolores Del Rio—one more appetizing than the other. I pointed them out to Salvador, a delicious lucky combination.

"They must have excellent kidneys," Dali concluded wisely—logical, but so anatomical.

Jack invited Dali to have lunch in the executive dining room at the studio. He ordered ham and eggs. I went into the kitchen and prepared a surrealistic plate: a piece of raw liver, half hanging outside the plate, the other half held up by toothpicks, a raw egg, and my wristwatch wrapped around the perfect roundness of the egg. When served, Dali was delighted.

Jack was furious. "It's in bad taste, Johnny. I don't like to embarrass my guest."

Harry Kurnitz ventured, "Jack, it's Mr. Dali's favorite still-life subject."

And Salvador came to help the situation as the waiter removed the plate: "What a way to serve a watch."

Hollywood was a completely different way of thinking, a fresh and valuable experience. Words like "magic" and "genius" and "miracle" were used easily, never leaving a mark on your day.

Here I discovered that "conceit" was mistaken for "confidence," "work" for "opportunity," "knowledge" for "charming ability," and "sex" for "love." "Friendship" was replaced with "usefulness," "help" for "compensation," and "enthusiastic youth" for "bearded arrogance."

After *Coffin for Dimitrios*, retitled *Mask of Dimitrios*, was released, Hal Wallis, one of Hollywood's better producers, chose me to do a film called *The Conspirators*, a story in the vein of *Casablanca*; and in addition it had the glamour of Hedy Lamarr.

Trouble began for the film—in what would seem for anyone who did not know just how strange Hollywood's ways could be peculiarly. That year Hal Wallis' work got most of the Oscars—with *Casablanca* and *Dark Victory*—which would seem to indicate how fortunate I was to have Wallis as my producer on *Conspirators*.

During the festivities of Oscar night, the repeated calling of the name of Hal Wallis aroused long applause and laughter.

This was regarded as a covert slap at Jack Warner. Wallis was fired the next day.

He was replaced on *The Conspirators* by a minor producer. The script was changed. The film that had already been shot under the supervision of Wallis was discarded. Location and the pace of the story were changed. Stars took advantage of the situation, especially Lamarr. Their demands were granted. My job as a young director became a nightmare. Secretly the film became known as *The Constipators*, with "Headache Lamarr" and "Paul Hemorrhoid." The professionals—Greenstreet, Lorre, and Victor Francen—gave me their sympathy; but the just valuation of the film was given by Max Steiner, who was called in to do the musical score. We saw the finished product together. After the show, the lights went on. Hopefully I waited for his comment. It was short, just one word: "*Ouch!*" Brief and to the point.

After the press preview, the critics murdered the film—and me. It seemed a good time to decide to withdraw from cinema and return to painting. At the very moment of decision, there arrived a letter. It was from a respected friend and brilliant director, Edmund Goulding. Here are excerpts from his letter:

Dear Jean:

I am sticking my chin out to send you this note because, in one way, it is presumptuous and extremely pompous. It is only because I have a feeling of affectionate friendship for you that I am going to say to you what I said to myself this morning out loud when I read another bad notice on *The Conspirators*.

I beg you not to take *The Conspirators* to heart. You are only as good as your story, and you had a bad break. You took it over from one producer and another; the thing was changed while you were working on it; and no one knows better than I do what nerve-racking experiences can come out of such a situation. You hit very hard with *Mask of Dimitrios*, and you have a good one now. I had a feeling that the little smacks in the reviews might be creeping into somewhere in your insides, and I would be very sorry if they did. As a matter of fact, you should thank your lucky stars; it should actually be a lesson to you. . . . no one is any good without a story. Take the advice of an old pal and sweat, from now on, on the script. Stall, delay, do anything . . . get the script right.

I couldn't tell you this without sounding pompous and opinionated, so I have to write it. I had an experience exactly like *The Conspirators* once and out of it came a nervous breakdown. Everyone has them and they hurt. And you, essentially a painter and artist, are probably hurt more than the man who entered the business via the real estate business.

Don't be cross with this thought that I'm sending you—and a kiss.

Eddie

A sympathetic letter from an old friend to a young man in a moment of defeat? Yes, and precious as such. Surpassing this kindness was the understanding shown. More than I could ever put into words to my friend, this letter was helpful—in my career, in life. I hope that Eddie Goulding's counsel can go on helping a few honest beginners who make their life a challenge to aim for perfection.

In 1947—after four pictures in a row made and released in 1945 and 1946—I made my last and best picture for the Brothers Warner. I owe this assignment to the bizarre conduct of J.L. and to the strange behavior of Errol Flynn.

I was given the choice plum of directors' assignments at the studio—*The Life of Don Juan*, with Errol Flynn: big budget, lavish production, long schedule, the works. But my idea of the character of Don Juan as a person—a man who is a victim of women (couldn't say no to a beautiful lady) instead of a man who victimized women—didn't agree with Errol Flynn's idea of Don Juan. He wanted to maintain his public image—that of hero-lover, the dashing Romeo who jumps out of a high castle window and lands on his fierce running horse, leaving behind a delicious satisfied lass and an irate husband shaking his hopeless fists at the vanishing Errol. Nothing wrong with this, but . . .

So inevitably, after weeks of quarrels, J.L. called me into his office.

"I have bad news, Johnny. Errol wants to do the picture, but not with you as a director. I'm in a spot. I can make the picture without you, but I cannot make it without Errol Flynn."

"You're right, J.L.," I said, disappointed. Losing a picture—and especially *Don Juan*—was an unpleasant blow to my pride.

Jane

Left: *Belinda*. Right: *The storm*.

Top: *J.N., Charles Bickford, Jane Wyman*. Bottom: *Belinda and her baby*.

"Why don't you go and see our busy producer Jerry Wald," J.L. said. "He always has a few scripts ready on the loose. You may find one you like."

Jerry handed me three scripts. I read their titles, and *Johnny Belinda* intrigued me. Not because I knew anything about the story. I hadn't seen it as a short-lived play on Broadway. But I had just begun to smoke cigars, and Belindas were my favorites. Maybe it could be a suspense action story in Cuba. When I read the story, I was deeply moved. It was a story of tolerance, the story of a girl child, deaf and dumb, a young animal becoming aware of life around her and of her own feelings, the rebirth of consciousness.

That afternoon a plain deaf and dumb girl replaced the glossy Don Juan as my new assignment; and Wald-Negulesco were a happy team.

Before leaving for Europe, J.L. dictated the cast: Jane Wyman for Belinda. For the country doctor we liked the test made in New York of a young actor, but the boss didn't.

"He doesn't talk, he mumbles. Get the young actor who plays Dr. Kildare."

So, Lew Ayres, who played the doctor in the Kildare series, was signed. He was excellent and was nominated for an Oscar. Only the mumbling actor from New York happened to be called Marlon Brando.

Most of *Johnny Belinda* was shot on location, at Fort Bragg in Northern California. The working conditions were in perfect harmony. Stars, crew, technicians, met every night after dinner to talk about the next day's shooting. It was the only time in my experience that an actor (Charles Bickford) argued against his scene: "Unnecessary to the story—a silent mood shot of Belinda's day's work on the farm will be more significant." The still photographer got up very early the next morning and on his own composed a haunting photograph-shot as a suggestion for the mood scene. Teamwork to remember.

Jerry Wald was fighting the front office, trying to keep them away from our location. They felt I was indulging myself in too many pictorial shots. They actually took the camera away from me.

I needed an extra long shot for the end of the picture.

"Tell the son of a bitch to forget about it. He has enough shots" was the note sent to Jerry Wald.

Without Jerry's fight, I couldn't have finished *Johnny Belinda*.

"Fire the Rumanian jerk," J.L. cabled to Jerry on location.

"If Negulesco leaves the picture I leave the studio," Jerry cabled back.

Jane Wyman was calm through all this: "No matter what they do, the Oscar is mine this year." We all agreed, smiling at her confidence. But she was right. The Best Actress Oscar of 1948 was awarded to Jane Wyman.

When J.L. saw the final cut of the picture, his first words at the end of the film were "Sorry, boys, I have to take a leak."

It's hard to answer this kind of final comment. When the Great Man returned—relieved—he spoke memorable words: "It's always in the men's room that I get my best ideas." It was his excuse. Then, pointing his accusing finger at us, "We invented talking pictures and you two make a picture about a deaf and dumb girl. Only one thing could save it. Narration

Top: *J.N. and Jerry Wald.* Center: *Wyman, Bickford, Lew Ayres.* Bottom: *Wyman, Bickford, J.N.*

over her silent close-ups to tell the public what she was thinking."

We fought the decision, and the picture was released as shot.

The next day Jack Warner called me into his office. Though there were still three more years in my contract, I was officially fired.

I was working at the 20th Century–Fox studio when the year's nominations for the best five productions were announced. Each and every department in *Johnny Belinda* was nominated.

To top all impudence, Jack Warner called me long distance: "Kid, we did it again! We got twelve nominations. Next time we'll get thirteen." (*We?*)

"I have news for you, J.L. There are only twelve nominations in every picture," I replied, delighted.

"We will invent one extra. And *we* will get it."

I never went back to work for Warner.

JERRY WALD
THE "DOER"

I N the course of so many years working with producers, I met all kinds of them: the "careful" producer; the "let's not run into it blindly" producer; the "I like to weigh it from every angle" producer; the "listen, kid, no sex, no violence, no murder, means no box office" producer; the "if you can tell the whole fucking story on the back of a fucking mail stamp" producer; the "here is a property every director wants, but you're the only one who will understand the fucking subtleties and the shitty studio's problem" producer; the "forget it, kid, if you don't have Garbo and Gable, you have no

The director: All in a day's work

picture" producer; the "ach!" producer, generous and a dreamer until you talk money ("Ach! I'm so broke"); the "real understanding, professional, out-of-writers-and-directors-ranks" producer; the "family ties or tycoon's relative" producer (though the capability of Richard Zanuck proved the contrary to my fears); the "lucky one owning what the public needs and wants at the precise time" producer (Broccoli-Saltzman with the James Bond series); the "you and I know this story will be a fucking smash but first let's show it to the boss" producer. And then the most valuable asset to a studio: the passionate doer producer. Jerry Wald was a *doer*.

Reasonable to a point, he could sell himself on anything. A personality drawn by a caricaturist with a character composed by a dreamer, no one ever knew what made him tick or what made him succeed. With unlimited zest in everything he did, he'd pick people's minds and wind up with a production he'd claim as his own. An article in a newspaper, a bestseller, a smash play, another producer's successful picture, or just a simple social conversation would end up as a "Jerry Wald Production." And often as a smash.

Here is an example of how his mind worked: One evening at dinner I confessed to him what Romain Rolland's *Jean-Christophe* meant to me as a young man—my growing up to manhood.

"Would you like to do it?" Jerry asked.

"Do what?"

"*Jean-Christophe*."

"Would I like to do it?"

Next day the front page of every film daily announced:

A JERRY WALD Personal Production of Romain Rolland's masterpiece, *Jean-Christophe*. The awakening of YOUTH to MANHOOD. Alain Delon and Charles Boyer have been already set as principal stars. In a screenplay by the prize-winning Romain Gary. In addition, Jerry Wald has assured the collaboration as set designer of the famous Hungarian painter Vertes, who did such an outstanding job in *Moulin Rouge*. Jean Negulesco—of *Johnny Belinda* fame—will direct.

Just a dream, but to Jerry a cold fact. His telephone rang all day—agents, actors, friends. Questions, denials, threats, and warnings were accepted with the same gentle answer: "Wouldn't 'he' be wonderful in it?" So interest was created, and a few people read the book with renewed hopes. A full scenario treatment was written, sets and locations were discussed and chosen, money was spent. Unfortunately, this fabricated dream of Jerry's was abandoned.

I've been connected with Jerry Wald in three pictures: *Humoresque, Johnny Belinda,* and *The Best of Everything.* Each was a clearly defined step in my profession as a director, and each had a side story to tell.

Humoresque was the brain child of Clifford Odets, distinguished American dramatist. He was signed by Warner Brothers to write *Rhapsody in Blue,* the life of George Gershwin. Odets knew, loved, and admired Gershwin. After months of exciting work, he presented the studio with a scenario 900 pages long, a masterpiece. But Jack L. Warner didn't agree with him, as 900 pages meant three long pictures. Odets was fired.

And *Rhapsody in Blue* was taken away from Jerry and given to another producer.

Clifford Odets begged Warner to let him cut the three scripts to the normal length for a musical—for no salary. But J.L. was adamant. He didn't want Odets in the studio. Another writer was called in to do a completely new job on *Rhapsody in Blue,* and the Odets script was shelved.

Jerry Wald sent me the three voluminous scripts. I read them in one day. I was ecstatic.

Warner Brothers owned the original story and the title *Humoresque,* an old picture made in silent times. We adapted the Gershwin story to a violinist, and with a new writer— Zachary Gold—*Rhapsody in Blue* became *Humoresque.* We worked hard to cut the three volumes to the normal feature-length script. J.L. was pleased to charge the cost of an unproduced scenario to a future production. We got the go-ahead. Stars were Joan Crawford and John Garfield; violin recording was by Isaac Stern; the musical director was Franz Waxman. The friend, commentator, and supplier of cutting remarks on art and talent was Oscar Levant.

Oscar ad-libbed most of his dialogue in the picture. His stinging sarcasm usually hurt. He was bright, wise-cracking, with a touch of vicious humor, but always brilliant. To June, his wife, after their first date: "You have an unawakened face, but your mouth has possibilities." To Joan Crawford, who knitted continuously while rehearsing, eating, arguing, looking at rushes: "Do you knit when you fuck?" There were icebergs on the set for days.

Hollywood stories sound at times phony, cheap inventions. Yet this incident was true and worthwhile telling: John Garfield had never held a violin in his hands, yet through the picture he had to play very elaborate, tricky violin concertos. In faraway shots a double, a real violin player, would replace our star. After meeting with the technical brains of the studio, Jerry Wald and I decided to have a mask of Garfield's face made to be worn by a real violinist for closer shots. Perce Westmore, the head of the makeup department, picked up a musician from the orchestra the size and build of Garfield and adapted for days a rubber mask to the real musician until it fitted to perfection. We were ready.

The morning of the shooting, J.L. was there. Oscar Levant was at the piano. And there were Joan Crawford, John Garfield, Jerry Wald, reporters from the daily papers and international music magazines, along with guests and friends. Hundreds of extras in black tie and long dresses filled the concert hall. Technical and special-effects people looked on. It seemed that the whole studio was there to watch the miracle of make-believe.

The double was brought in and placed in front of the hundred-piece orchestra. A violin and bow were handed to him. Three cameras were focused on him.

"Watch him, Johnny," I told Garfield, standing next to me.

"I'm watching, I'm watching," he answered attentively.

"*Action!*" I shouted proudly.

Cameras rolled. Orchestra and Levant attacked the first musical phrase of Tchaikovsky's violin concerto, and we all waited breathlessly for the violin solo. The sound track came in perfectly, prerecorded by Isaac Stern, but the musician double for Garfield didn't move.

"Cut," I yelled. "What's wrong?"

Franz Waxman, the conductor, showed the musician the score and pointed to the place where he should start. The double nodded vigorously. Again, *"Action!"* Cameras rolled.

Johnny: From Humoresque *to* My Old Man—*burning the candle at both ends*

Levant and the orchestra came in on cue. The double was motionless.

"Cut. For Christ sake, what's the matter with him?" I yelled furiously. He came toward me mumbling incoherently under the mask and handed me the violin and the bow. The makeup man removed his rubber mask. He was coughing and covered with sweat.

"Well?" I asked.

"I don't play the violin. I'm a piccolo player."

Westmore had picked up a musician from the orchestra the size and shape of Garfield without asking what instrument he played!

My prop man saved the day and the budget. The elbows of

Garfield's tuxedo were cut enough so that his arms hung out.
The arm of a real violinist went in to hold and finger the
violin. The same procedure was used with another violinist
providing the arm to hold the bow. Both real violinists disappeared behind Garfield's back. Photographed in a close shot,
above the elbows, the illusion was perfect. When at the end
of the take the two appeared from behind Garfield's back, the
sight was uncanny and comical. "Why don't the four of us
stay together and play concerts around the world?" Oscar
Levant cracked.

John Garfield confessed that, for years after the picture was
released, in many countries where *Humoresque* was shown he
got offers to play concerts, or he was asked just as a favor to
play something. Of course, his refusal was vague, but fortu-
nately definite.

One afternoon at the beginning of the picture Jerry called
me into his office. "Trouble with Crawford," he said.

"What's wrong?" I said.

"She just left here crying."

"What is she crying for?"

"You don't talk to her."

"Talk about what?"

"The scenes."

"What scenes?"

"Her scenes. She wants to know what's behind every scene.
She says you don't tell her what her scenes mean, what the
motivation is."

(There goes method acting and that fucking word "motivation.")

"Look, Jerry, I'm not the kind of director that has to play
mood music for the stars before we shoot a scene. I have to
see a scene being rehearsed and hear actors going through
their lines. That's when I get my ideas. Besides, we didn't
have any important scenes with her yet worth commenting on
or analyzing."

"Just the same, Johnny, you should talk to her. Flatter her.
Make her feel she is part of the project."

"But she *is* the project. She's getting an enormous salary,
and she knows how to read and judge a part."

"Please, Johnny, be clever. You'll be married to her for the
next three months. So it's better to be friends."

I went home worried. Shit! What now?

Dusty Anderson, the beautiful Cherokee Indian cover girl I was engaged to marry, had two dry martinis ready for us. I told her about my Crawford worries.

Dusty was on her side: "She's right. Why don't you tell her what her character is all about? Show her." (Not one, but two dames against me!)

"Show her, show her! Show her what?" Suddenly I had the answer. I drew a very flattering portrait of her character in *Humoresque*—Helen Wright—with eyes closed, but exuding an inner feeling of controlled passion. She had a shadowed forehead (she liked that), prominent cheekbones, offering a generous mouth. It was drawn in a pleasant sanguine pastel color, with a mat and frame to match. The next day I presented it with a note and a single dark red rose. (Mushy?) The note read: "Dear Joan, This is the Helen Wright I see and dream of—and only you could give her to me. Jean."

There were tears in Joan's eyes as she whispered, "Thank you, Johnny. Now I know."

The picture ended on schedule. Joan Crawford had won the Oscar for *Mildred Pierce* (the picture before ours, which helped the box office of ours). My salary went from $350 a week to $1,500. I gained the friendship of John Garfield. *Humoresque* was a lucky association all around.

In 1959, Jerry Wald was producing for 20th Century–Fox. After *Humoresque* and *Johnny Belinda*, it was then that we connected again for our last film, *The Best of Everything*, a story of New York girls working in publishing.

Rona Jaffe, the author, felt deeply and emotionally about this book. It stayed on the best-seller list for five months. "The most important thing about *The Best of Everything* is that it is real, real, real. Or it should be," Rona told me again and again. She was a very valid collaborator during the preparation and rewrite of the scenario. And better yet, a true believer in details—sets, clothes for the girls, their way of living. "There is never enough closet space in a New York apartment. Particularly if three girls live in an apartment which is designed for two" was one of her anxious notes to me.

Casting the picture, Jerry Wald wanted Joan Crawford to

play the head supervisor, the mother-hen of the girls.

"But it's a nothing part, Jerry," I argued. "She'll never do it."

"Not after I put in the scene that every actress will sell her soul to play."

The scene: A smoky small bar, almost empty, late in the night. A black man plays the blues softly on the corner piano. Joan, at the bar alone, a date the man forgot, tells the story of her life to a patient and considerate barman. A classic schmaltzy scene.

"It's a good scene, Jerry. But it doesn't belong to the story," I told him after I read it. "Besides, you had exactly the same scene in *Humoresque*."

"It didn't hurt the picture," Jerry answered.

"But it belonged there. It doesn't belong here," I tried again.

"It's a good scene, Johnny. And it may get us Crawford." It did.

When in New York for location work, I went to see Joan. Her apartment was fabulous—white everywhere, shoes off at the door. The *Time* magazine people were taking pictures of her. Her late husband, Alfred N. Steele, the chairman of Pepsi-Cola, had died only two months before. She was voted vice-president of public relations for the company. Joan was barefoot, wearing black Chinese silk pajamas and a dressy flower hat. "They wanted to photograph just my head," she explained about her strange outfit as the *Time* people left.

We went from room to room on a tour of the apartment. And Joan recounted with the just right broken voice the death of her husband. It was a superb performance. She drank vodka continually. I noticed she never carried the glass with her. There was a new full glass in every room in a convenient spot.

Joan Crawford was a *star* in everything she did. She received friends as a star. When I asked for a cracker and a piece of cheese for my drink: "Press that white button behind you, Johnny." I did. The kitchen door opened and a maid rolled in a double-decker wagon with pounds of fresh caviar, smoked salmon, smoked trout, sturgeon, dips of every kind, crudités, Polish and Russian vodka, champagne. "A feast!"

Her bedroom was a showplace. A button was pressed, and automatically the drapes closed in slow motion. Subdued lights came from somewhere. And waves of soft, insinuating music filled the voluptuous temple: a star at work.

One evening at Jerry's house in Beverly Hills, Joan had a real diamond pasted on her forehead above the left eye. The whispers had it that Joan was launching a new fad in wearing jewelry.

I had to find out. I pointed at her pasted diamond: "Why, Joan?"

"Johnny, don't you see? Nobody has noticed the bags under my eyes."

Jerry Wald wanted a test made of a talented girl who played a minor role in the picture. She was very young, extraordinarily good-looking, with a mobile face and golden hair—very beautiful. Jerry asked Joan Crawford to introduce her in the test, and he hoped to incorporate it in a Fox newsreel, which meant enormous coverage. Joan accepted—only if I directed the test.

Flattered, I stayed to do it after the day's work. I picked up a good setup—an office window. Both girls were watching the New York skyline. When the camera slowly started moving in, Joan would turn, make her introductory speech, and bring the girl to face the camera. Joan would exit and the usual procedure of questions would complete the test. Everything was ready—lights, sound, camera.

"Action," I said. Joan turned to face the camera and started her speech. Only Joan was holding prominently in her hand a *bottle of Pepsi-Cola*, the name visible right in the center of the shot.

"Cut," I interrupted. Turning to the prop man, I said, "Bob, will you help Miss Crawford get rid of the bottle."

"Oh, *no*," Joan insisted. "Jerry has promised I can hold the bottle of Pepsi-Cola in the test."

"But, Joan, nobody will listen to you or look at you, but look only at the bottle. Besides, it is unfair to the young lady."

An impasse, a short silence.

"No Pepsi-Cola bottle, and Joan Crawford goes home," she said with finality.

"No, Joan," I answered quietly. "Pepsi-Cola stays but Negulesco goes home." I got up and left the stage.

Crash, tragedy, hysteria. Joan put on menthol tears. The still man took many tragic close-shot photographs of her crying. And combined with old commanding stills of me during the picture, they resulted in two pages in *Life* magazine under the caption "Once friends, Joan suffers miseries from tyrant director."

Jerry welcomed publicity in *Life* for our picture. Only the poor young lovely girl lost her chance to be discovered.

When the bar scene was shot—and well covered—I made the mistake of whispering to the script girl, "Good scene. Well played, but—"

"But what?" she said.

"Ten to one it will not be in the picture," I said.

"Why do you say that?" she asked.

"Because it doesn't belong."

I was right. The scene was not in the picture. The script girl talked. She was a good friend of Joan's. Joan was not my friend that year.

Jerry Wald's sense of humor was continual—healthy, sometimes naive, often inspired by his enormous collection of filed jokes. But the temptation of a miracle and impossible dreams were Jerry's everyday hard work and harder fun. Enthusiastic as a child—devoted friend, slave to publicity—he was sublime and horrible.

Jerry died young, suddenly. I heard the news in my car radio coming home from a party. I went to his home. Two more friends were there: Oscar Levant and Clifford Odets. We spent the night talking.

Jerry Wald was a great loss to the survival of a golden period of the industry and the splendor of Hollywood.

NUNNALLY JOHNSON, THE SAGE OF THE PICKLED PINE DESK

N UNNALLY did not like directors. He felt they took too many liberties with his scripts. He liked The Word. Producer, director, writer of over one hundred scripts, Nunnally was a master. His word would be the right one. But he

Among top class pros. From left: Finlay Currie, Nunnally Johnson, Jack Benny, Irene Dunne, Alec Guinness, J.N.

could fool you—it wouldn't be the expected one. Often in the projection room as we watched the day's rushes, he would say, "*You* look; *I'll* listen."

We were teamed for four pictures: *Three Came Home, Phone Call from a Stranger, The Mudlark,* and *How to Marry a Millionaire.*

In a Nunnally Johnson script, I would find dialogue that bound characters and story together. Nunnally was always on guard against those words that drag a story off course: "That's a great line but not for this story." He would go off by himself and come back with the right line. He was his own sour-faced editor. He even looked sour when he wrote something funny on the set. His dialogue brought characters to life and kept them breathing.

He was not given to athletic sport, not a bit. He would get tired carrying his typewriter from his desk to the table on the porch. From the magazine section of the *Los Angeles Times* I cut the picture of seven muscle-bound beach boys and sent it to his office: "Nunnally, keep the photos of your body out of Dusty's bedroom. I found them under her pillow this morning."

He returned it with scribbling across the page: "Don't worry. These are last year's pictures. But it was nice of Dusty to recognize me."

When I was in Greece doing *Boy on a Dolphin,* he wrote: "You've been gone so long I'm glad you sent a picture of yourself. I have forgotten what you looked like. I remember Dusty in every detail, but not you. You're the one with the dark gray hair, aren't you? P.S. Do you know what the hypochondriac had put on his tombstone? 'You see, I told you I was sick.' "

The stream of letters flowed on, with Nunnally's playfulness leaping up like trout in the stream, from wherever he was working to wherever I toiled.

From Hollywood, Nunnally sent a report to me in Greece:

Greg Peck and the Corporation responsible for *The Big Country* gave a whopping big party Friday night. (The only matter that might be of any interest to you was that Jayne Mansfield came with her clothes on. I couldn't see that this was any improvement.)

For the first half, *The Big Country* promised to be the perfect Western. Standard stuff but beautifully handled. Then the whole fucking thing flew apart. Everybody kidnapped everybody else and then had to be rescued. And you know how long it takes to rescue a girl who doesn't want to be rescued. The final scene was those two fellows walking toward each other, very very VERY slowly. Shot the shit out of each other, both of 'em. I don't mean to be unfair to the picture. It's really very good. But it started out to be wonderful. Wyler now uses THE METHOD in directing. Nobody says anything. The camera keeps popping from one to the other, hoping to catch SOMEBODY saying something. But the actors won't talk. Finally the camera—to hell with 'em—cuts to a mountain. At least you know where you stand with a mountain.

About art: One morning he sent me a reproduction of a very sensual nude painting: "Why can't you drop all that nonsense and paint strictly from life and invite me over sometime while you are at it. I'll bring the whisky."

Exchanging ideas about my film *Jessica*, we touched on the relevance of *Lysistrata* to the film. Nunnally wrote: "Miriam Hopkins played Lysistrata in New York in the version I think was by Brian Hooker: The women banded together to protest the men going off to war all the time. So okay, no nooky until you buggers make peace."

Here is his comment after reading the script of *Jessica*:

> There is one point that I think might have an electric effect on everything thereafter. The point is this, that when the resolution is made to have no more babies, it should immediately be made clear that this long-range plan necessitates a very immediate decision—no more fucking. (No more fucking? That's exactly what I said: No more fucking! But you don't mean NOW, do you? Yes, NOW. From this moment on, n-o-m-o-r-e-f-u-c-k-i-n-g!) I think this point ought to be made crystal clear, in language as close to fact as the law will let you get away with.

A note complaining of the release of his previous picture: "I haven't heard a word from anybody anywhere about *The Man Who . . .* etc. It opened in London and Leslie sent me a couple of pretty good reviews. But from the studio, NOTHING. When I'm feeling very low I assume this is because it's

just too embarrassing to mention—'Like a fart in church' . . ."

His ironic comments about the decisions the executives at the studio are afraid to take:

> I've finished another version of *The Colors of the Day*, now titled *The Man Who Understood Women*, and will mail it to you if I can find out where you are. As usual, I hear nothing about it around here. Schreiber [20th Century casting director] said he thought it would be difficult to cast the male lead. He also said it would be difficult to cast the two male leads in *Flaming Lance*. And it would be next to impossible to find the right kind of fellow for *The Wandering Jew*. Each of these parts calls for a male with one head, two arms, and two legs. Not easy to dig up a type like that, you know. Buddy [Adler—new boss of 20th] he don't say nothing. Nobody's going to boobytrap him, boy! Many's the time I've wished that Darryl hadn't preferred Greco to 20th Fox. Right or wrong, he always said something!

I was on location out of town. Dusty wrote me a letter and asked Nunnally to add something. He did: "P.S. This is written from the sofa on the left of the fireplace. The door is locked. Dusty and I are very comfortable and happy. Better luck next time, pal."

The World of Suzie Wong was a picture from which I was removed as director. Ray Stark, the producer, and I disagreed on cast and shooting. This is the note I received from Nunnally:

> We saw the *World of* . . . last night. Obviously you lied like a dog. You weren't sacked. You realized what you had got yourself into and took to the hills. I can't believe that you wanted to have anything to do with a picture in which the leading man was either a eunuch, or had only ½ ball. And Bill Holden having to live in that cathouse against his principles and having to hold both hands between his legs day and night to prevent a fate worse than death.
>
> At any rate, when the lights went up at the end, there wasn't a dry eye in the house. Plenty of dry seats—but no dry eye. Holy jumping Jesus Christ. Congratulations.
>
> [And signed] Nunnally (A man of tremendous integrity).

These letters are a commentary on the pretenses, maneuvers, and chicaneries of Hollywood. They are also a self-portrait of Nunnally. He turned his rages into hilarity. He turned everything into hilarity. Including man's most sacred subjects—himself and sex. The Nunnally wit was different.

One of his last letters (Nunnally was already quite sick):

What a pleasure it was to hear from you and Dusty and how I loathe you for the heavenly life you live. I must say I simply don't understand God. You've been a cad your whole life long, deflowering little girls, betraying your best friends with their wives, and never once attending chapel. And you wind up in a heavenly spot with a beautiful wife and two lovely daughters and no longer sought by the police.

Meanwhile, I have patted 750 children on the head, I have spoken kindly to widows and orphans, I have remembered my enemies in my prayers, and what's my reward? Sitting in a corner and incapable of any vice whatever. If I had to do it all over again I think I would live my life differently.

Do you know that I wouldn't trust you with Doris as far as the front door?

I also got a nice letter from Norman Krasna, who envied Dusty. He said Dusty had really made it big, being married to a combined lover and chef cook. Norman wasn't very much interested in you as a lover, but he did wish he had you in his kitchen. So do I. I could entertain Dusty in the living room.

From the *Herald Tribune*, March 28, 1977: "LOS ANGELES, March 27 (U.P.I.)—Nunnally Johnson, 79, who started out as a reporter and later became a prolific short story author, columnist, and screen writer of about 100 movies, died Friday . . ."

My memories of Nunnally are rich from so many years we worked and spent together. They are good memories, grateful memories.

When people would praise me for a picture, I would protest, "Did you listen to Nunnally's dialogue?"

His last letter to me arrived one week after Doris' cable announced his death. It seemed natural to hear from him. Nunnally will always be alive with me, and with a happy laugh.

D.F.Z., DARRYL FRANCIS ZANUCK, THE FOX WHO MADE 20TH CENTURY-FOX

I worked for Darryl Zanuck, an association of many years that had its zigs and zags for me. But it was never dull or secure or monotonous. He made every project a challenge, every assignment a bold statement.

As a filmmaker, he was the most spectacular and one of the most courageous figures of the cinema's golden period, a pioneer leader of action with a genius intuition of showmanship.

In Hollywood D.F.Z. was a symbol of significance, without doubt one of the most powerful executives, with a staggering reputation for successes and failures.

A swollen egotist with a smooth sneer, Darryl Zanuck talked as if he believed everything he did and said, not allowing a chance for argument or doubt. Stubborn in his convictions and intoxicated by his own shouts and dynamic ideas, he easily convinced his listeners that he was right. And most of the time he was.

Our first meeting was no different. In 1948, after I was fired from Warner Brothers for making *Johnny Belinda*, I decided to go back for good to painting. My friend Brian Aherne lent me his bungalow at Indio in the Palm Springs desert. I started to work on my Mexican drawings and to try to convince Dusty—my wife for the past two years—that Hollywood was not for my sensitive soul. She listened patiently but knew better. That year my agent Frank Orsatti died, and when Charlie Feldman my new agent called to tell me that *Zanuck* wanted to see me—my car didn't move fast enough.

I already knew so much about D.F.Z. People said he was a bantam and at the same time very much a rooster. He grew up in Los Angeles and on his grandfather's Nebraska farm, and he enlisted at fifteen and served with the army in Mexico and France. Back in Hollywood, he worked as a writer at Warner Brothers, doing stories for Rin-Tin-Tin, the famous dog who was a money-maker in serials.

From then on, everything Zanuck touched turned into excitement. He did scripts for *Little Caesar* and *Public Enemy* and started the gangster cycle in films. Then Warners boosted him from a $125-a-week writer to a $5,000-a-week executive producer. He was a fast worker, kept the budget in line, and got a jump on the rest of the industry with new ideas—like sound, with Al Jolson in *The Jazz Singer*.

When I was trying to break down the cinema walls in 1933, this man of my own age had stepped up to the tycoon level by forming 20th Century Pictures with Joseph Schenck (the promoter who had shown his movie financing genius by bringing together Mary Pickford, Douglas Fairbanks, Charlie Chaplin, and D. W. Griffith to form United Artists). Zanuck and Schenck brought Spyros Skouras in, and the combine rolled up $10 million a year in profits.

So, the big man summoned me. He was seated behind his desk smoking an enormous cigar as he read a script. A quick pencil note and this little man acknowledged my presence with a soft handshake. He spoke slowly and quietly: "I saw your last picture."

"*Johnny Belinda?*"

"No. *Deep Valley*. A good job. I asked my people in the studio to see it—the way pictures should be made on location."

He picked up a script and handed it to me. "Here is a script that four directors refused to do—good directors. Only they couldn't see what this property offers." His voice suddenly got loud as he stood up. "I know its potentiality, and I'm sure you will, too." He started to walk the length of his office.

"We made this kind of picture at Warners for years— James Cagney, Ann Sheridan, and Pat O'Brien. Focus on the girl's tits, and if somebody drops a hat, start a fight." He stopped by the door.

"When you finish reading it, we will talk." I got up, and again I received the soft handshake. "By the way, Negulesco,

I admire your talent. But you have a terrible reputation as a man," he said.

"Why, Mr. Zanuck?" I said.

"You're a playboy," he said.

"I was. Now I'm a married man." I defended my reputation.

"Still, it is said that no woman is safe with you." No smile.

"Thank you for the compliment, Mr. Zanuck. But rumors have it that many a starlet has had to break her sprinting record around your desk," I said with admiration.

He grimaced briefly, what was supposed to be an amused smile. "I'm the boss." Again a grin, this time more genuine. "You play croquet?"

"Not well."

"I'm sending you two balls, a wicket, and a mallet. Improve. You will spend every weekend at my place in Palm Springs, playing with professionals."

They were already painting my name in the parking lot. Two car spaces away from D.F.Z. My salary was twice what Warners paid me, and my office suite was impressive. That afternoon I got this note from him: "February 10, 1948, My dear Negulesco: It is a pleasure to know that you are on the lot and I look forward to seeing a lot of you. D.F.Z."

But I wondered what that soft handshake represented. Zanuck did not need to crush your hand as a proof of physical strength, which he had. He let you know with his soft pressure that your gifts were now under the guidance of a great conductor of the cinema art—and the cash registers. Now you were to figure in the fast play of his mind.

Well, he had me. I had been welcomed and already was a devoted fan. That first picture was *Road House*, with Richard Widmark, Ida Lupino, Cornel Wilde, and Celeste Holm—a solid success. It featured two outstanding songs: "Again" and "One More for the Road." No-voice Ida Lupino sang them and placed them first on the Hit Parade of the year's best songs.

Like most of the great producers, Darryl appreciated talent and courage: "I want new ideas, dangerous ones. But I beg all of you, before you bring 'em to me, think hard and for a long time about the chances for success. Study each idea from every angle. Measure its potentiality in today's market. Is it what the public wants?—here and everywhere? Then bring it to me. I'll get twice as excited as you, all the way. And if it's a failure, it will be twice as big, because I went overboard."

That was the Zanuck approach—no deceit in studio deals. When the picture was a flop, he showed how fair he could be. I made a picture in England, *Britannia Mews*, a disaster, insane casting. The critics murdered us. I sent a note to Darryl assuming all the blame. "I liked the story, accepted the cast, enjoyed making the picture." I promised that somehow I would make up for it.

He wrote back: "Don't try to be a hero. You're not the only one to blame. I okayed the story, the script, cast, rushes, answer print. If it had been a success, I would have grabbed the credit. [And other times he did.] But a flop . . . of course you're to blame, too, but don't be a hero. And try not to do it again."

Croquet the hate game. The king of "Desert Croquet" was Darryl and his court at Palm Springs. He constituted the Palm Springs Croquet and Yacht Club. The club had stationery with a coat of arms: a crossed mallet and a D.F.Z. cigar with three balls on top and the motto "By Wicket Deeds Shall Ye Be Known." The organization was dedicated to "the promotion of clean sports and the elimination of all croquet barriers, including Moss Hart." (It was said that Moss Hart, the playwright, introduced Darryl to croquet.)

My introduction to Palm Springs croquet was unusual. I was Darryl's partner against Louis Jourdan and my compatriot Fefe Ferry. Fefe started first, went through the first and second wickets, and took a bad position for the third wicket. I followed. I passed the first and second wickets, and as I prepared to hit my ball for the third wicket, the earth started to tremble. The worst earthquake in Southern California records caused sudden undulation of the houses. The swimming pool was dancing, water splashing over on both sides, an eerie ghostly sound.

"The girls," Darryl shouted. We dropped our mallets and ran for the guest buildings. In my rush, by mistake, I stumbled over a wicket and fell. I looked back. Fefe with his foot was gently moving his ball for a better position (a Rumanian touch).

The girls, all in bikinis, were running for cover in the bar,

led by Collier Young (married to Ida Lupino). They were trying to hide under the big coffee table. Of course Collier was the first to get under. Dusty, Ida, and Virginia Zanuck had place only for their heads and shoulders. Three colorful asses were springing from under the table like an enormous plucked daisy. Rita Hayworth, nude, ran from Aly Khan's room to hers (they were just engaged). The enormous wall mirror behind the bar split right across. Glasses, bottles, and paintings were trembling and singing.

When, hours later, the fascination of green lawn drew us back to the game, Darryl commented sharply that Fefe's ball now stood in front of the third wicket.

"No violation of rules." Fefe shrugged. "An act of God."

At Palm Springs, Zanuck surrounded himself with his court of jesters, who included:

Howard Hawks: brilliant director, slow talker, and a genius of an imaginative liar;

Top: D.F.Z. Bottom, *from left: Louis Jourdan, J.N., Charles Lederer.*

Charles Kenneth Feldman: handsome, best agent in Hollywood (and mine), friend of every tycoon, a collector of modern art, wives, and scatterbrained beauties;

Prince Mike Romanoff: the emperor, erudite, bombastic, with perfect manners, one of the greatest impersonators of our time;

Louis Jourdan (Lulu): handsome, suave actor, and (unfortunately) the best player among us;

Fefe Ferry: Rumanian, chic agent, the darling of lonely ladies, and taken-for-granted cheat;

Gregory Ratoff (Grisha): Russian, fat actor, colorful, talent to fit two lives;

André Hakim: Egyptian, Darryl's son-in-law, always laughing, count your fingers after a handshake;

Casey Robinson: screenwriter, Roman senator profile, wicked and dangerous wit;

And Yours Truly: Noisy loser, stubborn, and selfish.

These were the regulars. There never was a time like "then." Our childish fun was genuine. Weekends at Palm Springs were full of practical jokes and pranks and mischief.

Virginia Zanuck, a handsome frail lady, was totally devoted to Darryl and her three children. Her sophistication was naive, but her devotion to friends was genuine.

One evening, Lord and Lady Boley, an English cinema mogul, were dinner guests at the Zanucks'. Virginia Zanuck told us at lunch, "No foolery this evening." The Zanucks had been guests at the titled couple's castle in Scotland, and our kind of jokes would be frowned upon. "Try to be, for once, grown up and civilized." We promised.

On the court Darryl held a small conference. "Virginia has to be taught a lesson. How dare she lay down the law against our fun. Tonight before dinner I'll throw her into the pool." We all agreed. And our game was played that afternoon with carefree anticipation.

At night, when Virginia appeared at the bar, dressed to kill, she had on all her jewelry—pearls, diamonds, rubies. Charmingly she acknowledged the expected compliments. Darryl secretly whispered to us, "We can't do it. All those valuables. I can't push her into the pool. Too bad!"

Fefe, my Rumanian compatriot, whispered suddenly, "Throw *me* in, Darryl. You pick a fight. I'll argue noisily and you push me in. The rest of the crowd will jump in." Agreed.

Lord and Lady B. were charming and very English—monocle and hah-hah type. We behaved splendidly until dinner was announced. As we were passing the pool, Virginia and the honored guests in front, Darryl and the court jesters following, Darryl bellowed, "Fefe, you are a miserable and unmitigated liar. I never said such a thing."

"You did, and all of us heard you," Fefe shouted back.

"When?"

"Tonight."

Splash. Fefe and his Rumanian accent crashed the quiet water. The guests and Virginia turned, surprised and shocked.

Virginia was furious, fit to be tied. "Darryl, damn it, I begged of you. You promised. I asked you all to behave tonight, for once not to disgrace me. Damn it, damn it, damn it," she shouted crying. "I'm so mad, so furious, I could scream. You . . ." She looked at us, ready to kill. Then hysterically she jumped into the pool, dress, jewelry, and all.

"Boys, what are you waiting for?" Darryl screamed as he joined Virginia and Fefe. And one by one we were in, fighting through the melee.

Lord and Lady B. were watching, with no definite expression, the Hollywood *wet* behavior. Methodically the lord put his monocle away, folded his coat, removed his shoes, and grabbing Lady B. around the middle, dragged her into the pool—where the fun was at its peak. "Yippee!" His Lordship screamed.

Darryl was always the first to get up and have his breakfast by the pool, clad in the briefest shorts. I was next to join him. Usually he was lost in his checking of the financial pages of the morning paper. We were quiet, respecting each other's silence and my appetite.

But this special morning the financial figures were generous to him. "Aha!" said he.

"That good?" said I.

"Good? Great. Three points."

"Three points of what?"

"The stock. I bought it last week."

"How many do you have?" said I.

"Of what?" said he.

"Shares."

"About twelve thousand."

"So you made thirty-six thousand dollars," I said.

"Just about," he said.

"So, what are you going to do with it?"

"With what?"

"The thirty-six thousand dollars you just made."

"Nothing. It stays there. If it goes up, that makes more. If it falls, there's money to cover."

"But Darryl, what about today?"

"What about today?"

"Look, Darryl. Yesterday you did not have these extra thirty-six thousand dollars. Today you have these thirty-six thousand dollars. Aren't you going to use them for something? Give these thirty-six thousand dollars a reason for being. Not just a figure. Buy a painting, a new car, a sculpture, well—*something?*"

Darryl looked sadly at me, not grasping one shade of my logic. "Johnny, you'll never be rich!"

I knew I had trespassed beyond my limits. I, who only *once* in my lifetime had made a stock investment, putting all my savings in Cuban-American Oil shares, just before we split with Cuba. Yet, every time I bought something I couldn't afford, it always came out right. Rich? Maybe not. But happy? Oh, *yes.*

After Darryl Zanuck proclaimed the crushing victory of the West croquet team over the East, there was a letter from Moss Hart of the East team, which he sent to Hollywood trade-paper columnist Edith Wilkerson:

Dear Edith,

I am by nature a peaceful fellow, and what small share of indignation I possess I usually save for Presidential campaigns and World Wars. But two recent items appearing in your much-admired column have exploded such deep wells of anger that I am breaking an old vow and "writing a letter to the papers."

As you may guess, they are those items referring to Darryl Zanuck and Croquet. To come to the point harshly: I don't know what Darryl Zanuck is doing, but he is most certainly NOT play-ing Croquet. Croquet is a noble game; its basic element is skill, but its first requisite is a right code of ethics. Played correctly, it is a game of savagery, passion and deep, almost mystic, fulfill-ment. To find it sullied by such tomfoolery as "peaked caps," a gaping throng of goons, and such players as Fefe Ferry, Clifton Webb, Tyrone Power, et al. is more than I can take. I came up in Croquet the hard way and for long summers was only allowed to watch. After this I was placed on a scrub team in the late after-noons when the big games were over. And even then I would have spit on Clifton Webb as a partner. So you can see it is not only offensive but shocking to have this neophyte foisted on your readers as an authority. And on you too, dear girl, for Darryl Zanuck's cupidity has already made you the laughing stock of anyone in the East who has ever sent a ball through a wicket.

I think it would be wise to let Mr. Zanuck know he is trifling with more than grandiose film spectacles when he makes up his own rules for Croquet and allows Gregory Ratoff to so much as set foot on a Croquet lawn. It's more than maddening to find my name linked in a Croquet game in which Charlie Feldman was referee. I doubt if Feldman knows the difference between a dead ball and Howard Hawks. Or vice versa. And to think that Darryl Zanuck (according to his own words) had an obstruction removed from the course! Why, a natural hazard on the fields is the very essence of the game! His arrogant posturings at Croquet affect me the way Toscanini might feel were he to find Jimmy Dorsey play-ing *Parsifal* at the Salzburg Festival. Tell him if he continues to despoil the fair name of Croquet, I'll come out there and make him crawl through every wicket. Does all this sound churlish and angry? Well, you bet your acid little column it is! Yours for more ethics in Sports.

Moss.

There was fun at Palm Springs, but once the weekend was over the contests were transferred to the 20th Century–Fox lot, where basic and serious problems were fought out.

In 1953, all over the world the movie industry was faced with threats of collapse. Something was needed to save it. Again Darryl came to the help of the industry. He brought in CinemaScope. In the past he had stirred the public to re-newed interest in films with the "gangster cycle," with his probing into anti-Jewish discrimination in *Gentleman's Agree-*

ment and anti-Negro discrimination in *Pinky*. The saga-of-the-farm depression was examined in *The Grapes of Wrath* and *Tobacco Road*.

CinemaScope was a medium different from anything we had before, anything the audiences were used to, a new experience. The medium in itself was an important star, overpowering. But the problem we faced was a classic one: the law of success. If the public was too conscious of the technical perfection or imperfection of the new medium, then the story and its entertainment values were lost.

The Robe was a perfect vehicle for the first CinemaScope picture. It had magnitude, breathtaking pageantry, Christ on the cross. In almost every scene the screen was filled with hundreds of people carrying wine urns or palm branches.

I was assigned to the second CinemaScope picture, *How to Marry a Millionaire*, produced and written by Nunnally Johnson.

The challenge we faced with *How to Marry a Millionaire* was to show the paying public and the other studios (which were reluctant to buy the new process) that CinemaScope could be used normally for a simple story. In *How to Marry a Millionaire* our special breathtaking scenery was feminine beauty—Marilyn Monroe, Lauren Bacall, and Betty Grable—three girls who would rather marry rich men than poor men. Could this comedy be told in the new medium? Both Nunnally Johnson and I felt the answer was yes. Our conviction was that this tale should be told simply. Let CinemaScope add to the dramatic impact instead of being a distraction.

Although Darryl did not agree with our determination to use the new medium flexibly, we were proven right. The critics raved. *How to Marry a Millionaire* confirmed the new techniques—an exciting plus and a box-office bonanza. It led to my new assignment, *Three Coins in the Fountain*.

I gloried in the possibilities this story had. Rome itself could be the star—Rome and Venice and the Italian countryside—and the Italian spirit of noisy joy-of-living, and Neapolitan songs and *amore*. All painted in vivid Italian colors for masses of people who had dreamed of seeing Rome, or perhaps had had a brief holiday there without really seeing the Rome they had dreamed of.

The producer, Sol Siegel, and I agreed that this story had

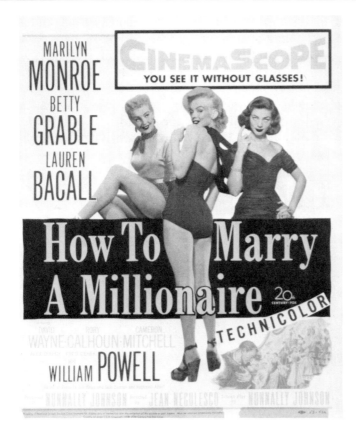

to be shot in Italy with the principal actors. There we could catch the bubbling human spirits and the theatrical quality of laughter and love that we wanted, and capture the ancient grandeur as well.

"Do the long shots with doubles in Rome. Film the story with the principals in the studio, with process keys" was D.F.Z.'s decree.

I wrote to him: "We are convinced that you will be amazed at the possibilities of the location."

D.F.Z. sent back a memo: "We have already decided exactly how we are going to proceed with the production of *Three Coins in a Fountain*. If you don't like the way we are doing it you should ask to be relieved of the assignment. You take care of your side of the business and let me take care of mine."

Sol Siegel burrowed beneath the tycoon's throne and asked
Sid Rogell, head of studio production, to make a cost study of
my schedule—thirty-five pages of script filming with principals
in Rome—compared with building sets and shooting the same
pages in Hollywood.

Rogell laid the results, a matter of cold economics, on
Darryl's desk. Shooting in Rome would cost only *one third*
the price of an all-Hollywood film. Money talked. Darryl sent
us to Rome.

With love from the Champion to the novice —
Darryl (3 Ball) Zanuck —

The brilliant musical team of Sammy Cahn and Jule Styne wrote the title song and Frank Sinatra recorded it.

When we were ready to show our rough cut, for three nights we had private showings at the studio—for our friends in the industry, for the crew and studio people, and for an audience of teenagers. Unanimously the reaction was great.

John Patrick, the Pulitzer Prize–winning writer (*The Teahouse of the August Moon*) who wrote the script of *Three Coins*, commented: "The only wrong thing is that the dialogue interferes with the beauty of the film." Not so. The dialogue had just the right spice and romance needed. Sol Siegel and I felt good, elated.

The night we showed the picture to D.F.Z. and Spyros Skouras—20th Century–Fox president—cockily I said to Darryl, "I think we have a winner!" He looked long at me. No smile. Chewing on his long cigar, he sat down. At the end, when the lights went up, after a long silence, Darryl abruptly got up and left the room. Not a word was spoken.

Skouras left after him. Later he called Siegel and confessed that his disappointment in our picture was painful.

Next day we were summoned by D.F.Z. to his private projection room. The cutter sat to his right. Usually he nudged the cutter at places where he wanted changes. That night the nudging covered all scenes and every reel. At the end he explained to the cutter the changes and cuts he wanted. Finally he said to us, "It's a sick baby. It needs hard work," and he left the room.

We saw the new version. A butchered job. A long short with nothing of the magic we thought we had achieved. A letter went to him: "Dear Darryl, This morning we saw the new cut version of *Three Coins*. We are aware that you are one of the greatest cutters in the industry. But if you decide to release *Three Coins* as it is now, we insist that our names will not appear in the credit titles. Sol Siegel, Jean Negulesco."

That evening he asked us to dine with him. "For God's sake, boys, let me see the new version before you blow your tops" was his welcome.

Dinner was pleasant. Darryl entertained us with amusing stories of his vacation. During the projection of the new butchered version there were no grunts or any whispered com-

Spyros Skouras

ments. When the lights came up, again a silence, this time
shorter. Then Darryl turned to the cutter: "Put it back as it
was and ship it."

New York exhibitors went overboard in glowing accolades,
with the certainty of smash business ahead. This didn't stop
Skouras from sending Darryl the following telex: "Dear
Darryl, Everybody here wild about *Three Coins in the Fountain*. I want to congratulate you on the *almost unbelievable
cutting job* that *you* did. Spyros."

In a moment of humorous loyalty, Darryl sent me a copy
of Spyros Skouras' message with a note: "See what kind of
idiots you have to work for?"

Darryl F. Zanuck was an S.O.B. He was a great S.O.B., but
he was OUR S.O.B., and I loved him.

Under his inspired leadership I delivered to 20th Century–
Fox studios, from 1948 to 1970, twenty-two pictures: *Road
House, The Forbidden Street, Under My Skin, Three Came
Home, The Mudlark, Take Care of My Little Girl, Phone
Call from a Stranger, Lydia Bailey, Lure of the Wilderness,
The Last Leaf, Titanic, How to Marry a Millionaire, Three
Coins in the Fountain, A Woman's World, Daddy Long
Legs, The Rains of Ranchipur, Boy on a Dolphin, The Gift
of Love, A Certain Smile, The Best of Everything, The
Pleasure Seekers, Hello-Goodbye.*

Darryl's senses of values and humor were often diabolic. I
remember one Monday morning, after long and animated
croquet games at Palm Springs, Darryl put me indefinitely on
suspension for not accepting his decision about how a certain
script should be done.

One hour later he called me: "Johnny, now that you're not
working, pack your things and let's get down to the desert for
some croquet a day earlier!"

Yes, that was Zanuck too. No thought that I was minus a
paycheck (with three mortgaged houses) for an indefinite
time to come—just that we were old buddies heading off for
a nice crooked game of croquet.

Of course, the boss is always an S.O.B. But the fact is that
Zanuck kept his place at the top by getting good work out of
us at the studio. We were his winning team. I will always be

grateful to him for picking me up for that team; and for giving me for many years security and luxury; and for helping me make my place in this racket I love. But, I had to deliver.

SAM GOLDWYN

I never worked for Sam Goldwyn. (His real name was Sam Goldfish.)

In his high-pitched voice, he used to tell me, "You get yourself a great story, the best writer available, a first-class cast—the right cast—a great cameraman, and you have the chance to make a great picture."

The first time I heard this I laughed. He looked surprised and serious. "I mean it. It is the only way."

A Hollywood legend, Sam Goldwyn achieved the envied status of making distinguished pictures. He made certain never to insult the public intelligence. He knew his limitations, and his instinct for perfection resulted in "quality" films.

The foremost credo of Sam was "Goldwyn is the boss." He was absolute owner of "Sam Goldwyn, Inc. Ltd." Supreme authority, tyrant, and monarch, he decided and controlled every detail in his films. Rebel, great showman, greater salesman, totally and completely independent, gambling his own money, with no board of directors, no banks involved, Sam Goldwyn achieved art, distinction, quality, taste, and box office in his productions. His instinct, given such free expression, combined with his passion for details and disregard of budget, made for the famous "Goldwyn Touch."

This instinct for perfection was savage. He had to have the best, *at any cost*. And sometimes he would pass the limits of friendship, courtesy, or just simple decency: "Never let that S.O.B. in my studio again—unless I need him."

For diplomatic safety, Sam Goldwyn never committed himself immediately. On many evenings at his home we would see new films in his projection room, pictures of other producers. When the lights came on at the end of the film, he inevitably would ask, "What did you think of it?"

And after everyone would give his or her honest opinion, someone would say, "Sam, what did *you* think of it?"

With a mischievous smile he would answer, "Considering this from every angle, I don't think it is fair for me to make any comment about other people's films in my own house!"

Crafty, convenient, and safe: a tycoon never loses.

He was a genius when it came to murdering the King's English. A champion at using words improperly, incongruously, he gave to his well-known blunders a supreme comic authority that became part of his fame: "Include me out." "Toujours Lautrec." "Tea and trumpets." "I can answer you in two words: Im possible." "A verbal contract isn't worth the paper it's written on." "This atom bomb is dynamite."

Was he unconscious of his delightful variations of the language? Or was he deliberately using them to add to the Goldwyn legend? I often wondered.

One Sunday at Jack Warner's, Sam asked Dusty to take a walk in the garden before lunch was served. They arrived at an old Roman stone sundial. Sam stopped. "So what is this?"

"A sundial, Sam."

"Sundial? What is it for?"

"Well, as the sun moves around the sky, the shadow of the sundial moves around the numbers and tells the hour." Dusty was patient.

Sam thought for a moment, then shook his head. "What will they think of next?"

One time, at 3 A.M., Goldwyn called producer Sam Spiegel: "Sam? This is Sam."

"What? What is this—a joke?" Spiegel mumbled.

"This is Sam Goldwyn."

"Oh, hello, Sam." Spiegel sighed, irritated.

"Sam, we both have a problem."

"Which one?" Spiegel awakened, alert.

"You have an actor, and I need him."

Spiegel snapped pleadingly, "Look, Sam, can we talk about this in the morning? Do you know what time it is?"

Goldwyn turned to his wife in bed: "Frances, Sam Spiegel wants to know *what time it is.*"

Sam Goldwyn, like every tycoon, had to win, even if he had to cheat. Spilling a bottle of ink over a losing scorecard or trying to light a cigarette only to set fire to a scorecard at gin rummy were some of his more obvious devices.

One afternoon on his croquet court, when no other player showed up, we played a very boring single game. Boring for both of us: Sam cheating and I winning.

"Let's play one hand of gin rummy," Sam suggested, not accepting an afternoon of defeat. By luck, he got three gins in a row.

"Hey, I can beat you without cheating," said Sam, high-pitched, delighted.

According to one book, "Croquet is a gentle game. A simple, amiable sport that brings out the happy nature of the contestants and relieves them from all tensions and cares. One of the liveliest features of the game of croquet is the trial of wits to settle delicate questions." This is what the book stated in 1830, when "croquet was devised at a French sanatorium to exercise and entertain patients. English visitors introduced the game in England, where it became the pastime of Victorian society."

Now, just what was different when this graceful therapeutic exercise crossed the ocean and the continent to end in the croquet courts of Sam Goldwyn and Darryl Zanuck? After all, it was still a game of balls, mallets, wickets, and stakes. All of us were governed by the simple "rules" we subscribed to when we became life members of the "Goldwyn Croquet Club":

1. Don't get excited.
2. Correctly remember balls you are dead on.
3. Have patience with fellow members who are not as good as you are.

Even tempers, polite memory, and noble unselfishness were our guiding spirits. Until we walked onto the court. Then the spirit of Hollywood croquet exploded. George Sanders wrote a song about it, entitled "Hymn of Hate."

We never bet any money on the game. The hate was

enough of a reward. Goldwyn's court was on two lots. So when we wanted to destroy an enemy it would take him two hard shots to return to the game.

One time when the venerable Sam's ball—this preacher of calmness—was about to be sent flying into yonder by George Sanders, Sam pleaded, "If you don't do it, George, I'll buy you a Rolls-Royce."

"I already have one." George laughed and banged Sam's ball with vicious delight.

Hollywood croquet was for the long-ball hitters. As we played it, the game required the wallop of polo, the concentration of chess, the silence of a tomb.

One afternoon only one player showed, Charles Lederer, the brilliant writer and famous wit. Sam waited for half an hour. "Let's play a single game until somebody shows up." Charlie agreed without much enthusiasm.

At one moment at the beginning of the game as Sam was ready to hit one of his balls (they were playing with two each), Charles stopped him. "Before you go with your blue ball to the third wicket, Sam, I want to remind you that you are still for the second wicket."

"You take care of your balls, and I take care of my balls, please," Sam snapped angrily.

"Look, Sam," Charlie said quietly, "I love this game. But it isn't any fun if you cheat. I could explain to you why your blue ball is still for the second wicket."

"I'm sick and tired of everybody telling me what to do on my court. I'm going to the third wicket," Sam shouted with finality.

"Sam, you go to the third wicket," Charlie said, still quietly, "and I walk out of this court and *never* come back."

Sam stopped with his mallet in midair and looked around. No other players were there for a game. So, high-pitched with indignation: "What's the matter with you? Are you for Stevenson or something?"

(It was not an election year, but from Sam's point of view Adlai Stevenson was too intellectual to be President of the United States. So anyone who was for him was too intellectual to have common sense.)

Sam Goldwyn, a perfectionist about his films, was totally devoid of any talent or even the slightest ability as a croquet player. To be his partner was to suffer, swear, and wish that you had never played the game.

He was better at making pictures, but that seemed a secondary talent when we were keyed up about the game. Still, we never forgot that he was too important to leave out of the game. He owned the court.

No, I never worked for Sam Goldwyn. Yet he had peculiar behavior when it came to his games or his ways of getting what he wanted, what he had to have. As one talked about him, it was often in jest, repeating his latest blunders, his last grammatical disaster. Yet he was respected and envied. I had for Sam profound admiration.

Best Years of Our Lives, Wuthering Heights, The Pride of the Yankees, Arrowsmith, Dodsworth, Stella Dallas, Dead End, The Westerner, The Little Foxes, Guys and Dolls, Porgy and Bess . . . His pictures had a marked and definite impact on my struggle for growth as a director and for achievement of better quality in my films.

DAVID O. SELZNICK, THE EXUBERANT PRINCE OF MOVIES

A California winter day in the late 1950s, the funeral of Buddy Adler, the late studio head of 20th Century–Fox. (D.F.Z. had left in 1956 to become an independent producer.)

Buddy Adler's reign was short. A distinguished producer himself, he made many friends in the studio among producers and especially directors. He understood the problems of a director and the complications. Always impeccably dressed,

gray-haired, handsome, he could have fitted any of the re-
fined parts of his films (*Love Is a Many-Splendored Thing,
Anastasia, From Here to Eternity, South Pacific*).

At a church in Hollywood, the studio employees were
gathered, along with family, agents, friends, and important
people of the industry. A short, impressive service and the
smooth golden voice of Tony Martin singing "Love Is a Many-
Splendored Thing" closed over us the sadness of a lost and
missed friend.

Intermixed with the sadness there was a question in many
minds: Who would be the new studio head? The studio
hadn't been functioning well since Darryl Zanuck had left.
Spyros Skouras, the president of 20th, was worried.

The crowd gathered outside the church. Most of us were
at a loss for conversation. Spyros Skouras signaled me: "Walk
with me, *compatriote*. I want to talk to you." (I had had four
box-office hits in a row, so I must have been way up in his
valuation.)

His limousine was following us. He walked silently for a
while. There were a few acknowledged greetings, a few ignored.

"*Compatriote*, I'm in trouble and I need help—from everybody. I need to make a decision, and quick. I have to name
somebody as the head of the studio. Darryl refuses to come
back. Who then—Wald, Brandt, Blaustein, you, Siegel,
Charlie Feldman? Or a new man? Who, *compatriote?*"

(When a big executive asks you to help him make a decision, he has made up his mind long before; but he plays
around with the thinking processes of the people he rules,
affecting humility and a need for help.)

I held the right pause, and then in a quiet voice: "Spyros,
all the names you mention are good men, some better than
others. With the exception of me. I don't have the mind or
the stomach for this kind of job."

"So, then, *compatriote?*"

"So, then, there is only one name you didn't mention, one
man who fits this place to perfection—David O. Selznick."

Spyros stopped walking. "Why him and not the others?"

"Because David Selznick is respected and admired by directors, writers, producers, and stars. They *want* to work for
him, and with him. Great talent wants to work for David

Selznick as they wanted to work for Darryl Zanuck." We started walking again.

"They will, Spyros, if the head of the studio is a man like David Selznick. Any executive who could produce single-handedly *Gone With the Wind* is the man for you. And with him, you'll have the best creative talent in the industry working for you, for your studio."

"Some people don't like him."

"Who, Spyros? Besides, David will know how to handle and cope with distributors and directors and writers, because David is a producer who reads and feels and writes and thinks."

"All the others do the same, *compatriote*."

"Maybe they do, Spyros, but they didn't bring Hitchcock from England to do *Rebecca*, or Ingrid Bergman for *Intermezzo*, or discover Katharine Hepburn in *Bill of Divorcement*, or help Joan Fontaine and Gregory Peck and Fred Astaire and Joe Cotten and Louis Jourdan, and many more to advance their careers."

Spyros was silent. He stopped walking, motioned for his limousine, and got in alone.

"Thank you, *compatriote*. I'll certainly think about it."

I walked back to my car. It was a long walk. I wonder if I made any impression on him, I thought. So he is going to think about it?

He did. He had his mind made up who he wanted before he talked to me. We got as the new head of the studio a man called Peter Levathes, a Greek TV distributor. During his "vice-president-in-charge-of-production" term, few pictures were made. Many were started, few finished.

When a picture is finished, cut, and previewed, it is impossible to explain what makes it a success or a flop. I always thought that the making of a picture is the result of a close collaboration among the co-workers involved in the project. But for David Selznick, picture-making was the outcome of a series of conflicts and disagreements between the co-workers actually making the picture and the one person who had complete and total authority for the final decisions.

During the preparation of *Gone With the Wind*, George

Cukor, the director signed for the film, made tests for months of the possible stars and most of the scenes.

One day David had some misunderstanding with George Cukor about the way a scene should be shot. "Your ideas may be great, George. But if the picture fails and I break my neck, I want to be sure it is because of my own doing."

"So?" Cukor questioned.

"So, you're fired, George." (Victor Fleming directed G.W.T.W.)

And so much for collaboration the Selznick way. Yet good people, including George Cukor, wanted to work for him.

David was one of the *best* in proving that classics could be respected and shot entirely with all their beauty and integrity. Witness *Little Women, A Tale of Two Cities, David Copperfield, Anna Karenina, Little Lord Fauntleroy, Adventures of Tom Sawyer*—all critically praised and solid box office.

In the early 1930s there was an absolute *taboo* on making pictures about Hollywood. David O. Selznick maintained that there was no such thing as a forbidden project if the story was good. His proof? Producing *A Star Is Born*.

His greatest adventure, of course, was *Gone With the Wind*. Three years before actual shooting, it became the subject of many conversations and the focal point of meetings— the production that would set a standard for all future films. David said, "Anything that we will make after *Gone With the Wind*—no matter how well done or how important—will look tame and be insignificant."

He used more than a dozen writers, always went back to the original book. Selznick had to have his say, to control, to rule. Thousands of memos went to all departments. He was an obsessed, haunted one-man show.

One evening Brian Aherne and I were having a drink with David at his home. Only one subject was mentioned: *Gone With the Wind*—"majestic, miraculous, towering. Nothing could compare or come close to it!" He placed before us photographs of the planned film, color slides, enormous transparencies, color stills of costumes, sets, shots of actions and scenes. It seemed there were thousands.

Driving home, Brian said, "Looks great, but how could a man be that sure?"

But how right David was. *Gone With the Wind* was and

still is everything he said—a classic, a grand example of the
art of filmmaking. No praise or shouts of admiration or ova-
tions were exaggerated.

The opening night reception was held in a nightclub near
Sunset Boulevard in Hollywood. I was Olivia de Havilland's
escort. There was a general exuberance; spirits were elated—
that wonderful feeling everybody has after an astounding success, a sure winner. There was gaiety around us, and that was
the way the whole industry felt after the showing of *Gone
With the Wind*.

David asked Olivia to dance. I went and invited Vivien

*Two sisters from Hong Kong, a
Rumanian gigolo, and a pink
Russian. From left: Joan Fon-
taine, J.N., Olivia de Havilland,
Anatole Litvak*

Leigh. On the dance floor it was madness—too many interruptions from people congratulating her, too many anxious photographers flashing their blinding lights. Finally a moment of quiet.

"Vivien, how wonderful to know that Scarlett O'Hara is the miracle you dreamed of."

"Yes, it is," she said quietly.

"Then why so sad?" I said.

Vivien said nothing. I waited. Then, "What's next after Scarlett O'Hara?" she said.

For me, it was the one clearly marked memory I have of that evening: a beautiful young girl lost by success, insecure and dazed by praise and homage.

David O. Selznick

"Live beyond your means!" Lewis J. Selznick, David's father, a Russian immigrant, advised his sons David and Myron when his own millions vanished and he was forced into bankruptcy. "Luxury not security. Throw money around if you have it or not. Give it away deliberately, insanely. It will give you confidence."

They did. They both ended on the top—David as a producer, Myron as an agent.

David was a gambler. He once covered every number at the roulette table, just for the fun of it.

David's last production, Hemingway's *Farewell to Arms*, was done after almost nine years of inactivity as a producer. Jennifer Jones, his wife, played the part that Helen Hayes had originated, and Rock Hudson the part of Gary Cooper. The company was shooting on location somewhere in the north of Italy. Hundreds of memos went out hour by hour—memos from one page to twenty or thirty pages. Most of them were aimed at the film's director, John Huston—not only what the scene was about but how it should be played, how certain lines should be read, what special lighting used to obtain the right effect, what makeup and props and sound. John read most of them and ignored some. One day he had enough.

Rumors had it that in the middle of a take, as another thirty-page fresh memo was delivered to him, John Huston stopped shooting, called an early lunch, and dismissed the company.

John asked one of his assistants to get his suitcase from the hotel and call him a taxi.

When comfortably installed in it, John calmly faced the Italian taxi driver as he turned with the exaggerated smile of his trade: *"Dove vuol andare, comandatore?*—Where do you want to go, chief?"

"Paris—Paris, France."

"Parigi, signore?"

"Si, Parigi."

And they drove away to France.

Charles Vidor took John Huston's place. They say he too ignored David's memos.

The remake of *Farewell to Arms* did not have the magic of the original one. Maybe John Huston and Charles Vidor should *not* have ignored David Selznick's memos.

My bungalow office on the 20th Century–Fox lot was a marvel of comfort and luxury. Besides the big office plastered with my collection of original Bernard Buffets and my own sepia portraits of stars of my last pictures, it contained old English farm furniture, a studio-bedroom for an afternoon siesta, a bathroom with a hard shower, a completely equipped electric kitchen with Steinberg wallpaper, and a dining room with a built-in cabinet to contain over a hundred vintage wine bottles and every kind of liquor.

David called me when I was in London. He was preparing a picture for Fox. "Could I use your bungalow for a few weeks?"

"For months if you want," I said right away. "And by the way, the key to my liquor cabinet is pasted with Scotch Tape on the back of the Bette Davis portrait. You're welcome to it."

David used the office but never used the key to the liquor cabinet. As a gift, he left two cases of Dom Pérignon and a note: "Johnny, it's a great place to write memos. I didn't dare not work with those Buffet creatures staring at me so hungrily. . . . D.O.S."

Generous, enjoying life beyond its norm and living beyond his means, stubborn with an insane confidence in his every

impossible dream, a gambler, a brilliant charmer with an
ironic smile beyond his unlighted cigarette, David O. Selznick was a friend, a prince among producers, a giant who
revolutionized the cinema industry.

HOWARD HUGHES,
THE AMOROUS TYCOON

Howard Hughes was an eccentric. He showed all the signs
of being a lunatic or a genius. No one could ever explain his extraordinary behavior, his fantastic decisions and
brilliant accomplishments. He knew what he wanted and he
knew how to get it. He used your services, your brain, your
talent, and took your friendship or your girl to achieve his
singular wish. He had the means to do what to us would only
be a fairy-tale dream.

Once he wanted to meet Jean Simmons. As the story has
it, she refused to meet him or have anything to do with him.
Informed that she was under a long-term contract at the RKO
studios, he chose a simple solution: He bought the studio and
became her boss. What followed is not clear. The boss had a
studio, the star got married to somebody else, and the budding
romance stopped there. But the consequences of this purchase
of a studio were staggering and unexpected.

When the news broke in the morning papers that Howard
Hughes was the new boss of RKO studios, the executives,
producers, directors, and writers who had long-term contracts
became jittery. Howard was known to be unpredictable. His
decisions were rash and without explanations. The top RKO
people changed their habits. They arrived at the studio before
10 and stuck around after 6 P.M., waiting to meet the new
boss. But Howard did not show up—not the next day, nor

Hughes and Jean Peters

the day after, not for one week, nor the next. A month passed
and no sign of the new master. The jittery crowd relaxed.
Nobody talked with or met Howard Hughes. "He may never
take possession of the studio." The tension slackened. Everybody breathed easier and the leisurely working hours were
back.

Then one night close to midnight a small dirty Chevrolet
drove up to the RKO entrance. A horn blast awakened the
guard. "Open the gate," the tall, gaunt driver shouted.

"Studio is closed until tomorrow at eight," the guard
shouted back.

"Open the gate," the young driver insisted. "I own this
studio. I'm Howard Hughes."

The gate was opened.

"And call everybody to meet me in the courtyard right away. *Right away!*"

For the next half hour the guard was busy phoning. The calls were urgent, desperate. Howard parked his car in the center of the courtyard but stayed inside munching hungrily on a cheese sandwich he carried in a paper bag.

One by one the executives, the producers, and the heads of departments left their parties, their gambling games, or their beds and surrounded in a quiet, embarrassed circle the little Chevrolet. Howard did not open the door or acknowledge their presence. Calmly he finished his snack, washed it down with a pint of milk, and waited.

Finally the production head of the studio arrived out of breath and full of excuses and spoke to the man in the car: "Terribly sorry I was unaware of your arrival. We would have been here to welcome you. We all will do our utmost to help the new boss accomplish any changes, obey to the limit any decisions he will take . . ." and on and on. Howard did not hear or listen. The pregnant silence was broken by the studio head's lame offer: "Would Mr. Hughes like to look over the studio?"

Howard opened the door of the car, came out, and faced his employees.

"What would you like to see, Mr. Hughes?"

Howard looked at the speaker and all around, slowly, coldly. *"Everything."*

For hours they visited every stage, every department, and every office, stars' dressing rooms, actors' and extras' cubicles, dining rooms, toilets, garage, projection room. There was no door, no closet, no stairs, no storage or parking place that Howard missed that night. He was alert, bright, observant. The crowd followed, exhausted. No comments were exchanged. Just information as to the reason for and the usefulness of everything. Howard had to know where his millions had gone.

It was early morning when the baffled group stepped out into the courtyard. They were still waiting for the great man to speak. But he didn't. As he was getting into his car, the studio head man questioned him weakly: "Is there any instruction or comment you may want to make about the studio?"

Howard turned to him and uttered only two words: "*Paint it.*"

For the next two months the whole RKO spread was painted from top to bottom, inside and outside. Eventually Jean Simmons starred in some inferior roles. She was forced to buy out her contract and leave the studio. Howard personally produced some successful box-office pictures. He sold the RKO studios a few years later at an enormous profit.

Everything he touched turned to gold. When a projection room containing the negative of an unfinished picture was destroyed by fire, the insurance was more profitable than the lost film.

A fight with Howard Hawks, the director of one of his personal productions, forced Hughes to complete and direct the picture. It was a blockbuster—*The Outlaw.* He bought homes for his amours and their mothers, only to sell the real estate a few years later at an enormous profit.

He moved from country to country and from east to west, frequently reserving whole floors of secluded hotels for him and his entourage. At one such time he was occupying the whole top floor of a big Las Vegas hotel, running his empire from his rooms. He had his own cook, his servants, his guards, his lawyers.

As the story was told, the hotel manager, after a couple of months of such occupancy, asked to see him—a serious matter. Howard came into the meeting hall with his whole entourage. Embarrassed, the hotel manager explained that "because Mr. Hughes is not using the facilities of the hotel—restaurant, bar, servants—and is not doing any gambling [which they were expecting him to do]—this singular situation has inflicted on the hotel huge losses. The top floor of the hotel is always reserved for big gamblers. Gambling providing the largest profits of the hotel. And because Mr. Hughes insists on occupying indefinitely this floor, the management will be grateful if Mr. Hughes will vacate the premises. And if possible in as short a time as Mr. Hughes can."

"I did not hear you. What did you say?" When Howard did not like something, he assumed a convenient affliction. He was hard of hearing.

The manager repeated his demand, self-consciously but more definitely. Howard listened patiently. But he did not

answer. Instead he turned to go to his quarters. As he passed
his lawyers he just said quietly, "Buy it."

That afternoon the hotel became the property of the
Howard Hughes empire for an undisclosed number of millions. Later he realized that the acquisition was such a profitable affair that he bought more than one hotel. And much of
the available territory of the State of Nevada.

I had the unique pleasure of giving Howard Hughes many
gourmet dinners—duck à l'orange, cassoulet, stuffed grape
leaves and *mamaliga*, apple strudel. I always took care that
he was surrounded by beauty and beauties.

One evening he called: "It is my time to reciprocate." I
put on my best blue serge suit. Full of expectation (a billion-
aire's orgy!), I arrived at his home. The house was brown,
Victorian, and dark.

Howard was busy on the telephone. The old servant asked
me if I wanted a drink. "A whiskey and water." Quietly he
disappeared and came back with a small glass of whiskey and
water—no ice—and waited. I studied the furniture, the paintings: burnt-sugar color, smoky brown, gilded heavy broken
frames holding sentimental and moral subjects, comfortable
red plush couches, old and ripped around the wood, and an
ordinary uncovered mattress in a corner of the room (dog or
guest?). I finished my drink. The servant came and told me
Mr. Hughes would be out presently—long-distance calls. I
asked for another drink.

He took my glass and came back a minute later empty-
handed. "Sorry, sir, no more whiskey," he apologized.

"I didn't want another anyway," I answered feebly.

Howard drove me to a place where "the best steak in the
whole of California sizzles." It was an abandoned streetcar
set on its old rails somewhere on Wilshire Boulevard, up a
quiet alley, adapted as a one-room restaurant. The steaks were
good and *big*, sizzling on a round wooden board, with baked
potatoes and sour bread.

"And only eighty-five cents," Howard noted triumphantly.

Howard often wanted to meet and "have" your girl. And if
by chance one claimed exclusivity, he became obsessed and
insisted frantically on achieving his wish.

In 1938 I was dating Miss Luise Rainer. She had unusual beauty and a brilliant mind. And, as if that were not enough for one woman, she was awarded two years in a row the Academy Oscar (1936 and 1937) as Best Actress in *The Great Ziegfeld* and *The Good Earth*. All these enticements and the fact that she led a very quiet, reserved life made Howard unreasonably foolish.

"Johnny, could you give me Luise Rainer's telephone number?" Howard called in the middle of the night.

"I can't, Howard. She does not wish to have her telephone number known."

"But you have it?"

"Yes, I do."

"So give it to me."

"I can't, Howard. But tomorrow I'll call her and ask her if I can give you her telephone number."

"Call her now."

"It's three o'clock in the morning, Howard. Tomorrow I'll tell you what she said."

Before 8 A.M. Howard called again. "What did she say?"

"Howard, I've not spoken to her yet."

"Why?"

"It's too early. I'll call around ten, O.K.?" I hung up.

When I phoned Luise, she just said flatly, "I don't want to meet him."

"But, Luise, he is an important man. In spite of his fortune, he could be exciting company."

"I still don't want to meet him."

"Maybe dinner with both of us?"

"No, definitely not." Luise had her own mind.

I rang Howard: "She doesn't want to meet you."

"What do you mean she doesn't want to meet me?"

"Just that, Howard. She doesn't want to meet you!"

"You're joking."

"I'm not."

"But why?"

"She is a strange girl, obstinate and pretentious. Forget it."

He kept me busy talking for an hour. Finally I convinced him that there was no sense on insisting. When he called back every fifteen minutes with more arguments and suggestions, I lost my patience.

"Look, Howard, there is only one way. In one week on the twenty-eighth of February I'm giving a party. It's my birthday. Actually my birthday is on the twenty-ninth, but this isn't a leap year, so I celebrate on the twenty-eighth. Luise will be the hostess. I'll introduce you to her and you'll be on your own after that. O.K.? Only, it's black tie. So be at my home around eight. Black tie, remember?"

"I'll be there."

He arrived at the party in white tie yet.

"Luise, this is Howard Hughes."

"Hello." Luise acknowledged the introduction, turned her back, and went away.

"How—what did I do?" Howard was puzzled.

"Don't worry. The night is young." I tried to encourage him.

It was a good party, with Rumanian and Japanese food and good wines. When it broke up late in the night there were only three persons left in front of the fire—Luise, myself, and Howard. And somehow Luise was doing most of the talking. The drinks, the compliments, and the presence of an anxious famous man on the make gave her eyes the sparkle of feminine coquetry.

I don't remember how, but we were talking about Christmastime, the past holidays. "There is nothing here comparable to Christmas in our country," Luise was remembering. "The vacation started long before the holidays. Our home was close to a lovely lake. Father had a little boat and he took us across the lake. In the moonlight it was so beautiful."

"I have a boat." Howard broke off the monologue.

"You do?" Luise snapped at him. "Where do you keep it?"

"Close by—Long Beach. Would you like to see it?" Howard was happy to be in the conversation.

"Yes I would," Luise said.

"When?"

"*Now*," she challenged him.

Howard dialed a number, mumbled a few orders. "We're ready," he announced triumphantly.

I was tired and bed was tempting. "Look, darlings," I explained sleepily, "why don't you two go along and I'll see the boat another time. I had a hard, complicated day. I'm really tired. I would be stupid company."

They went. What happened I heard later, much later, from Howard. As he told the story, there was very little talk on the way to Long Beach. Howard tried to impress Luise with technical terms and numbers as to the speed, performance, and unusual perfection of his boat. Luise listened indifferently and sarcastically repeated his technical extravaganzas. When they stopped by his boat, it was an *ocean liner*, flooded in lights, the whole crew lined up at attention, the captain running to welcome them.

"Your boat?" Luise found her voice.

"One of them," Howard answered quietly. They went on board. Luise was impressed, speechless.

"Would you like to see the engines?" Howard asked eagerly, and conducted the baffled Luise down the ladders to the engine room. It was impressive—not romantic, but impressive.

"You know, Miss Rainer, if I just start the engines and move the boat only around the bay it will cost nineteen thousand dollars," Howard explained.

Luise smiled and ordered mockingly, "Move it."

"But I said it will cost nineteen thousand dollars."

"And I said *move it*," Luise repeated.

He looked long at her. Then: "If I move the boat, I may not go just around the bay."

Slowly Luise turned and with her famous sidelong glance said "Move it!"

They came back two weeks later. Howard had his way.

During his courtship of Jean Peters (later Mrs. Howard Hughes) they spent a weekend in Santa Barbara, a delightful Spanish-type town not far from Los Angeles. On the way back, traveling in his old broken-down Chevrolet, they stopped at an out-of-the-way gasoline station to fill their tank. The attendant said, "Six dollars and thirty-five cents."

Howard turned to Jean: "Pay him."

"With what? I don't have a penny."

"But Jean, you know I never carry money."

Jean shrugged, and he turned to the tough attendant: "I'm Howard Hughes. I happen not to have money on me. So would you—"

"Six dollars and thirty-five cents," the man interrupted.

A helpless silence, then Howard tried again: "Look here, this is Jean Peters, the movie star."

The man looked at the star's faded jeans, her old sweat shirt and dirty tennis shoes—and at Howard dressed the same way. He leaned across them and took out the starter key. "Six dollars and thirty-five cents, or you and your jalopy don't move."

"You don't know what you're doing," Jean said, exasperated. "This is Mr. Howard Hughes."

"Tell that to the cops, ma'am," and the attendant walked away with the key.

"Why don't you call Greg?" Jean suggested. (Greg Bautzer was Howard's lawyer.)

"Sure. Do you have ten cents for the phone?" A helpless shrug from Jean. Howard got out of the car and approached the sulking attendant.

"All right. You don't believe that I'm Howard Hughes or that she is Jean Peters. You're wrong. So lend me ten cents to make a phone call and you'll have your money."

The gasoline man said nothing for a while, then reluctantly handed Howard ten cents: "I've lost six dollars and thirty-five cents. I'll lose ten cents more. But that's all."

Howard called, gave a few instructions, and joined Jean in the car. They waited—not for long. Two black Cadillac limousines were there within half an hour. Men in dark suits rushed to the Chevrolet, got their orders, paid the bewildered attendant, and got the Chevrolet ignition key. Howard and Jean waved to him and the whole convoy left with screeching tires.

It is said that somewhere in an out-of-the-way road by the sea between Los Angeles and Santa Barbara there is a gasoline station with a tough attendant who has developed a curious twitch.

During the shooting of *Three Coins in the Fountain* on location in the north of Italy, all the city telephone lines in Merano, near Cortina del Pezzo, were totally and completely out of service each night from six to seven. Not for Howard Hughes. This was the hour when he called Jean Peters, our star. Her dialogue was always the same. Monotonous and repetitious: "Yes, Howard. . . . No, Howard. . . . I will, Howard. . . . I will not, Howard. . . . Of course, Howard. . . . Yes, Howard," and so on for a whole hour. As a joke we always asked, "Who called you, Jean?"

The power of money! Even Italian officials were unable to use their own national telephone during the Hughes-Peters calls from 6 to 7 P.M.

When we returned to the studio, Jean confessed to me one afternoon that she had given Howard a three-month time limit. If he didn't marry her in that time she would marry somebody else. And she did—"a younger and weaker Howard Hughes type," she explained, from a good Philadelphia family.

It is said (and this is without benefit of any information from the bridegroom) that on the wedding night, somewhere in Florida, Howard arrived with his bodyguards. Jean was put on a boat or plane for some unknown destination. The bridegroom was rewarded with a generous, important job in one of Howard's companies. A quiet, rapid divorce was obtained for nonconsummation of the saintly marriage.

Some time later, 20th Century–Fox was shooting a costly picture, *A Man Called Peter*, with Richard Todd and Jean Peters, in New York and Philadelphia. When the troupe was ready to go to Philadelphia, gossip rumors had it that the jilted bridegroom called Jean and asked her a big favor in some words like these: Would she mind when in Philadelphia, instead of staying at the hotel which the studio had booked for her, could she stay with his family? It would soften the stigma of their marriage failure. And his parents, who were very fond of Jean, would be so proud to show her off to their friends.

Jean answered that before she could say yes or no she had to call Howard. She did. Within five minutes of her telephone call, a plane carrying Jean Peters left Philadelphia for Los Angeles. At the same time, another plane with a double for Jean left Los Angeles for Philadelphia. All the scenes in this town were shot with the double. It cost the studio a fortune to build sets in Hollywood and complete the scenes with the principals. Did Howard pay for it? I doubt that. Zanuck and Skouras and the whole industry were powerless when Howard wanted decisions to meet his wishes.

*   *   *

Howard broke many beauties' hearts. But, not knowing, he killed the dream of the young girl he loved and married. This is the story:

Errol Flynn's pictures in the early 1950s were below the quality of his earlier ones. What was even sadder for him and the studio was that his box office as a star attraction was over. Warners couldn't recoup even the negative cost of his last three heroic adventures. He still had four commitments on his old contract—each a sure lost gamble. When Errol asked for an appointment with J. L. Warner it was granted immediately.

"You see, old boy," Errol started after the cold welcome, "you have been losing a fortune with my last films."

"Not that bad, Errol. We made some money in Turkey and Zanzibar." Warner tried to be funny.

"You won't, and you'll lose at least a million with each of my next four pictures. Four million dollars, if not more."

"Well, Errol, we spent too much on your films—too big productions. Now a small Western, some simple stories—"

"J.L., you know it's suicide," Errol interrupted. "You built me up as a heroic figure. Nobody will accept me as a simple Joe. I'm a liability, a bad one. I'll make you a proposition. You give me two million dollars and you'll be ahead two million out of the four million you'll certainly lose if you insist on completing my contract. And you can have my contract. The fastest and best two million you made for the studio this morning."

Jack Warner was furious, mad enough to fight. But Errol's logic was so simple and convincing that it is said Jack made a compromise. Not for two million, but not far from it, and Errol was free.

What Errol needed at that point was a good adventure story. So when I got an assignment to make *Lydia Bailey* (the invasion of the island of Haiti by Napoleon's army), I thought that Errol would be excellent as the hero of this epic. I made a date to see him that morning at his home. On my way to him I met Jean Peters in the parking lot. I suggested to her that she might be the right love interest with Errol in the picture.

"I've loved Errol Flynn since I was a little girl," Jean confessed eagerly. "Making a film with him is a dream come true."

Errol was already drunk, and only 11 A.M.

"Of course, old boy. I am free now to do an outside picture, but first I want to read the script."

"It's being written, but you can read the book. I'll send it to you."

The telephone rang. It was for me. Howard Hughes calling.

"Why don't you take it in the bedroom," Errol suggested.

His bedroom, the famous love altar, had mirrors everywhere, including on the whole ceiling.

Howard's voice came over the wire: "Jean tells me you want to cast her with Errol Flynn." *Click.* An unmistakable noise came over the wire. Errol was on the phone extension. "Now you know what I think of this combination."

I stopped him. "Howard, I'll call you as soon as I return to the studio." I hung up.

"Howard wanted the telephone number of a girl," I told Errol when I returned to the living room.

"Of course, old boy. You gave it to him?"

Again the telephone rang. Back to the bedroom's mirrors and Howard. "She wants to do it badly. But the combination of Flynn and Jean is a disaster for her." *Click.* Errol was back on the extension. "I'll have to read the script and—"

"Howard, I can't talk to you now. I'll call you in fifteen minutes." I hung up.

And it went like this for half an hour. Howard arguing, Errol picking up the extension, I trying to keep some form of secrecy. Finally I left, promising Errol to send the script of *Lydia Bailey* as soon as I had the first draft.

Back at the studio, a short note from D. F. Zanuck: "Cast set for *Lydia Bailey*. Do not approach Errol Flynn or Jean Peters."

Howard kept Jean away from her childhood dream.

The last time I saw Howard socially was soon after his marriage to Jean Peters. We gave a party at our home for the newlyweds. The Who's Who of the industry were there to meet them. Howard was wearing a dark suit, white shirt, and tie. Quite a change from crumpled dungarees, unpressed shirt, open collar, the usual tired tennis shoes, and a two-day beard.

He felt uncomfortable, and the gay, noisy friends made him even more nervous. Just before dinner he was gone.

"Where is Howard?" I asked Jean.

"Couldn't stand the collar and tie," she answered gaily.

"Anything wrong?" I said.

"You know Howard. He has to have everything his own way," she said and turned away a little sad and lonely.

Among the exciting lunatics I met in my life, Howard Hughes could do and did everything. He had limitless power and a limitless fortune. He was a genius, a restless pioneer. He was a fickle lover, an impossible husband, a wavering friend, and—sadly—a terminal victim of a dull commodity: cleanliness.

ANATOLE LITVAK, THE SUFFERER

ANATOLE Litvak's skin was pink. He was pink when he was mad, pink when he laughed. His ears were transparent pink, especially when he was standing against the sun. As his hair got whiter, his face seemed to get pinker. He was also Russian. Meaning his love affairs were disastrous, his marriages turbulent and short-lived. Always in love, but once he was sure of the lady's true affection, he would do everything to destroy it—so he would be free to complain and suffer, especially *suffer*, in all shades, forms, and intensities.

After the worldwide success of *Mayerling* in 1937, Hollywood lured him. On the ship to New York he met Miriam Hopkins, the vivacious, brilliant blond bombshell, star of stage and screen. And of course, as a matter of normal behavior, he fell in love with her—deeply, seriously. "Will you marry me?" was his song on the last day of the crossing. Miriam, an explosive fun-loving girl, laughed. A shipboard romance was just that—a temporary interlude of shared fun, but nothing to be followed through. Her parting words: "Tola, darling, you're sweet. When you arrive in Hollywood try to meet a young man, Jean Negulesco. He knows me well. He can help you."

Tola was furious. When friends introduced us, he was deliberately sarcastic. "So you're Jean Negulesco?"

"Well, yes, I am," I answered, a little baffled. "Why?"

"I crossed the ocean with Miriam Hopkins," he continued.

"Lucky you," I said.

"I asked her to marry me," he said.

"Good God, why?" I said.

"Because I love her," he said.

"I still ask you why," I said. (Just then I was divorcing my first wife, Winifred.)

"Haven't you ever been in love?" he said, still ironic.

"Sure, many times. But not to marry."

"Never been married?" he said.

"That's another story," I said.

"Miriam suggested that I meet you. That you can show me ways."

"Ways?"

"How to change her mind—to marry me."

"That's kind of Miriam. I loved her for years, and I don't pretend to know one thing about her. She's one of the most exciting ladies I ever loved. She was kind to choose me—temporarily—among so many admirers. But to know her, never."

"Then why did she say that you can help?"

"Miriam talks too much—and talks, and talks. As a matter of fact, you have to wait until she takes a breath through her ramblings before you jump in to say yes or no. You don't get another chance for a long time."

"I still don't know why she asked me to meet you. And I still love her," Tola insisted, puzzled.

"Tola," I began kindly, "one phase I am sure about. Miriam loves life, and people, and knowledge. You have every asset she likes in a man, but don't ask her. Don't tell her what you want or how you feel. One night after much champagne and caviar and laughter and you're absolutely sure you've really had a good time together, order one more magnum of champagne and one pound of caviar. Put 'em in your car and put Miriam in your car too. Carry her if you have to. She is petite. And stop at the first marriage place (of course you got the marriage license days ago). Open the magnum and ask the mayor and the witnesses to drink to your happiness. And get *married*. She'll love it. Not much of a script, but it usually works—particularly with Miriam."

Tola listened and looked at me as if Hollywood had softened my brain. But he tried it, step by step, and it worked. They were married.

And it was a *disaster*.

He built a magnificent home at Malibu Beach but lived in her house up in the Beverly Hills Canyon (first mistake). He did not offer to pay for her servants, liquor, and food (second mistake). Miriam was doing a picture. Tola visited her on the set and commented how the director should have handled the scene he had witnessed (third mistake). So the inevitable happened. Miriam took residence in Reno, Nevada, for a quick, quiet divorce.

Now the second phase started for Tola: *suffering*. We walked on the beach, long, exhausting walks. He talked constantly and cried and hoped for reconciliation.

"I'll give anything to have Miriam back: ten thousand dollars, twenty, twenty-five, my Picasso, my contract. I must not lose her."

All offers very tempting for a man out of a job for two months. Finally, I had one suggestion: "Tola, you want Miriam back? We engage a helicopter and fly over her villa in Reno, each of us carrying a magnum, and we will parachute into her garden. 'Miriam, this is stupid, let's go back home,' you tell her."

"No, she will never do it," Tola whispered, shaking his head.

"What can we lose? Maybe a broken neck if the parachute doesn't open in time," I said.

Of course we didn't do it. After the divorce was final, they remained good friends for a long time.

In the months after World War II, we still had to have coupons to buy meat, sweets, or any luxuries. An ex-major in the army—Signal Corps Photographic Service—Tola had access to better coupons. One Sunday he was going to give a lunch for forty people in honor of Olivia de Havilland, his new star and his potential heart throb.

The Saturday before, he brought home the most glorious ham, a rhapsody of fragrance and juices. His domestic couple roasted it to perfection with mustard and honey and cloves and slices of pineapple. It was a beautiful picture. What satisfaction could be anticipated!

Ludwig Bemelmans—brilliant writer, painter and illustrator, gourmet, bon vivant, a delightful host and precious friend—was living on the same floor with me as a guest of Tola's. That afternoon, walking on the beach a few houses away from Tola's, we visited Doris Duddley, a lovely lady who had a good crowd of beautiful young people visiting—sunburned, happy, healthy, and hungry. We joined them and soon the vin ordinaire was floating in our veins with warmth and brotherly love. But peanuts and potato chips were not the answer to our appetites. Bread and onions were in abundance, but no butter, no cheese, no sausages, no ham.

At the word "ham," the rubicund, bold round face of Ludwig took on rainbow shades of mischievous planning. And his triumphant voice was the war cry before the attack. "Let's go, Johnny," he shouted with glee.

"Where are you going?" Doris asked.

"For the *miracle*, Doris, the *miracle!*"

The tide had come in, so we were up to our navels in water. Giggling with pleasure—a good joke was in the making—we arrived by the back way to Tola's house. It was past midnight. Everybody was asleep. The house was in darkness, but we knew our way to the kitchen. There it was in the icebox, the glorious ham—the *miracle*.

Proud of this brilliant idea and the enormous joke, we waded eagerly back to Doris', Bemi holding the plate of ham gingerly.

"Wait until you see Tola's face tomorrow when the guests arrive!"

Stupid joke, but we didn't think so then. Next morning we were awakened by deafening knocks on our doors. Tola was foaming at the mouth, trembling with fury. He was not pink but magenta.

"*Out*, out of my house, you monsters! Thieves! Out, out, *out*. And *now*."

Our angelic looks didn't seem to soften his fury. How had he found out?

It seemed that first thing in the morning dear Doris Duddley returned the big plate on which we had carried the ham to her house, and thanked Tola in the name of all her friends for the generous king's present—the ham. "It was delicious. Moist and perfectly cooked."

That was the end of our ménage à trois. We even offered to cook hot dogs and sauerkraut for his guests, and serve it, but we were refused, ignored, thrown out. Time softened Tola's fury, but never were we trusted or invited to spend weekends at his home again. A pity!

Tola was given to strange jokes. At one time during World War II a particularly awkward joke bounced back the wrong way and became an alarming national scandal.

He was having dinner with beautiful Paulette Goddard, Charlie Chaplin's discovery, at Ciro's, a better restaurant and nightclub. That same night, I was dating Alice Eyland, Miss "Chesterfield," and was seated at a table next to his. Both girls were hot news, dressed to kill. The photographers were having a field day shooting us from every angle. Returning to the table from the dance floor, Paulette dropped one of her earrings under the table. Tola—quite drunk by now (as was Paulette), but still the perfect gentleman—disappeared under the table to find it. But how long does it take to look for an earring? The silly joke grew to be phony acting. Tola's disappearance under the table lasted beyond the time limit of a prank. Paulette began to moan convincingly. Friends, waiters, and photographers became voyeurs. They laughed and whispered encouragement to Tola. They felt they were witnessing a free and bold Hollywood scandal.

When finally, fifteen minutes later, Tola appeared from under the table, to the applause of the amused audience, he straightened his hair with just the right amount of embarrassment. Flashbulbs popped on and off rhythmically, and the rumor spread through the night and filled the gossip columns. For days, syndicated newspapers and cine-magazines carried the story enlarged and distorted out of proportion.

"What did Paulette Goddard say when Tola Litvak went under the table? Dial 387 (?) for the answer!" A game and a laugh. When you dialed that number, a series of short moans of ecstasy was the answer.

For poetic justice, Tola got a mouth infection at the height of the scandal and had to paint it dark lavender (it matched his pink face). But the joke became a deeply serious matter. The State Department in Washington was flooded with protest letters from American mothers: "Our sons are dying on battlefronts, and this foreigner, wearing the American uniform of a major, plays at home and fights his war in nightclubs. A disgrace. An outrage. A shameful display." Such expressions of strong feelings moved the State Department to action.

I was East doing a training film for the U.S. Army when I was summoned to Washington by the State Department to give my version of the incident. I treated the whole matter as an unfortunate joke. The officials were not convinced.

Cherchez la femme. A woman got Tola into this trouble, and the woman he found to get him out of it was the same one—Paulette. Averell Harriman, the ambassador to the Soviet Union under President Roosevelt, liked Paulette. Liked her enough to intercede in the "Litvak Case" and have it killed.

Strange as it may seem, Tola enjoyed the widespread reputation.

Perhaps Tola's greatest romance began when the "Oomph Girl" came into his life, Ann Sheridan. She was a young sexy blonde, a simple, delightful comedienne, given to raucous laughter and straightforward, often coarse, language. She appeared as partner for Cagney, Bogart, George Raft, Cary Grant, and Ronald Reagan in Warner box-office pictures like *They Drive by Night, The Man Who Came to Dinner, King's Row, I Was a Male War Bride.*

Top: *Anatole Litvak*
Bottom: *Ann Sheridan*

Annie really fell for Tola, as deeply and seriously as a simple girl could fall for a foreign charmer. And then the usual Tola pattern: late for dates, inconsiderate and abusive, or simply forgetting to arrive at all.

One night Sammy, Tola's butler, called me frantically: "You better come over, sir. Mr. Litvak is not home. Miss Annie is drinking hard. She's throwing our best dishes out into the ocean."

"O.K., Sammy, I'll be right over."

Annie was drunk, drunk as a skunk, with a vocabulary to match. She was standing on the terrace, a stack of Tola's best dinner plates on the table next to her.

Swish—a plate flew expertly toward the night tide. She saw me: "Where is he? Where is the pink jerk?" she yelled. *Swish*—another plate went to eternity.

"Annie, baibee, just listen—" I tried.

"You listen to me. [*Swish*] I've been waiting here for three hours. [*Swish*] The dirty pink bastard, fink rat. [*Swish*] Good-for-nothing worm. [*Swish, swish, swish*]

"*Wow, wow, wow*, did you see that? Three in a row. Like beautiful fucking seagulls! There goes the last one. [*Swissshh*] One of these days, I'm going to tell that phony two-timer to go and—"

"All right, Annie. One day you'll tell him." I tried to calm her. "Now, why don't you—"

She put her arms around me and interrupted my argument: "Now why don't you be a good boy, have a drink with Annie, and wait for the *skunk*?"

I stayed. I had a drink, and one more for the road, and another.

It was past midnight when Tola arrived, wearing a pure-rose-angel look and offering no excuses. "And how's everybody? Did you have any dinner?"

I hiccuped.

"So where were you?" Annie bellowed. "We had a date at eight, remember?"

"Busy, Annie, busy. Sorry I couldn't make it. I apologize."

"See, Annie, he apologized," I shouted with relief, getting ready to go home.

"I don't buy it, Buster." Annie stopped me and turned a steely glance at Tola. "Lover, I'm not going to tell it to you tonight, but sometime I'll tell you to go and fuck yourself. Not tonight, but sometime—"

"You're vulgar, Annie. I'm tired. Good night." He started from the room but turned to me at the stairway. "Close the door quietly, Johnny, when you take her home."

A sullen silence, then Annie burst out laughing, her raucous, earthy laugh. "What a ham! And what a stinking, lousy performance!" Imitating his voice: " 'Close the door quietly, Johnny, when you take her home.' Ha! Can you believe it? I hate the creep."

"No you don't, Annie. You love him and admire him. We all do. But he's peculiar." I put my arms around her. "Now go upstairs and make up? Be the clever one."

She didn't give me much of an argument after that. She was lonely. They made up. And fell in love all over again.

But this new reconciliation didn't last long either. The Tola suffering pattern erupted with imaginary suspicions, one-way questions, and fanciful pains. Ann Sheridan finally told him one day "to go and . . ." She married George Brent, the polished, handsome star.

A young, promising starlet committed suicide over her turbulent affair with Tola.

The big female star of his last picture was left stranded in Honolulu waiting for him and a promised heaven.

Ludwig Bemelmans

Tola was a good friend—complicated but devoted, considerate but selfish, primitive and sophisticated. It all depended on how you fitted into his ways and interests.

The last time I saw Tola was almost thirty years after the Sheridan romance. It was in Paris. He had a magnificent apartment on the Seine. He was building a new villa in Saint Tropez on the Riviera, was newly married to Sophie, a famous Paris model. He had lost some of his Russian sparkle, and his asthma was bothering him seriously. We talked the whole afternoon—reminiscences of old times, of fun and work and future plans. Dusty was returning to California for the usual inventory with new tenants for our home there.

When we left, Tola asked a strange favor. "Johnny, could I come and spend some time in your flat in London? I may find some of my sanity."

I called his Paris apartment from London two weeks later. His faithful secretary, Anne Sallepenko, told me that he had gone to Vienna for a possible deal.

He never made it. The deal or London.

HOWARD HAWKS, EXAGGERATED DREAMER

"HOWARD, I need an opening for my new picture, "I said one afternoon.

"What kind of a story do you have?" Howard spoke quietly.

"The story of a sadist. A bowling-alley king gambler in love with the same girl his young manager wants."

"And the girl?"

"A nightclub singer: hard, a sparkle-plenty facade, yet a lonely, unhappy soul."

"The young manager?"

"Simple, uncomplicated, athletic."

Howard lighted a cigarette meticulously. He took his time, inhaled deeply, then mumbled almost to himself:

"Early morning . . . the office of the young manager . . . he walks in whistling, takes off his coat, hangs it up, sits at his desk . . . opens the daily work sheet . . . when his eyes focus on something draped over the back of a chair—a silk stocking . . .

on the couch another one . . . a bra . . . a matching pair of lace panties . . . further, two provocative red shoes . . . and suddenly is aware of the sound of his shower running full blast—"

"But he doesn't have a shower," I interrupted.

"Build one!" Howard snapped, and continued right on: "He approaches the door of the shower . . . it opens and a naked, round, sexy, wet arm stretches out. . . . 'Will you pass me a towel?'—a husky girl's voice . . . of course she is the singer the boss engaged. From here on it's easy going."

I liked it. It was the opening of my first picture at 20th Century–Fox, *Road House.*

Six years later I was going to Italy to shoot *Three Coins in the Fountain.* I went to say goodbye to Howard.

"Howard, I need a new opening for my picture. The story of three girls, three working girls, Americans, secretaries in Rome, in love with three men—an Italian prince, a successful writer, and a handsome Italian working with one of the girls in the same office."

Howard lighted a cheroot meticulously, inhaled deeply, and started to mumble:

"Early morning in Rome . . . the handsome Italian boy enters his office . . . takes off his coat . . . hangs it up . . . when his eyes focus on a pair of silk stockings draped over the back of his chair—"

"But, Howard, I had this opening in *Road House,* six years ago."

"Did it hurt?"

"No. It helped."

"So use it again. Change the sex. *He* takes the shower. *She* comes into the office. *She* hears the shower. *He* asks for a towel. New time, new people, new sets. Keep things happening fast enough and nobody has time to notice the resemblance to the old picture, or care about the logic of events. Change the sex. That is the key."

With *Front Page* Howard changed the reporter, Lee Tracy, to a woman, Rosalind Russell, and called the new version *His Girl Friday.*

"A stroke of genius," Ernst Lubitsch commented when he heard of the change.

I did not use this opening in *Three Coins*.

This was Howard Hawks, a giant in the film business, who got his first chance in a silent feature with *The Road to Glory* in 1925 and continued to make important pictures in the 1920s, '30s, '40s, '50s, and late '60s. He was one of the few great directors covering half a century of filmmaking—silent and talkies.

Born in 1896 in Goshen, Indiana, Howard W. Hawks had a university education, experience as a mechanical engineer and prop man, and had spent time in cutting and script departments. His appearance was as distinctive as his films: gray hair, blue eyes, tall, with a low-pitched civilized drawl. He was an inveterate gambler and man-about-town, dressed in expensive and sharp tweeds, and led a busy and turbulent social life. He was also a preposterous, imaginative, and inspired liar. In his films Howard was often concerned with the relationship between male friends—companionship rather than love.

His film women were as hard as the men. They moved and acted like them. Howard was intrigued with their masculine integrity. They were not women in love but rivals—cynical, tough-minded, indifferent to sentimentality, and sexy. And yet his women were sexy and seductive, with an air of having just come out of bed or inviting you into it—not the usual gentle, easy-to-hurt, well-combed characters.

Howard Hawks could crowd a world tragedy, complex human relations, heavy drama, light comedy, a chase, a suspense thriller, an epic, and delightful small events into one normal-length feature, set in one location, one room.

He created an atmosphere of enclosure—packed emotions in a small space and a short time—while studying sarcastically the lowest human instincts and the lunatic humor of little guys. Comedy remained his passion. He showed unusual talent for mocking and destroying pompous dignity and for making a parody of romance.

I knew about Howard Hawks long before I came to Hollywood. I admired his films. Later I met him socially and was impressed with his patience and simplicity. He could explain a complicated card game to me with humility, the humility of a wise man, the humility of knowledge.

I've mentioned that he was an imaginative liar—exaggerated, extravagant.

His agent, and mine—Charles Kenneth Feldman—loved him but suffered the tortures of hell when he heard his exaggerations.

One time Howard was summoned to the small claims court to answer a suit brought against him by the gasoline station and the supermarket he used for non-payment of his bills. Charlie Feldman, who was a lawyer before he became an agent, and I drove him to court.

"Now, Howard, remember you'll be under oath. So any fibs, mistakes, or exaggerations you make can be used against you. I beg of you, let's pay the bills, let's make a settlement, and let's hurry to Palm Springs for the weekend. A promise?"

"Of course, Charlie, don't worry!"

But Charlie Feldman was worried.

The judge, a kind, tired old face, was a friend of Hollywood. He knew and admired Howard's pictures. For a full five minutes he read and carefully studied the voluminous file of the suit brought against Howard.

"Mr. Hawks, according to the papers before me, you owe the gasoline station eighteen hundred dollars?"

"Yes, sir."

"And you owe the supermarket thirty-four hundred dollars?"

"Yes, sir."

"Do you intend to pay them?"

"No, sir."

"I see. For what reason, Mr. Hawks?"

"They've been cheating me, Your Honor."

"When did you notice that they were cheating you?"

"Right from the beginning, about six months ago."

"Why didn't you tell them then, in the beginning?"

"I wanted to find out how far they would go, Your Honor."

"So if they hadn't brought suit against you, you would have continued to use their services?"

"Yes, sir."

"And not pay?"

"Yes, sir. Not pay a cent!"

Charlie Feldman was sweating and twisting in his seat.

"Mr. Hawks, how much do you think they've cheated you?"

"Well, Your Honor, about twice as much as the regular price."

"Which means that they actually cheated you of half of what you owe them?"

"Yes, sir."

"Mr. Hawks, the gasoline station and the supermarket are willing to make a settlement and accept half of what you owe. Are you prepared to pay them half of their losses?"

"No, sir."

"But why, Mr. Hawks?"

"They should be punished, Your Honor."

Poor Charlie. Now he knew that there was no hope.

The judge was thinking. He turned a few pages in the file—slowly.

"Mr. Hawks, remembering that you are under oath: What was the salary you received for your last picture?"

"Four hundred thousand dollars."

"Mr. Hawks, how much are you worth?"

"Real estate, Your Honor? Painting collections? Stocks? Investments?"

"Everything, Mr. Hawks."

"Hard to say, sir."

"About, Mr. Hawks, a round figure?"

"Well . . . I would say . . . between seventy and eighty million."

"Dollars?"

"Yes, sir, dollars."

Charlie Feldman crossed his arms, closed his eyes, and seemed to die slowly of embarrassment.

The kind judge didn't show any change in his calm expression. "And *cash*, Mr. Hawks, actual cash?"

"Again, it is hard to say, Your Honor. But as a wild guess I suppose between two and two and a half million dollars."

"That is quite a sum, Mr. Hawks. And in spite of these astronomical figures, you are not willing to settle this suit for *half* of what you owe—a meager twenty-six hundred dollars?"

"No, sir. They don't deserve a settlement."

The judge closed the file with a bang. "It is the judgment of the court that you, Mr. Hawks, should pay the *whole* amount you owe or go to jail. Case dismissed."

After Charlie settled the whole claim, Howard was in excellent humor. In the car on the way to Palm Springs, I kept quiet.

Charlie was fit to be tied. "You promised, Howard. You *promised* not to lie. Why did you?"

"I didn't lie, Charlie. I told the truth."

"So what about the eighty million dollars you're worth?"

"What about it, Charlie? You know as well as I that my real estate alone is worth half of that. And what about our gold mine?"

"Our gold mine, Howard, is a fake, a joke, a ridiculous investment, a *disaster*."

"No it isn't, Charlie. I know. They told me."

"They? Who, Howard?"

"The people who sold us the stock. They called me last week to buy some more. As a matter of fact, I wanted to talk to you about it. We need to get a specialist—a C.P.A.—from Washington to fix our taxes. This year our income will be enormous."

Charlie looked at him, then turned away.

We drove a few more miles, Howard whistling, I quiet, Charlie wanting to forget. But he couldn't.

"How did you arrive at the two and a half million dollars cash?"

"Simple, Charlie—all the safety boxes I have in banks around the country."

"In that case, you can pay me back the fifty-two hundred dollars I just settled for you in court?"

"No sense, Charlie, disturbing the safety boxes for such a paltry sum. Take it out of my next assignment."

"Which one, Howard?"

"The *next* one."

This was Howard Hawks—a poet, a liar; magnifying to the extreme; building, stretching, and overdoing; distorting and embroidering. And yet if one took the trouble to dare him, to call his cards, one would be the loser.

Howard wanted to build a ranch house on a piece of land he owned. He was preparing a picture with Katharine Hepburn and Cary Grant, *Bringing Up Baby*, so he had the studio build a set for the picture exactly like the house he wanted, outside and inside—and change it whenever he felt that the proportions weren't what he wanted. Slim, his wife of that period, would drive to the studio, and together they would design their dream house. For three months they lived in their home before the home itself was built, eliminating and adding—another window here, higher ceiling there, an addition, an experiment. When the picture was finished, Howard had a complete set of pictures of their dream house, and a complete set of plans for the construction of it drafted to the tenth of an inch. And he didn't spend one cent for the films' set over the agreed budget. Ideal way to plan a home: no mistakes, no additions, no changes.

Slim Hawks, a classic beauty—real style, with a perfect elegance that passed without being noticed—was more than a partner to Howard. She was an inspiration to this exciting, difficult talent.

A girl on the cover of *Harper's Bazaar* caught Slim's critical eye. She met her; they became friends; Slim brought her to Howard. And Howard Hawks's new picture, *To Have and Have Not*, gained a star. Thanks to Slim, Lauren Bacall was the discovery of the 1940s.

My admiration for Slim Hawks had no limits. I considered her to be perfection. I trusted her instincts and her judgment. One afternoon I went to see her in Palm Springs. "Slim, there is a girl—" I said.

"There is always a girl—" she said.

"No, this time's a little more than just a girl. She could be *the* girl." I sat down.

"You are in trouble," she said.

"I want to marry her," I said.

"You are in serious trouble." She sat down too.

"Slim, please don't joke."

"Sorry, Johnny. How could I help?"

"This girl is staying at the Racquet Club. She'll be there for two more weeks. I'd like you to meet her and watch her. Talk to her. Find out if she's the right kind of girl."

"For what?" she said.

"I told you. I want to marry her," I said.

"Well, Johnny, don't you think this is somehow stupid?

One doesn't marry just because a friend tells him she is the right girl. You have to make up your own mind."

"I've made up my mind. I'll marry her. Only—"

"Only what?"

"I'll feel better if you O.K. her."

"But why me?"

"Because . . . to my mind you're perfect."

"That's flattering. But what happens if I don't like her?" she said.

"I'll marry her just the same," I said.

"Well, that's better," she said.

Slim met Dusty, Dusty Anderson. That was *the* girl.

"You better catch her and quick," Slim told me a few days later. "You're not the only one in line. And when you do, I'll give you the wedding at my house. She's quite a girl!"

Slim and Howard gave us the wedding. Howard was best man. José Iturbi was Dusty's self-appointed godfather. In the back garden on a natural hilltop surrounded by four tall trees, hummingbirds darted around the flowers—a perfect background for a marriage ceremony. Everything to make the operation less painful.

We called Howard the "Great White Father." He was that. He was great. He looked white. He *was* old and wise, but he was also the youngest among us: young, imaginative, courageous, and mostly an exaggerated dreamer.

JOHN HUSTON, ARTIST WITH A PUNCH

For a man who creates a crisis, a storm, everywhere he goes, he is a quiet talker, almost whispering his sage knowledge. He is tall, over six feet, gaunt, looking like he's always hunched over his script. With a broken nose, big strong road-digger hands, he is an artist to the limit, interested in everything and everybody, friend to people and animals. He'll never answer your questions immediately. There is a sidelong look, and just the right length of silence to give weight to his answer. John Huston is the center, the roundup, the respected authority. This is how I see him. I admire and love him. And envy him.

There are so many sides of John's unexpected behavior.

Eric Ambler, author of A *Coffin for Dimitrios*, told this story about John:

Near the end of the War, John and Eric were in a bar by the waterfront. It was filled with sailors, tough-looking and hard-drinking. John wanted some action, a fight, so he turned to a big sailor on his right: "My friend here"—pointing to Eric—"says he knows you."

"So what?"

"So he says that you abandoned your station in your last battle."

"He did?"

"Just whispered to me."

The sailor came around and tapped Eric on the shoulder. "You know me?"

Eric blinked. "No, I don't."

"Then why do you tell your friend that I am a deserter?"

Baffled, Eric looked at John for help.

"I beg your pardon." John pushed the sailor aside. "Are you bothering my friend?"

And the fight started. Eric came out of the melee with two black eyes and a broken wrist.

Eric went to bed for three days. John and the sailor ended the night together good friends.

It was said that at one time he had a fight with Errol Flynn. There was no contest. Two punches and John was flat on the ground.

Errol helped him up. A splash of cold water and a whiskey brought John back to life. He started throwing wild punches at Errol, and again John hit the ground.

Again Errol helped him to revive, and again John was back punching and hitting Errol.

Back to the ground.

Errol dumped a whole bucket of water on him, and when John came to, Errol whispered to him kindly, "John, you have no chance. I was a professional fighter. Please don't be a fool."

It was told to me that John ended this story with: "When Errol said that to me, I knew I had him!"

My favorite assistant—Peppi Lenzi, the handsome Italian— was John's assistant in many of his pictures. While on location with Huston shooting *Heaven Knows, Mr. Allison*, Peppi told me that one hot afternoon John told him to relax for a while and told the stars (Deborah Kerr and Robert Mitchum) to do the same. "I have to rewrite the scene." He went out of the way, under a tropical tree, with the script and a big glass of whiskey and water. Hours passed. John was still staring at the open script, making short notes from time to time and quietly sipping his whiskey. When he finally closed the script, it was too late in the day to resume shooting. The company was dismissed and sent out to dinner. John joined them.

Peppi studied the new rewritten scene in Huston's script. Not a new line was written—nothing. But a paperback mystery book lay between John's script pages. John had to relax too somehow.

In 1947, three of us directors had a super anniversary of our marriages at John's ranch: Kendal and Lewis Milestone, with ten years of married bliss; Evelyn and John Huston; and my Dusty and I, with one year of trial and error.

Two hundred guests—friends, important enemies, famous beauties, and especially shining talent—filled John's Tarzana ranch by midnight. I provided Rumanian food—lamb shoulder with sauerkraut cured in champagne and caraway seeds. The Milestones brought Southern fried chicken, ham, and roast beef. The Hustons spread a generous hot selection of Mexican dishes, salads, fruits, and imported cheeses. There were drinks for every taste, beers and wines for gourmets and gourmands. A lively new orchestra had a beat hard to resist. The party lasted until late in the morning, when hot plates of *pipérade* and strong coffee greeted the morning chill. It was a bang-up party, with a lively display of top entertainment, including Judy Garland, Frank Sinatra, Danny Kaye, and Oscar Levant. Athletic beauties dressed in shimmering long gowns dived from the second-floor balcony into the lighted pools. There were a few inconsequential fights of jealous lovers, lost wigs, and scattered around the floor a few pairs of falsies—some scratched cheeks and quickly covered slaps. All in all, a beautiful normal Hollywood party of the period.

Every Christmas for years we adopted a war orphan through the Foster Parents Plan. Each year on the first of December we sent a letter to our friends: "This year again we are not going to send Christmas presents. Instead we will 'adopt' a fourth child. In this way you, too, will share in the happiness brought to a needy family. . . ."

John Huston resented this arrangement:

It's all very well for you to adopt a Polish orphan, but I'm used to getting Buffets and Jean Pauls [paintings] from you on Christmas. I feel that I should have been consulted in this matter, and as I wasn't, I would now like to know just how much the monthly checks are for. I do feel you must be coming off a lot better than you did in the old days when you were making fine gifts to your friends.

In case these remarks don't find their way to your hearts, I would like to present myself for adoption. I am forty-nine years old; would love to come to America. What I mean is none of this monthly-check and gift-letter business—I want to be taken right into your home.

As ever, John

It was during the war. John was preparing a new film. The star, George Raft, borrowed from Paramount, was not happy with certain scenes. So a meeting was arranged in John's office. George Raft—surrounded by his sidekick pals, his agent, and his lawyer—began his complaints. The usual: "Georgie is happy to do a picture for another studio . . . and Georgie is proud to be directed by John Huston. . . . But, the scenario, as it reads, is an *insult* to George Raft's *image*—the image he has created with his films. . . . Some of the scenes could distort and destroy the George Raft that the American Public and the public all over the world want." And on and on they talked. George talked. The agent talked. The lawyer talked.

John listened. Hunched over his desk, he drew continuously (John is an excellent draftsman). He sketched people, nudes, horses, flowers. Once in a while he gave an indifferent grunt—not agreeing or arguing, just a reminder to let them know he was there listening.

After one hour of one-sided arguments and muffled grunts, John closed the script and put it under lock and key in his drawer, raised himself to his full height, walked slowly to the door, opened it, and turned to them:

"Gentlemen, take your time. Settle these problems to your satisfaction. I'm going to war. The U.S. Army Photographic Service has given me an assignment." A short pause. "I really don't know what the hell you're talking about. So, good luck, gentlemen. Goodbye, Georgie. While I find what the war is all about, you take care of your fucking *image*."

And John Huston went to war. The picture was never made.

After dinner, John often loved to fight just for the pleasure of fighting—when usually people relax with a brandy, talk, or a social game ahead. One night at his ranch in Tarzana, California, John suggested to two of his friends present—Charles Grayson, a writer, and Collier Young, a producer—some exercise in punching. They went in his bedroom for a free-for-all slaughter. There were no war cries, no hard breathing, no rules. Half an hour later they joined the party in the living room, with black eyes, loose teeth, body bruises, swollen pink cheeks, and one bloody nose: just a hobby.

Then they got down to some heavy drinking. A young stage director from New York with his first film assignment was dazzled by the strange behavior that evening. He sat next to John.

John smiled at him. "How is it going, kid?" John said.

"Not too well, John."

"Directing?" John asked.

"Not yet. But actors—they don't listen. They don't understand. They argue with every scene. What do I do?"

A silent pause. A problem we all faced at one time or another, and found the answer to. Or ignored. We looked away.

"Tell him, Johnny?" He turned to me.

"I don't speak good English, John," I said, cowardly.

"Collier?" John turned to Collier Young, busy holding ice over his bloody nose.

"I'm just a producer, a wounded producer. Difficult to make sense," Collier answered.

John turned to Grayson. "Can you help him, Charlie?"

Charlie Grayson was holding his ribs. He talked heavily, out of breath: "I think I broke a rib." Turning to the young stage director, he said, "I don't like actors. They murder my lines. But John—he can tell you. He knows!" And Charlie stretched out on the floor.

John lighted his cheroot slowly, with pleasant anticipation. "You're wrong, kid. Actors listen. They understand. But they want to argue. They want to be convinced."

"About what? They know how to read." The young man was impatient.

"And most of them are well-read," John said quietly. "They collect good paintings. Some even paint—not bad either. They listen to classical music and have the latest recordings."

"Most of them are spoiled—spoiled children. I give up," the young director said.

John continued quietly: "They are children like you and me. And don't ever forget that they are the most important commodity in your film. It's success or failure. And they do their job. You? You just do yours—your job."

The young man was quiet for a moment, still lost, but timid. "Then, John, how do I handle my actors?"

"Talk to them about things they don't know. Try to give them an inferiority complex. If the actor is an American, speak to him in French or Spanish. If the actress is beautiful, screw her. If she isn't, present her with a valuable painting she will not understand. If they insist on being boring, kick their asses or twist their noses"—and John finished with a flourish—"and that's about all there is to it." We all applauded.

The young man smiled. "Twist their noses? Does it work?"

Evelyn Keyes, John's wife at that time, furnished the explanation: "It happened in Mexico. It was during the last days of shooting *The Treasure of the Sierra Madre*. It had been a long time on location—hard, hot, dirty, sweaty. Bogie had enough. He was bored. He wanted to go home, back to California. So he bothered John for days. John insisted he get the best of the location. The best of the story.

"'You want a masterpiece, eh, John? A perfect film. A gem. An artistic triumph?'" Bogie gravel-lisped.

"John listened to this kind of dialogue every night. Then one time at dinner when Bogie went too far, John leaned across the table, took Bogie's nose between his two strong fingers, and twisted hard for a full minute. No words were spoken. Only tears of pain ran down Bogie's cheeks. But then, no mention was ever made of returning home. Until the location work was completed."

The rest is history. *The Treasure of the Sierra Madre* gathered two Oscars, and it is a classic mentioned in many discussions of "Cinema as Art."

The young stage director never forgot John's wise explanations. At least I hope so, for his own good.

One thing that John has achieved that many of us directors would like to try—to be in front of the camera and be *good*. He is. We all want sometime in our life to make faces in the mirror, to laugh and die beautifully. John has succeeded in playing that character in a picture one remembers. Not because of the length of his role. But because of its unusual quality. A part to remember. That's John. John, the all-around moviemaker and man.

And this is why I envy him.

GRETA GARBO, THE TIMELESS ENIGMA

ORLY *Airport in Paris, Air France.* We were traveling first class on a 20th-Fox expense account.

Dusty and I boarded the plane having a what-kind-of-art-collection-did-we-buy? quarrel. I had invested too much in young painters (Bernard Buffet, Gen Paul, Pierre Bollaert), she said, and I had bargained too long over a superb Degas that both of us had wanted.

"Only five hundred dollars difference," she argued. "You like it. I like it. You wanted it. I wanted it. Why let a few hundred dollars upset your happiness?"

I closed the argument: "We will be back in Paris soon. The Degas will be there."

Of course she was right. A week later the painting wouldn't be there. (In fact it went to London's Tate Gallery.) I knew I was wrong, but I wouldn't admit it. And I also knew it was going to be a long trip to New York in silence.

The plane was full. We were seated in the second row. Both seats in front of us were unoccupied. I asked the lovely French stewardess if I could use one of them.

"Sorry, monsieur, they are reserved."

The hour of take-off was close. The moaning of "The Last Time I Saw Paris" soothed us. We had our seat belts fastened, and everybody was relaxing for the flight.

At the last moment, a lady in a black shiny raincoat and a slouchy hat, a large leather bag in hand, sat down alone in front of us. It was Greta Garbo, the last-on passenger.

Airborne, when the straps came off, I leaned toward her

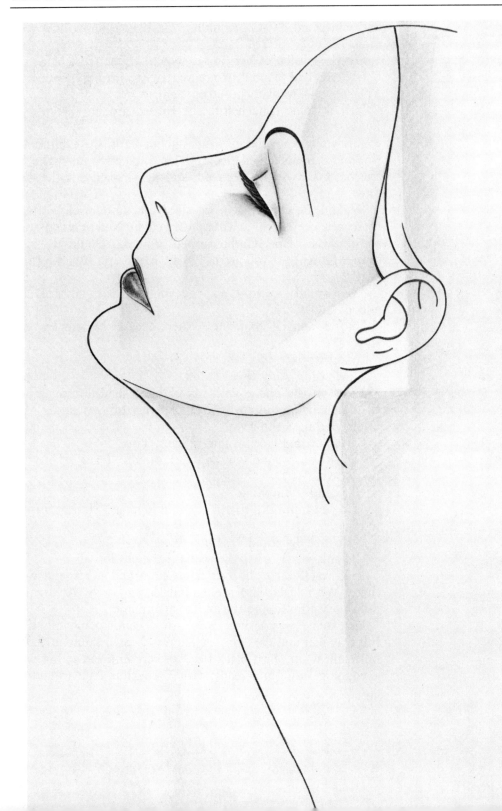

and whispered, "G.G., wouldn't you like to know how your orange trees are doing?"

(In the garden of her house, which we had bought a year before, she had planted two orange trees with her own hands. We knew she was very proud of them.)

It took some time before she turned around: "Jean . . . Dusty, how nice!"

A few pleasant brief exchanges about Paris, the exhibitions, the house in Beverly Hills, and we discreetly ended the intrusion. Garbo slept, ate, read, and just looked out the window.

We did the same and forgot all about our quarrel. Nothing more was exchanged until we arrived in New York. Before she left the plane, Garbo turned around. "Could we have dinner tonight? If you are not busy. *My* party. Just the three of us."

"We would love to, G.G., but you'll be our guest," Dusty added quickly.

"No, I want it to be my party. Please. Where are you staying?"

"Saint Regis."

"I will call." And we separated.

I was on the phone with my children in California when the hotel operator interrupted the conversation, excited: "Miss Greta Garbo is calling you."

"Thank you. I'll call you right back, Tina."

G.G.'s voice came low and unhurried: "I am asking you two a favor."

"Of course. Anything."

"Do you mind if a friend of mine joins us? He just arrived in town."

"We'll be delighted."

"Thank you. We will pick you up at eight-forty-five."

And exactly at eight-forty-five Garbo and her friend were there. We relaxed into a chauffeur-driven Rolls. As usual, I didn't pay attention to the exchange of names.

Her friend was a short, sunburned gentleman, with rich, full gray hair and dark glasses. He was dressed safely in classic blue suit, white shirt, black tie. Not very impressive, but with a winning smile and ready with friendship. We went to a small Hungarian restaurant famous for its goulash and strudel and the wines of the country.

I was amazed at Miss G.G.'s varying moods: a brief and sudden burst of gaiety, almost naive and childlike. In moments, she was restrained, cautious, and reserved. It all showed under her dazzling beauty.

When her friend suggested as entertainment after dinner a nightclub in Greenwich Village, "where a passionate gypsy beauty belts out Rumanian laments," Garbo refused brusquely. "Just because she sings all her songs to you and only to you," G.G. snapped at him.

"Not when I'll tell her that our friend is Rumanian. She will probably sing only to him. Besides she has a great voice."

"Like a horse," Greta burst out.

We laughed, and we ordered our strudel. She was jealous. Garbo was jealous. I was fascinated.

She suggested that after dinner we go to his house by the river. He accepted her decision gently, polite but not overdone. I believe he missed seeing his gypsy friend.

I had apple strudel and he ordered cheese strudel. We split half and half. There was richness in his friendship and kindness in his arguments. He was witty and ready with spicy anecdotes. When he paid for dinner, I mentioned that I would have liked to see and hear the Rumanian gypsy. He rejected the idea, to the obvious pleasure of both females— Garbo and Dusty.

His house, narrow and elegant, was by the East River in Sutton Place. Right from the entrance, and up the stairway there was hung on the walls on both sides an extraordinary collection of paintings: El Grecos, Gauguins, Van Goghs, Rembrandts. And there were more all over the house, priceless masterpieces that showed knowledge and perfect selection.

"What's the name of your friend?" I whispered to Garbo.

"Onassis—Aristotle Onassis. But he likes to be called Ari."

So the bargaining over the strudel—"I'd like a piece of yours if you'll take a piece of mine"—had been with one of the giants of world finance. Only this time I gained friendship, no crisis.

Later I saw Onassis often at the 21 Club in New York, lunching alone on the second floor. We talked about Maria, the Rumanian Gypsy in Greenwich Village, whom I had seen by then. "She reminds me of an exciting French singer—Damia," I told him. Onassis remembered Damia and agreed.

He loved his yacht *Christina*, named after his daughter. It had nine staterooms, each labeled after a Greek island. He would ask his guests to choose the island they preferred. Garbo chose the island of Lesbos.

I'll always remember him as he offered a bit of his philosophy of life: "If you're broke and have no place to stay, rent a room in the servants' quarters, but choose the best and most elegant hotel in the city. The gamble will always pay."

I first met Greta Garbo at the Feyders'—Jacques Feyder, the French director, and his wife, Françoise Rosay.

Françoise Rosay, one of the best French actresses of the time, gathered a delightful circle of friends in their house not far from Santa Monica. Writers Jacques Deval, Maurice Decobra, Yves Mirande, and Salka Viertel; directors Ernst Lubitsch, Willy Wyler, and Robert Florey; actors Arlette Marchal, Michele Morgan, Garbo, and Charles Boyer were the "usuals" in the Feyders' home.

I had heard so much about Garbo's lonely ways, about her self-imposed privacy, her strange, unexpected behavior. When I first met her I was ready to be confronted with some sort of bizarre performance. Instead, Garbo was simple, direct, in a good mood, comfortable, with a lovely sense of humor. The Feyders' home and its ambience gave her the comfort and security she needed.

At that time I wasn't yet working in pictures. I was still a painter and was making a portrait of Jacques Feyder. Garbo liked what I was doing. She posed willingly for some sketches and posed for photos I made of her and Jacques. She even snapped a photo herself of Jacques and me.

Soon I realized that to be her friend is to be simple and undemanding and discreet in your judgment of her and of her moods. One rainy evening at the Feyders' she was completely relaxed. She laughed heartily, listened carefully, then talked without interruption. One stranger, an English actor she didn't know, came in unexpectedly. Suddenly Garbo acted like a caged wild animal. She hurried out onto the terrace and walked alone in the dark, in the rain, to her home.

Garbo was shy, insecure. She felt that as a person she actually had nothing special or unusual for others to make a fuss over. She decided to be alone, to have a life of absolute privacy. The words were "I want to be *let* alone," not "I want to be alone." She created her loneliness and so protected her privacy.

The legendary stars have always counted, above everything else, on one special quality: their voice (Bacall), their beauty (Liz Taylor), their walk (Bardot), the atmosphere they carry along with them (Kate Hepburn), their marvelous ability to create a character (Bette Davis), their way of listening (Tracy), their body (Monroe). Garbo had no one special quality. She embodied all of them.

When I made her portrait, I realized that her beauty was a combination of marvelous but definite asymmetrics: a big forehead, one eyebrow higher than the other, a generous mouth with a much too liberal lower lip, a perfect nose slightly on the side in full face. Yet these asymmetrics—combined with that special sound of her voice, the body of a young warrior, the rhythm of her walk, the silent time she takes in answering—create the Garbo world she produces with her presence. This is unique, passionate, and profound. So she appeared then to me.

Years passed before I met Garbo again. My life had gone through changes and complications. Film had become my every-instant obsession. I had been divorced and was trying marriage again in a happier way. And I had become one of the millions who cried and laughed and grew enchanted by the spell of the most beautiful face of our century.

In dark theaters, in films on television, in color or black and white, Greta Lovisa Gustafsson (Garbo's real name when she was modeling hats for a big department store in Sweden) became Leonora in *The Temptress*, Felicitas in *Flesh and the Devil*, Anna Karenina in *Love*, Lillie Sterling in *Wild Orchids*, Anna in *Anna Christie*, Rita Cavalini in *Romance*, Susan in *Susan Lenox*, Grushinskaya in *Grand Hotel*, Christina in *Queen Christina*, Marguerite in *Camille*, Ninotchka in *Ninotchka*, Karina in *Two-Faced Woman*, and others.

After her last film, released in 1942, the M-G-M studios beat their publicity drums and shouted that *"Two-Faced*

Woman would give to the world a 'NEW' Garbo. A dramatic star of a different and special artistic quality."

Garbo did not think so. She did not like the film and simply and calmly announced that "she was retiring. She would never make another film."

Of course speculations ran rampant. It was a master stroke of publicity. Soon newspapers of the world would probably scream on their front pages, "GARBO RETURNS!"

The analysts knew publicity. What they did not know was the woman. Garbo was silent and withdrawn, determined about her announcement of retirement. And so ended one of the truly great careers in film history. The world lost forever another part of its beauty and luster.

Men came into her life and were soon gone. They all tried to marry her. But Garbo was and remained "alone." Books have been written about her in all languages. Almost every year there is a "Garbo Festival" somewhere in the world.

Picture after picture has been announced for her, with her. Thousands and thousands of photographs, studies and close-ups, have been published and displayed on covers and layouts. She bought and sold a dozen homes. She became rich, and rumors and stories, true and untrue, were told and retold. She became a legend, worshipped and imitated.

Why has Garbo retired from films? To answer this question articles have been written; explanations and speculations have filled books and magazines. Her silence and her decision have increased the curiosity, the mystery. My theory is the result of my knowledge of the actress, the star I worked with and I loved:

A star reaches such heights—dazzling, uncomfortable, uncontrolled adulation, immoral fortune—and all in the shadow of insecurity. Garbo loved picture-making. She loved film. How could she change and stay away from it when it meant everything to her—air, food, love, dream, integrity.

She meant it when she said she would never make another film again after the release of *Two-Faced Woman*—at that moment. But then it was too late to change. The decision went too far. She was committed to a decision—a temporary decision, but a decision. The rumors, the publicity, and the legend of Garbo deprived her of her only love—filmmaking.

In 1954 I produced the Academy Awards show. It was an

exhausting job, which I accepted on two conditions: One, that all the nominated stars and supporting stars would appear onstage to hand the statuettes to the winners for technical achievements. Millions of TV viewers would see their favorite stars whether they won Oscars or not. The second condition was that an honorary Oscar be given to Greta Garbo. The Academy Board agreed.

I knew that Garbo would never make an appearance to accept the Oscar, but would she let me come to New York and make a shot of her in her apartment, on her balcony, or any location she would choose? In a short speech she could thank the industry for this honor. Any writer would be proud to write the speech, which she could accept or reject. Also she would have the right to destroy the film and the negative if it was not to her liking.

"Let me call you in two days," G.G. told me. Her answer two days later: "Thank you. No."

I arranged to project a scene from *Camille*—the George Cukor masterpiece. The reception was extraordinary. Garbo received a standing ovation. Patricia Neal accepted the Oscar for her in New York.

In the summer of 1959, after I finished a picture for Metro-Goldwyn-Mayer, I gave my usual end-of-the-picture party at our house for the cast and the crew.

That afternoon G.G. came by—"Just to see my two orange trees." After two iced Polish vodkas, she was in a happy mood. I had an idea.

"G.G., this is still your house. The boys tonight are your friends. They worked with you and for you. Why don't you receive your friends in your house? Be the hostess. They will love to see you again."

For a moment she was serious, remembering. I insisted: "Cole Porter is coming too. He adores you."

She smiled again. "Maybe."

My sizzling Rumanian dishes in the kitchen called me. G.G. picked up her oranges and left.

That evening she was the first one to arrive. We went straight to the bar and helped ourselves to another double iced Polish vodka.

Dusty drifted away to meet the other guests at the door: "Garbo is here. Don't look surprised. Don't make much of it." And they didn't. They acted as if they had just left her at the studio that afternoon. Garbo was among friends. There was no tension from her. But there was held-in great excitement among her boys. What a story to tell friends: "We dined last night with Garbo."

There were two theories about Garbo. The first was that she was lonely. Her self-created aura of secrecy, her shyness, and her desire for seclusion were genuine. But she was not lonely. Her few friends were those who accepted her as she was, in the mood she was. They never expected her to conform to their way of doing things, or of thinking, or of living.

The other theory was that her ways were the obvious result of a self-made pose. Garbo knew that when people met her it was with fear and admiration. So her silence and her slow answering were parts of the pose which she knew would make her the timeless mystery she was.

Two theories, each containing elements that kept alive the publicity, each theory helped by the other. Both were true and legitimate.

Since 1941, Garbo has not made a film. What other famous living star has been able to keep out of film business for forty years and hold—and even see grow—her fame and popularity?

Many years went by before I saw Garbo again. I was doing location work in New York. One night I was dining at the Ahernes'. Brian of stage and film fame (*The Barretts of Wimpole Street, Titanic, The Best of Everything*) courted and married Eleonore de Liagre the same year and time that Dusty said yes to my wooing.

Eleonore called just before dinner: "Brian has a meeting at the Players Club. Do you mind having dinner with three ladies?"

"Mind? Of course not. Delighted, overwhelmed, and—"

"Be here at eight"—Eleonore interrupted the flood of my exaggerated schmaltz—"and keep your Rumanian charm for my two friends."

The other two ladies were Greta Garbo and Marlene Dietrich. What a jackpot of an evening! World glamour and

A woman of mystery even to my nervous Leica shots

maybe New York gossip of the highest discrimination.

Instead, G.G. complained about the neighbor living in the apartment over hers. He was building a new bath. Noise and copper pipes came through her ceiling. Marlene was comparing the rising prices from day to day on fruit and fresh vegetables. (Marlene shopped early and cooked for her man!)

Two of the most famous women in the world exchanging banalities and kitchen talk!

Was I going to be cheated out of special notes for my memory book? One doesn't dine every night with Garbo and Dietrich? I changed the subject: "G.G., when you were making a film, did you see the rushes every day?"

"I never liked my work," she replied.

"I've seen my rushes every day," Marlene added. "Not once but twice. Once with Joe [Josef von Sternberg] and once alone after Joe told me what I did right and what I did wrong."

"You worry after?" I challenged.

"Only one worry—that the film remains a Marlene Dietrich film."

I tried to pry into Marlene's work: "Joe certainly made the most beautiful close-ups of you."

"Yes, he did. But I helped." Marlene smiled. "I know my face and I know my photographic business—when to add a back light or when to kill two lights from the side to get the best of my face."

So the talk went like that during a gourmet dinner and in the company of limitless beauty. Marlene talked, argued. She was planning to fly to Australia for her one-man show, six weeks at an astronomic guaranteed salary.

Garbo listened. Serious. She told us the truth when she said, "I never liked my work." Blessed with rare beauty, she used it to buy privacy. Her own honest and, I believe, romantic nature bloomed in that privacy.

Two stars, two women of extraordinary fascination, yet giving opposite impressions. Garbo is insecure about publicity. Marlene thrives on it. Garbo is hard in the presence of sentimentality. Marlene will scrub the floor for her man and her grandchildren. But both of them are true professionals, two honest professionals.

A theater manager who had *Camille* playing to a full house for weeks observed that he had expected an audience of fans of Garbo's time. They did come, but with them a significant number of the new generation. They had never seen Garbo on the screen before. They were noisy and wisecracking about the exaggerated way their parents worshipped their idol.

"When they came out," the manager observed, "they were quiet and moved. They had experienced an artistic emotion unknown to them."

Garbo was the one star whom men and women loved unconditionally.

Garbo will get old. But her beauty will never diminish.

MARILYN MONROE, A VULNERABLE PHENOMENON

"SHE represents to men something we all want in our unfulfilled dreams. She's the girl you'd like to double-cross your wife with." (My comment to *Eros* magazine in 1962, nine years after I had directed Marilyn in *How to Marry a Millionaire*.)

It was in 1950, at the "Annual Sam Spiegel New Year's Eve Party." Sam was not the successful producer he became later, just a promoter with financial difficulties. For some reason, no one who was anybody would miss the Sam Spiegel (alias S. P. Eagle) annual party.

The famous and the unknown were there, maybe five hundred. There were two orchestras and two generous buffets. Beauties, the conceited and the hopeful, were mixed together, while a finance company was removing Sam's car from the garage. Yet there was an air of affluence, of pride and good feeling, knowing that we were there and belonged to Hollywood.

At one of the crowded bars on two stools a young man and a blond girl were touching elbows. They didn't know each other. No introduction was necessary. It was New Year's Eve, so they smiled. They toasted each other, and they talked about their work, their hopes. He was a writer-producer married to a star and somewhat discouraged by five years of frustration trying to promote a story he knew was great. She was a young actress doing small parts. Her option had been dropped that day by a big studio. She was yearning to get a break, *the* part, the *great* part.

They danced, and as midnight was tolled—the lights crazily flashing on and off to blasting music—the young man gently kissed the blond girl: "Good luck, honey. Things will be good for us this year!"

She hid a tear—"Not for me"—and ran away into the crowded garden.

The young man looked sadly after her: "Poor lonely Hollywood kid."

The blond girl that year played a small role that she made eye-catching in *All About Eve*. And Marilyn Monroe started her meteoric climb to fame.

The young man, Frank Ross, two years later got the chance of his life when he produced "his" story, *The Robe*, the first CinemaScope picture. And he was on his way to millions of dollars of profit.

Another Hollywood story.

Marilyn Monroe was sex symbol, love goddess, Venus. As a child she lived in orphanages and foster homes. Her father was never clearly known. She was raped at the age of eight by an elderly actor who paid her one nickel not to tell. A promiscuous mother eventually went insane. There was an early wrecked marriage, a smattering of only partially successful modeling, and a life of easily forgotten affairs. At the age of twenty, her walk had begun to call forth appreciative whistles. Cars honked, and lustful propositions came with every wiggle, every undulated step—the sound she loved that made her alive, completely secure, the robust masculine wolf whistle.

"That's the trouble. A sex symbol becomes a thing. I just hate to be a thing," Marilyn complained to an interviewer after her teen-age allurement had developed into a delightful national scandal. "But if I am going to be a symbol of something, I'd rather have it sex than some other things they've got symbols for."

My first confrontation with this phenomenon was when I

was assigned to *How to Marry a Millionaire*. Marilyn Monroe was working in Howard Hawks's *Gentlemen Prefer Blondes* when I went to present her the script. Howard introduced me. She was vague and did not want to accept the script until I told her that Mr. Zanuck had asked me to give it to her. She repeated, "Mr. Zanuck," with reverence and took the script. Then she wasn't there. No way to reach her.

After Marilyn read the script, her reaction was one of confusion: "Is it good for me? Is this the right and the best part for me?" she asked Charlie Feldman, also her agent. He suggested she talk to me. She didn't call to make an appointment. She just came. Wanda, my secretary, rushed into my office all excited: "*She* is here!"

"I beg your pardon?"

"M.M. is here. She actually talks and moves."

"Who?"

"Miss Monroe, that's who."

She was dressed in a polka-dot white silk blouse, silk black slacks, wearing sunglasses and red high-heeled shoes. Her childlike appeal was sincere and convincing, her vagueness persuasive, her humor seductive. The scene ran something like this:

Marilyn's voice quiet, childlike, out of breath: "Mr. Feldman asked me to see you."

"Charlie is a good and generous friend." (I made this into a compliment to her. No reaction.)

"Mr. Feldman said you'll explain to me."

"Explain?"

"My part."

(Now I knew there was some trouble.)

"Have you read the script, Miss Monroe?"

"Yes."

"And?"

"I don't know . . ."

"Miss Monroe, you read the script. It is a brilliant script by Nunnally Johnson. Your part is right for you. Shall I tell you what it is about?"

She took off her glasses and said in a loud voice, "I know what it is all about, but—" (Silence.)

"But what?"

(Still loud): "Who *are* we?"

(Wow. That's a good one. So answer the lady. Be clever.)

"Miss Monroe, you are three beautiful girls, Loco, Schatze, and Pola, wishing to marry millionaires. And the kind of girls you are, the contents of your icebox explains: hot dogs, orchids, and champagne. Does that answer your question?"

It didn't. She started to put her dark glasses back on but didn't. Finally she looked at me—not her uncertain sidelong look, but straight at me. And again she found her voice: "What is the *motivation* of my character?"

Now it was all clear. Her Russian coach, Natasha Lytess, had put her up to this. So this called for my most know-how voice: "The motivation, Miss Monroe? You're blind as a bat without glasses. That is your motivation."

Her eyes came out from under her drooping lids. The puzzled child had resolved the "if": "That's all?"

"Yes, Marilyn. That's all."

She put back her dark glasses and left—satisfied.

From the first day of the shooting Marilyn assumed one of

the prerogatives of the great stars. She came on the set at her own time and regarded schedule as an infringement on her civil rights.

Her co-stars were Betty Grable—a good professional comedienne with experience, smooth and accessible—and Lauren Bacall: razor-sharp wit, astute and definite, with a rare style of delivery, a great sense of humor, and an abundance of talent. Bacall and Grable, sympathetic to Marilyn, tried to help her, but their sympathy was sorely taxed after a while.

"She is terrified to step before the camera," Bacall explained to us. In those moments of indecision she tried to delay as long as she could the time to face the camera.

But once she faced it, an extraordinary unseen love affair took place between her and the lenses. A love affair nobody around her was aware of—director, cameraman, soundman. It was a language of looks, a forbidden intimacy. Only when the film was put together did this love affair become apparent to us. The lenses were the audience.

Not a beautiful woman as classic beauty goes, Marilyn knew how to make the audience see what she really wanted them to see—a desirable beauty.

All of us knew that she was preoccupied with being an actress—at all times. It drove us batty.

I met her at the start of a day: "Good morning, Marilyn."

She stopped with an absent-minded smile and breathed heavily: "Rockefeller!"

I knew she was sometimes witty and original, but her answer took me by surprise. I got ready for my daily worries.

Later in the day I had the answer. The three girls were stretched out on easy chairs drinking champagne and discussing whom they would like to marry.

Marilyn: "You know who I'd like to marry?"

Betty Grable: "Who?"

Marilyn: "Rockefeller."

There it was—the connection of this morning's greeting.

Marilyn was intent on rehearsing these stupendous lines, but after the girls had gone over the scene a couple of times, Grable turned to talk to Bacall.

Marilyn went right on: "You know who I'd like to marry?" Betty turned around surprised, but obligingly gave the cue: "Who?" and Marilyn said, "Rockefeller."

Grable went back to her private conversation with Bacall. But Marilyn went on: "You know who I'd like to marry?"

Betty paused in her conversation. Slightly exasperated, she shouted: "Sonny Tufts?" Marilyn, without batting an eye, repeated her line: "Rockefeller."

The only way she felt comfortable was nude.

"When I was a little girl, I often had this dream: I walked the length of the church with no clothes on. Naked and with no feeling of wrong, sin, or shame."

She was sexy, but not dirty—gay, carefree, healthy.

This honest joy in her body explains why she photographed so well. Richard Avedon, the fine producer, said, "What makes a great photograph is not the technique but the content."

One afternoon we were doing a silent shot of her asleep, dreaming. She was covered with a rich, shiny silk sheet. Her body was firmly defined under the undulated folds. Her eyes were closed, dreaming. I couldn't miss the opportunity to lean over the bed and fix the folds a little closer to her body. After all I was the director. As my knowledgeable painter's hands were doing the required job, gently folding and pushing the silk sheet under her, I realized that she was nude, completely nude.

"Marilyn, are you nude?" I whispered.

She didn't even open her eyes, she just gave a delicious "Mmhmm . . ."

"But what if there is a fire and you have to run out of bed?"

She opened her eyes. "The script says *nude*. So I am nude."

Embarrassed, I turned back to my crew. By the camera, two young priests, visitors on the set, their eyes bulging out of their heads, were leaning forward out of their shoes toward Marilyn. And certainly thinking, This is better than *heaven!*

Marilyn went back to her dreams. Her alluring face shone with divine anticipation. Of men, love, fame, the charming prince? No, the script. She was dreaming of a colossal, juicy CinemaScope-size *hot dog*.

As she became more successful, she grew more insecure. Marilyn was at times also timid. Full of complexes, she stuttered a little. She always tried to consult somebody before answering a direct question.

Classic beauty makes a story point: Lauren Bacall and J.N.

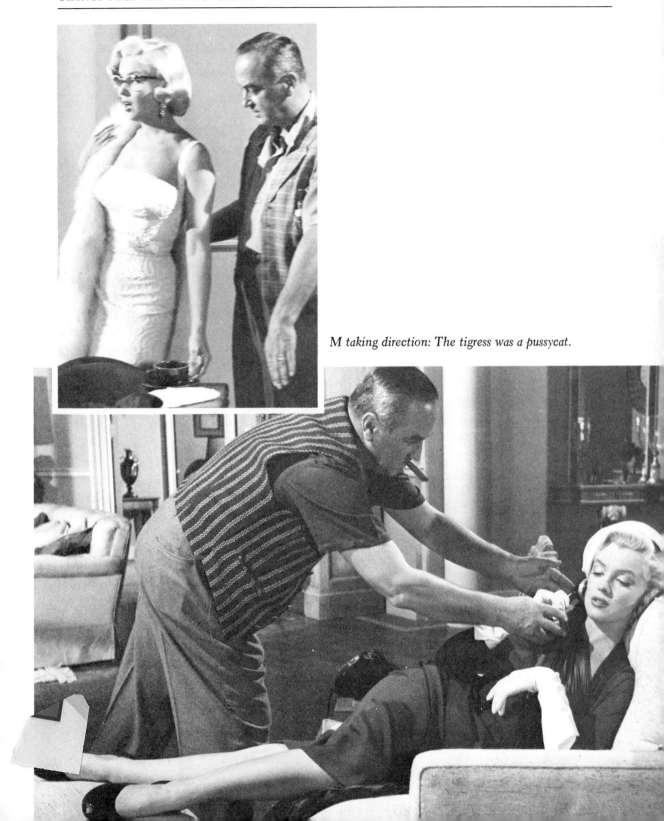

M taking direction: The tigress was a pussycat.

Once on the set a reporter asked her what was her favorite color. She excused herself and came to me: "Johnny, what should be my favorite color?"

"Don't you know?"

"You're a painter. What color do you think I should prefer?"

I thought for a few seconds. "I think *red* should be your color, Marilyn."

"Why?"

"Because red is violent, passionate, outstanding among other colors. It catches the eye—like you. You catch the eye, and that's all we see."

She quoted the answer to the reporter, word for word.

Everybody at the studio seemed to be happy with our film. Still we had to have the last confirmation from the public.

The Wilshire Theater was blazing with lights, feverish with microphones and flashbulbs and television cameras—and a smart audience. The industry and especially executives and studio heads were there that night. To see if a simple story in comedy vein could marry CinemaScope.

In front of me, Harry Cohn, Columbia's president, and Cecil B. DeMille were in animated discussion about the chances of CinemaScope. Tonight, they were saying, they had to be shown.

Suddenly there was a growing roar, like an approaching earthquake, a faraway stampede. "Marilyn . . . Mariiiilyyn . . ." I could hear it echoing over the pops of flashbulbs, the loudspeakers, the shouts and whistles, the welcoming screams of the adoring crowd: "Mariiilyyn . . ."

Four cops were carrying into the theater—over their heads—our star. Dressed in platinum and shining beads on white silk stretched to the extreme to emphasize every curve, every contour, of the sex goddess, she simply couldn't walk in her second skin. People stood up. Some climbed on their seats to see better. In front of me, Cecil B. DeMille was struggling to stand up on his seat. I witnessed beyond any expectation the luxury of her singular fame, the culmination of her triumph.

The show went over smoothly. The right laughs at the right places, and some extra we didn't expect. One hearty laugh was never intended: when the girls were broke, and, one by one, furniture pieces, lamps, rugs, and drapes disappeared. There remained one big enormous stark painting by Bernard Buffet to watch the lovely apartment. Then, in beat with the music and the mounting laughs, everything appeared in the right place again. Our lovely girls had captured a new provider, another millionaire sucker.

CinemaScope was accepted. The majesty of the New York skyscrapers did not seem a frightening background for the shapely beauty of our three lovely girls.

After the preview, a reception was given by us at our home for over a hundred happy guests. Marilyn and her sewn-in platinum and white-beaded dress were the focal point of every eye and every compliment. She was happy. She was loved. She had proved to everyone (and herself) that she could stand any competition.

Over the years I was called to make with her retakes or added scenes needed in pictures made by other directors.

We developed a rapport in that work. Marilyn would do what was called for. Sparkling, quick-witted, and all-around cooperative, she had the crew and her co-stars in love with her.

In 1961, after the unexpected failure of *The Misfits*, her divorce from Arthur Miller, and the premature death of Clark Gable, Marilyn became neurotic. Afraid to face reality, she wasn't strong enough to cope with life, and especially with failure.

The Fox studio lined up for her a remake of a successful picture, *My Favorite Wife*. It was called *Something's Got to Give*, co-starring Dean Martin and Cyd Charisse, to be directed by the favorite women's director, George Cukor. The writer was Nunnally Johnson.

"I'm working on a script for Marilyn Monroe," Nunnally wrote me, "but I don't know whether it will ever be made or not. They seemed to be too scared around Fox to ask her."

Nunnally met with her and told her the whole story and the way he was going to write the screenplay. After they finished three bottles of champagne, they were close friends. She adoring every word, every line he said, and Nunnally listening to and agreeing with every comment she made.

She was happy again—happy with the script when Nunnally brought it to her, and even happier when Dean Martin told her it was one of the best scripts he had read lately. The same thing was told to her by Lee and Paula Strasberg, her teachers from New York.

The picture started in a happy mood. Marilyn felt that this was the script that would recapture for her the adoring public, the whistles of the males. She told this to everyone who listened, to friends and lovers and to the studio people.

One afternoon I met her near my bungalow. She was barefoot, scantily dressed, and ecstatic, with shining cheeks and sparkling eyes.

"And where is Miss M. going barefoot?"

"The music building," she said. "They have a song for me."

"Be careful, Marilyn, there are bad stones on the road."

She raised her arms. "Carry me, Johnny."

I picked her up. She fit like a glove, a welcome cuddler. I felt strong and young and chosen. (Where are those goddamn photographers with their flashbulbs?) Reluctantly I deposited her with the musicians. She liked their company, she liked their talk, their jokes. They adored her. I always thought that a music man could have been her *right* marriage.

For a short time, the work on the picture *Something's Got to Give* was almost normal.

And then George Cukor brought a new writer in to polish the script and add new dialogue. With the first blue pages they lost Marilyn. The only thing she knew was that they had changed the script she liked—and were ignoring her opinion.

Marilyn went to bed, and the guiding spirit of Fox, Peter Levathes, fired her and closed the picture down.

Levathes was a tall, dark man, nervous and with the faraway look of a man with responsibilities beyond his understanding or ability.

"You are going to be put on the picture," Nunnally Johnson phoned me from London. "Marilyn has asked for you."

Levathes summoned me to his office: "The New York people have decided to have the Monroe picture roll again—with you as the new director."

I was happy to work with her again. "We should use the Nunnally Johnson script."

"Why?" Levathes was antagonistic.

"Because she liked it. And I believe it is important to have her happy at this time."

"Why should we? Marilyn has no script approval."

"But she likes the Nunnally Johnson script," I repeated.

"We spent money and time on the rewrite. We think it is better," Levathes insisted.

"Perhaps, but she doesn't think so."

"I have to call New York and see if they approve."

"Mr. Levathes, let me go and talk to her."

"You can't. We are suing her for seven hundred and fifty thousand dollars. She is counteracting by suing us for two million. Dean Martin has filed a plea claiming damages from Fox for eight hundred and fifty thousand dollars. Talking to her would jeopardize our legal position."

"Mr. Levathes, I know Marilyn. I'll find a legitimate reason to see her. I'll take her a drawing I made of her in *Millionaire* for her new home. We'll have a drink. Maybe a laugh. I'll promise her we'll go back to the script she liked, and you'll have a Monroe picture—which the studio needs."

Levathes was annoyed, impatient. "Johnny, I'm the executive producer of this picture. Weinstein is the producer. You'll be the director. But none of us can talk to her now. We shouldn't. Let the lawyers handle it. I have your promise not to approach her officially or personally—O.K.?"

So I didn't go.

Three days later Marilyn committed suicide.

Maybe I shouldn't have listened to Levathes and should have rushed right over to her home to see her. Maybe this was the chance to give her the hope she so badly needed—wanting to work, to be with us again.

Maybe. Maybe not. Maybe she would have ended her life anyway. Nobody will ever know the real truth.

Combining the ways of a child, a woman of the world, and a helpless mistress who needs protection, Marilyn represented at the time the slavery a man wanted—but also his freedom.

She owed everything to Hollywood. Fame, an adoring audience, limitless riches, a cult who zoomed her to heights she fought desperately to keep. She belonged to the *cinema* and only to the cinema.

She had such a right sense of knowing the character she was playing—the way to enter a scene, to hold singular attention as the scene developed, the way to end a scene—so that no other actor existed around her.

Her contribution to film was so rare, unique, and extraordinary that what could have been just a good picture became, sometimes, an experience of magic.

When she was dressed to impress, she was a hurricane of glamour. With a soft-spoken voice, helpless as a sharp knife, her eyes at half mast like a cobra watching its prey, she was a cruel child tearing off butterfly wings—gay, mean, proud, and inscrutable.

On my desk there's always a notebook binder with a rich brown cover of Moroccan leather on which my name is inscribed in gold. The cover is large enough to hold a complete script, but inside there is only a single page. There is an inscription to me:

WOULDN'T THAT BE WONDERFUL
IF YOU HAD THE THREE OF US
UP FOR DINNER?
———
These Pioneers
LOCO, SCHATZE, and POLA

The three girls were happy together when they brought me this well-chosen gift.

And now, after so many years, the biggest realization for me is that Marilyn achieved what she set out to do. She and she alone made herself an actress.

BOGIE AND BACALL

THE Garden of Allah was a colony of bungalows on Sunset Boulevard, Hollywood, where character actors, cover girls brought for one picture, or writers in trial for one assignment were living in contentment—all waiting to find out if their Hollywood contract option with considerable increase would be taken, or that their completed job was so outstanding that they might join the exclusive Beverly Hills or Bel Air colony. It was a warm afternoon in the forties, and we were in Roland Young's bungalow—the mannerly British actor with the comic flair—the first time that I met Humphrey Bogart.

He stood in the doorway drawing you into his magnetic field. He had a face of romantic ugliness, the eyes riveting, the cigarette angled in his hand so that the fighting knuckles showed, the voice gravel scraping on a dry creek bed. It was pure Bogart theater.

"Bogie, I want you to meet Prince Jean Negulesco"—Roland spoke most formally—"the royal Rumanian painter."

"What's all this royalty crap." More Bogart gravel. "Are you a good painter?" The eyes searched my face.

I tried to send a measuring stare back. "Painter I am. How good, I don't know. Prince I am not."

Roland, slipping me an approving wink, poured martinis. And more martinis. We had dinner at Lucy's Restaurant, then did more drinking in the Oyster Bar at Ciro's. There I made some caricatures of faces I liked. Two more martinis and Bogie and Roland got the idea to sell the sketches for one dollar apiece—autographed by both of them and signed by me.

Two pretty boys

The two theatrical voices announced the great opportunity: "For only one dollar you can have an original drawing by the personal royal painter of Queen Marie of Rumania." An interested circle formed. "We'll pay for everybody's drink," Bogie announced, playing the role of the hard-boiled gent with class. We had to dig into our own pockets at the end of the evening.

"You're good, kid," Bogie said. With that I was admitted to his special small group of friends.

Some people believed Bogie was a cruel trickster, a sadist. Actually he was a sentimental prankster. Bogie loved his friends with a possessive devotion. One night Roland had a formal dinner at the home of the studio's head for whom he was making a picture.

"How could he do this to us?" Bogie was annoyed. A number of drinks at Ciro's decided us to go to the Garden of Allah.

He wasn't there yet. Bogie went through the window and opened the door from inside.

"Let's see what the Englishman does when he finds his bed on the lawn," Bogie suggested.

We carried out most of his furniture, his bed all made up, with pajamas laid out carefully and slippers at the foot of the bed. We surveyed our work and hid behind the bushes to watch Roland's arrival.

Surprised he was—but tired and bored with us. He knew who did it. He sat down on a chair, lighted a cigarette, and just waited. The joke went bad on us.

Bogie made a sign. "Come, kid." We picked up the bed and put it back inside, and every other piece of furniture. Roland, absolutely calm, just followed us with his eyes. When everything was in the bungalow and in place, Roland picked up his chair, went inside, and closed the door in our faces.

On the way to Ciro's, Bogie suddenly roared with laughter. "Why the English codfish! Not even a fucking thank-you." When Bogie's joke was hurting a friend, he stopped and made amends.

As serious and dedicated as Bogie was about his work, he was as enthusiastic and fiendish at any chance to enjoy other people's discomfort. Especially if he had caused it. At that special moment, he assumed a foxy look and giggled, anticipating and relishing the explosion that resulted.

In 1952 I was lent to Metro-Goldwyn-Mayer for a picture. It was four days before the start of *The Town and Mrs. McCheshney*. We were having dinner at the Nunnally Johnsons' with Bogie and Lauren Bacall. Bogie was in great form. His jokes were fresh. He was making fun of himself and flirting with Doris Johnson and Dusty. I had the just-before-starting-a-picture blues.

Bogie snapped at me: "I tell you what you need, kid—the *Santana*. Three days on the boat, no calls, no dates, just calm sea, good air away from the smog. I'll pick you two up tomorrow morning and drive to the harbor. We'll swim and relax, sleep like babies. Don't take your script. Forget it. Bring you back Sunday morning. Start fresh on Monday. O.K.?"

"It'll be great for you, darling," Dusty said. "I need some rest too." Dusty loves to sail.

"I'm out," Bacall said quickly. "I'm staying home."

Bogie, Dusty, and J.N. on the Santana

"I stay with her," Doris said firmly.

"Can't leave town. It's in my contract," Nunnally mumbled.

I agreed halfheartedly. The joy in Dusty's face anticipating a weekend at sea convinced me suddenly that it *was* a great idea. (Why wasn't I struck with an instant short case of flu? Why didn't I collapse with my usual sacroiliac bends? Why didn't I break a toe or something? I could have stayed home!)

We went in my car. Bogie drove. He knew a shortcut to the harbor. We parked in a public garage and, with a small suitcase and my camera, got on the *Santana*.

Named after the Santa Ana, the desert wind, she was a fifty-four-foot sailing yacht. Trim, sleek, she was beautifully kept. Carl Peterson, the cheerful Danish captain, showed us to our sleeping quarters. Everything was friendly, everything shining. To me, it still had that special boat smell which makes me weak in the knees. I was seasick on the set of my film *Titanic*. Soon we were on the sea headed for Catalina Island.

Bogie, a scotch in his hand, looked completely relaxed. Dusty was holding on ropes, loving the wind and the spray from the waves. I went in the cabin to lie down.

Before we were even moored at Cherry Cove on Catalina Island, we were invaded by Bogie's yachtsmen friends. Suntanned, happy, noisy, they had a language of their own—sea language. How much "she does." How "dependable she is." How "she undulates" and "how she comes through." I knew a few lovely ladies in Hollywood to whom this language could apply—and with no change of terms whatever.

"You look great, kid," Bogie greeted me each morning. "You look relaxed. No phone calls from the big boss. No script to mix you up. Just a good relaxed time."

I was as relaxed as a stretched bow.

Sunday morning I was ready to go back to Beverly Hills. "Bogie, you promised to take me back Sunday morning," I reminded him with finality.

"Take it easy, kid. You don't want to spoil Dusty's fun, do you?" he graveled back accusingly.

"But Bogie, you promised."

"I'll tell you what, kid. Why don't you start ahead of us. *Walk.* You're not the *first* to walk on the water."

Dusty roared with laughter. Bogie felt that I needed some good advice.

"Grow up, kid," he said. "Try to mingle with our friends. Be a part of the fun. Relax. Don't be a stranger. Make a fool of yourself."

It was that phrase "Don't be a stranger" that did it. Sunday is the "day" of visits. Bogie was in a great mood and so was Dusty. The coffee smell was still in the cabin, the bacon and eggs were not washed from the plates when they had their first martini.

I decided in spite of everything to have a good time. I tried, and it worked. I had fun. Bogie provided Playboy-bunny hats; the boys and the girls wore them. We sang and danced and competed with the boys against the girls for the best chorus-line show. Fools, but happy fools.

I loved my Dusty. I liked Bogie. I even liked being at anchor in a boat. And that Sunday morning passed with more salty language and promises of "Next Sunday, O.K.?"

We left in the late afternoon. *I was going home*, home built on solid ground. With the night, we were back in the harbor. Bogie suggested a great chili place.

I stood my ground. "I want to go to Beverly Hills. Right *now*."

But happiness was not mine yet. I paid for letting Bogie drive my car to the harbor. He had not turned off the key in the ignition. The battery was dead. (Did you say dead? Yes, dead, d-e-a-d!)

It was past midnight when we arrived home. Bogie got into his own car. "Well, kid, wasn't this great?" he asked shrewdly.

"Bogie, it was the most boring, obnoxious, and hateful experience of my life. But I love you just the same."

With a mischievous, impish smile and his lisping, booming voice: "Baloney, kid. You're just a fucking ungrateful prick." And his car roared out of the driveway.

Next day, I started the new picture exhausted and seasick.

Lauren Bacall made a change in Bogie, and it was all for the better.

"*Humphrey*"—that was all she had to call when Bogie was ready to start a fight or in the mood to needle a stranger or

VOGUE

PARIS

DÉC./JAN. F 30

PAR
LAUREN
BACALL

was passing the limits of a joke. Bogie obeyed, apologized, and changed his hostile mood to a slap on the back and a laugh.

In their courting days, I used to meet Bacall walking her dog on Reeves Drive in Beverly Hills. The famous model of the *Bazaar*, she was provocative, tall, beautiful. She looked at you from the side of her eyes, the sidelong-glance bedroom look. Stubborn and decisive in her work, anything she started she remained dedicated to, surmounting any handicaps—physical or otherwise—to achieve just what she wanted.

Bogie had class; and hers is a kind that is distinctively her own. When one remembers what she did or what she said, what stands out especially is how she did it and how she said it.

The Shah of Iran and Queen Soraya were visiting Hollywood. The motion picture industry entertained them with a big dinner at the Luau Restaurant in Beverly Hills. All Hollywood was there: stars, producers, directors, writers, starlets, agents.

After dinner, during dance time, Bacall, watching the royal couple, whispered to Bogie, "She is so beautiful. Why don't you get up and ask Queen Soraya to dance?"

Bogie stood up. "If I'm going to dance, I'll ask the Shah. He's prettier."

Bacall, to avert an embarrassing encounter, hurried to invite the Shah herself. They danced beautifully, watched and admired. The Shah, obviously pleased and flattered, complimented his partner: "You're a natural born dancer, Miss Bacall."

"You bet your ass, Shah!" Bacall answered with hearty projection. Without missing a step.

In March 1956, Bogie had a major operation. He never was well again. I went to Europe to make a picture. By the end of the year I returned to Los Angeles for two days, and Dusty and I went to see him. He was watching television. I brought him two of the latest lithos by Bernard Buffet, signed and dedicated to him. When he became sentimental—which

Bacall: "Jean Negulesco thought I looked like this in How to Marry a Millionaire. *I hope he was right."*

he was—he usually covered up with a wisecrack and indifference. This time he was moved. He made us hold them above the fireplace that he might appreciate them better.

I still see him now—Bogie in a dark red robe, his neck grown thin, his crooked face studying the lithos and telling us in his gravelly voice where he planned to hang them in the house.

In 1972 (fifteen years after Bogie's death) I was in New York for a day. I called Lauren Bacall to get a ticket for her very successful play, *Applause*. The house was sold out, and she got me a house seat. I watched a miracle. One person holding a play together by sheer vitality, by rich ability, her own special magic. She didn't have a voice, but she sang. She had a bandaged twisted ankle, but she danced.

After the show, at "21" for a light supper, she talked and I listened. So many rich memories of Bogie. It was late in the night when we closed the place.

There were those who loved Bogie and some who·hated him. The percentage was overwhelmingly on his side. It would not have been so much for him if he had not had the luck to meet Bacall at the height of his career.

The first photo Bogie gave me was a commercial still from his film *Petrified Forest*, a Christ face, a look of loneliness, a man with a broken heart. On it, he scribbled, "Johnny, are you alive?"

Bogie was alive all through his life. But more, Bogie is alive *now*. It would be no shock to see him and hear his gravel lisp: "Baloney, kid, you're a pro or you're a bum. You're a man or you're a phony."

KATE AND SPENCE

I always wanted to do a Western. I had my cowboy suit, my hat, my boots. But producers would smile kindly: "Johnny, your pictures have a naughty touch, that foreign charm. Don't spoil it. Let Hathaway do the Westerns. Now, here is a story I know you can do."

And the Western would be put aside for a "naughty" story. With three wicked girls and three wicked guys, foreign charm and light music. And I looked with envy at Henry Hathaway's picture with good guys and bad guys, horses and gentle girls and gunfighters who could shoot a hole in a penny thrown in the air by another gunfighter.

One day, one of the better literary agents in Hollywood sent me a Western story, a good simple story.

I thought it would be great for Spencer Tracy. I called. Katharine Hepburn answered—her unmistakable voice. "Send us the story." I did immediately. Next morning she called: "Can you have afternoon tea with us?"

When I met them, they looked and were the way I imagined them to be—simple, warm, ready with friendship. She served a good cup of tea with homemade cookies, and he talked. I thought Spence was one of the most fascinating men I had ever met. His charm was the easiest. When he listened to you, he made you want to be at your best.

He liked the story and wanted to do it. That simple. That afternoon our friendship began. I was invited often for lunch, always cooked by her.

Their relationship was based on a very solid and ideal foundation: Kate was doing the spoiling and Spence simply

accepted. She was submissive. He was commanding. From the beginning she understood that devoting her life to him was the only course that would make caring for each other a lasting arrangement.

Their first meeting is now a classic tale. Cast together in a film that was about to be produced, they met for the first time in an upper corridor of M-G-M studios: "I think I am a little tall for you, Mr. Tracy." And from the producer, Joseph Mankiewicz: "Don't worry, Kate. Soon he'll cut you down to size."

Katharine is amazing: incredible, distinctive, and passionate.

In looks and voice, she shocks and surprises. She is a presence, a presence she carries with her in every scene. In every instant of her life.

She was always in good humor and usually of a dominating nature. The voice was loud and not apologetic for her outspoken convictions: "For God's sake, will you shut up and let Jean speak?" if Spence would interrupt her chatter.

During the making of a picture, Kate involved herself completely in every aspect of the project. She invaded other people's territory—producers', directors', writers', cameramen's. She could not keep still. A fusspot on the set, she pretended to be an expert on everything—wardrobe, sets, lighting—which was of course very much resented. But what all the acknowledged experts resented even more was when they had to admit that she actually did know everything and that she was right all the time.

Kate learned her lines to perfection and sometimes the lines of others. But, this was where Spence stopped and Kate just began. She analyzed the character she was playing, studied it from every aspect, tried to understand the "whys," argued, made changes, was never satisfied about her characterization.

"There must be one more way to do it better," she would say.

Spence's approach to a scene was just the opposite. Once he knew his lines, he counted on his instinct of the moment. He strongly believed that his first two takes were always the best. And yet, if he had to do it more than twice, he would do everything exactly the same as the first time.

Spencer Tracy knew how to listen. He talked with such reduced gestures and so calm a voice that it was a miracle to see how much more convincing he was than the actors playing with him. You never took your eyes away from him, as if he were the only one in the scene. In a long shot of a crowded scene, Spence was always a close-up.

In some of my discussions with him about acting—with a capital "A"—he hated the idea of being considered superior to other actors. His belief of happiness showed in his way of living and the quality of his acting: simplicity, always simplicity:

"A truly happy person finds his freedom not in how much money he has but in how much belief he has in himself." A moment of silence. Then he summed up his thinking: "It took me forty years to learn what I know. I'm a movie actor, and the only thing I have to do is to learn my lines. The rest will come."

The successful pattern of the pair's romantic comedies—*Woman of the Year, Keeper of the Flame, Adam's Rib, Pat and Mike, Desk Set*—was molded on the premise of two unsuited, inconsistent personalities at each other's throats—not polite but considerate, cutting and never giving a chance of surrender. These struggles built to love—and considerable box office. A story and a script were there, but the comedy or dramatic tension resulted from the combination of their special talents. They were without doubt, in my opinion, the most successful couple in the history of the cinema.

Spence and Kate seemed to have continued this formula in life. "I have had twenty years of perfect companionship with a man among men," she summed up their life together.

Spence loved gossip. He loved to hear it. He loved to tell it. Very often I played croquet at Sam Goldwyn's court with the "West Coast Croquet Masters": Louis Jourdan, George Sanders, Howard Hawks and his brother, producer Bill Hawks, Mike Romanoff, Herbert Bayard Swope, Charlie Lederer, and of course Sam Goldwyn. Sam was incredible. What he did to the noble game of croquet, his twisting of the King's English, his cheating and explaining, were precious marvels of hysterical behavior. I did a pretty good imitation of Sam's high-pitched voice, and Spence would delight in my stories.

"What did *he* say today?" Spence would ask with eager anticipation.

"Oh, not much. He made a good shot against Mike Romanoff." In a high-pitched voice I continued: "You know, Mike, I could beat you with my legs tied behind my back."

Spence, who knew Sam well, would roar with laughter, to Kate's delight at seeing her man so happy.

Once, in the absence of world-shattering news, Los Angeles newspapers decided to create with the help of film critics, theater exhibitors, stage and film editors, a contest: "Who is the greatest actor alive today?" After weeks of publicity, Sir Laurence Olivier was chosen the best—accolades, glorifying articles, and a golden plaque for the winner. Then the reporters had the idea to interview the runner-up. Spence was number two.

"They've just left, the reporters," Spence told us. "They came to ask did I think the selection was right. Is Sir Laurence the greatest actor?"

" 'Of course *he* is,' I told them. 'Look at his credits: great actor, great Shakespearean actor, great director, great successful producer in the stage and the cinema. Of course he is the greatest. And no one comes close to him.' They were amazed at my enthusiasm but also a little disappointed. Now here is the twist."

Spence laid back on his chair in contented ease. "When they left, I stopped them at the door. 'Oh, by the way, gentlemen, I forgot to mention one small detail. When Sir Laurence is talking with me he calls me 'Teach.' ' "

Spence was happy as a child telling that story.

Kate had simplicity and shocking honesty. Her approach to every moment of the day was with a sense of wonder and adventure.

One afternoon after an elegant lunch at our home, Kate left, only to ring the bell before I had time to turn around: "Give me a fork, Jean-Jean. I cannot stand the crabgrass between the bricks of your pathway." And in her beautiful loose gray slacks, striped blouse, and open sandals, she spent the afternoon pulling out *all* the crabgrass between the bricks of our pathway.

Kate did everything for Spence, anticipating his needs and wants. She would listen to what he said, agreeing, laughing at his jokes (they were good jokes). She would take anything from him, even his mockeries (some pretty hard to take), nothing from anybody else.

Spence was an impatient man, spoiled, loving to abuse his male authority.

When on a tour with a play or just on a pleasure trip, Kate would bring kitchen utensils—pans and pots, electric outlets, cups, plates, and silver—to cook and serve all the meals as if they were at home. For Spence, at the time to leave a place, he would be the first to sit in the car waiting impatiently and blowing the horn. Kate and Phyllis—her English secretary and constant companion—would hurry out, struggling with suitcases, overcoats, laundry, and all the kitchen paraphernalia.

"Christ, girls, can't you hurry a little? There is nothing I hate more than to sit and wait," that man among men would grumble.

I often would reprimand him on his assumed privilege to abuse kindness and devotion.

"I have the right to act like that, Spence. After all, in my youth I was a gigolo. But you, a real rugged, warm-blooded American through and through . . ."

One cold afternoon Kate came into the living room carrying a full load of heavy wood for the fireplace.

"Don't do that," he whispered impatiently.

I looked at him surprised: "Well, you're not all bad, Spence. You are considerate sometimes."

"No, nothing like that. I don't mind her doing it. But not in front of my friends."

In the fall of 1966, I was invited by the International Executive Service Corps, New York, to go to Turkey and help, if possible, the Turkish film industry raise its local production to international standards. I stayed in Turkey nine months, an adventurous time filled with Balkan promises. Of course everything fizzled out when the question of money arose.

I had a lot of time on my hands. I wrote Kate and Spence of my impressions of that extraordinary country, extraordinary where tourism is concerned, where masterpieces and blatant richness held hands with the lowest forms of misery and discomfort.

When I returned to the States, they were the first friends I saw. At lunchtime or tea, no matter who the guest was— male or female—Spence was always served first. But this time Kate served me first.

"You don't mind, Spence," Kate said. "He was away for months."

"Go ahead," Spence muttered. "I know where I stand when the Rumanian is around."

A precious compliment from a special lady.

Guess Who's Coming to Dinner was Spence's last picture. Kate knew Spence was not well. Rehearsing their scenes at night during the shooting of the picture, he'd forget lines, and he found it hard to remember cues in dialogue—a difficulty he never had had.

Every night she would leave a small light on in the kitchen, located at the far end of the corridor of their cottage. On the stove was a kettle of water; a cup and saucer were handy, and the tea Spence liked. He had the habit of getting up in the middle of the night, making himself a cup of tea, and going back to bed.

After the picture, Spence was tired. He slept alone. Kate slept in a small spartan room near the kitchen, waiting awake in the dark for him to have his cup of tea and go back to his room. Then she too could have her much-needed sleep.

That night, June 10, 1967, in the early hours of the morning she heard Spence's steps in the corridor. The rhythm of his walk was slow. Halfway down she heard him stop and lean against the table facing the entrance door. She heard the creaking of the table as he leaned on it. He took one more step, and again he stopped and leaned against the table—harder and a long, long time. And then the body gave up and hit the ground. And it was the end.

In the morning his legal family came and the body was taken away from "their" cottage.

The day of the funeral she saw him again, very early in the morning at the mortuary before they closed the coffin. She left a lifetime of perfect companionship with him behind her.

She wasn't at the funeral. They never were seen together at public places.

After the funeral a handful of friends met at "their" cottage. Kate was busy talking, busier than I had ever seen her. She jumped from one subject to another, almost afraid to linger too long on one line of thought. When she listened to somebody else talking, she became still, lifeless. It hurt to watch. There was an effort by all of us to talk naturally: just another day. Kate asked Chester Erskine to sit in Spence's chair. It shouldn't be there empty. ("Spence just went around the corner to buy the evening paper.")

Dusty and I left first. Kate took us down the front steps to our car. The three of us remained silent. It seemed it lasted so long, all afraid to speak or move.

I took her hand to say goodbye. "How could Spence do this to us, Kate?" I said, angry and unable to keep up the pretense.

With this she broke down and collapsed on my shoulder. All her poise forgotten, she sobbed hard, uncontrolled.

She was Spence's woman, and it was right for her to grieve.

SOPHIA AND A GREEK ISLAND

B OY *on a Dolphin* was a sensuous journey into an ancient Greek legend and its effect on love—love of money, love of art, love of country, and love of physical beauty. I was getting ready to fly to Paris to sign Gina Lollobrigida, who was there shooting *The Hunchback of Notre Dame* with Anthony Quinn.

In Paris, a reluctant Gina was hard to negotiate with. "I want a baby this year, not another picture," she argued. But one night at a famous restaurant where I invited her to dine— and helped by Sam Goldwyn, who happened to dine there too—she was persuaded to pass the baby for *Boy on a Dolphin*. We signed Gina to co-star with Cary Grant. Only to have next day a visit from Cary's agent to inform us that "Grant will do the picture, but not with Gina—only with Sophia Loren."

Sophia's romance with Cary during her previous and first film for a Hollywood company, *The Pride and the Passion*, was international news; and their off-scene amour burned the sober Spanish fields with "no pride but passion" (ouch!) and well-planted publicity.

Twentieth Century–Fox had difficulty cancelling the contract with Lollobrigida; but, as always, they could find a way out.

Sophia Loren was signed to co-star with Cary Grant.

A telex from Carlo Ponti, Sophia's Svengali, caught up with me that evening: "PROMISE PRINCELY WELCOME ON YOUR ARRIVAL ROME IF YOU BRING SENSATIONAL SCRIPT. CABLE EXACT FLIGHT. LOVE, CARLO."

GALLERIA SCHNEIDER
ROMA

RAMPA MIGNANELLI, 10
TELEFONO: 684019
DIRETTORE: DR. ROBERT E. SCHNEIDER

LA GALLERIA SCHNEIDER HA IL PIACERE DI INVITARLA
ALLA MOSTRA DEGLI ULTIMI LAVORI DI JEAN NEGULESCO.

A DIRECTOR ENJOYS LIFE
DOODLING IN PURE AND IMPURE LINES...

Negulesco
56

Lunedì 10 Dicembre 1956 - dalle ore 19

La mostra rimarrà aperta dall'11 Dicembre al 19 Dicembre 1956, dalle ore 10,30 alle
13 e dalle 16,30 alle 20. Chiusa la domenica.

*An invitation to the director's
doodles—Schneider Gallery,
Rome*

Director and star arguing violently about a scene

In Rome later in the week we met Sophia. She was on time and alone. No Carlo Ponti, and no agent, and no paparazzi. She was beautiful; she was big—big eyes, big nose, big lips, big body. It was Mother Earth in all her glory. She didn't pay special attention to anyone in particular. She had almost a timid voice, but warm, with a delightful accent, and nothing of the flamboyant Italian divá. I was impressed.

"What's 'she' like?" Dusty asked as I entered to take her out to lunch.

"Who?"

"You kidding? Sophià."

"Oh, Sophia . . . well! She is . . . she is Sophia."

And Dusty waited. Then: "I see. You were impressed."

"Impressed is not the word. Unbelievable, overwhelmed, bewildered."

"Let's have lunch." Dusty dismissed my downpour.

I felt good. Cary Grant, a romantic story, and an Italian beauty were ingredients for top entertainment. On this comforting thought I left for Athens.

Greece rises out of the sea, and from the sky the light on Greece is so unique and intense that poverty and ugliness are wiped out.

The art of Greece is timeless and unsurpassed. Athens is a city still intoxicated by the melancholy of a glorious past and baffled by modern times.

We signed Dora Straton's folk dancers, the Panegyris Group; engaged a Rumanian painter, Ghika, as technical adviser for sets and locations; and sent for the Ferrari from Rome to be used in the film—a gunmetal-gray 375 Type Sport Farina, twelve cylinders, 340 horsepower.

Most of the preparations for filming in Athens were done. What we needed now was an island, a small quiet island where we could work and live for eight weeks or more. The painter Ghika promised us one.

Hydra—"the port of donkey"—is a small town on the island of Hydra packed around the harbor in the form of an amphitheater with houses planted in the rocks in Cubistic rows of white and blue. The cobblestones on the twisted streets are whitewashed almost every day. Its people are mostly sponge divers, stern and courageous seamen barely hiding a crazy pirate past.

Hydra offered a wild purity. It was the sacred rock of bold heroes and daring madmen, with thousands of steps running up and down between small houses and little chapels. In the harbor, in front of wooden tables symmetrically arranged in even rows, fishermen were peacefully drinking Metaxas brandy, ouzo, and retsina wine. It was the ideal location.

Twentieth Century–Fox and Spyros Skouras gave a "welcome to Greece" party for Sophia. Everyone who was anyone in Athens was invited. Spyros delivered a longwinded speech about the *Boy on a Dolphin* project and wandered aimlessly trying to explain CinemaScope. At a loss, he repeated the same speech in his native language. Ghika whispered to me, "Funny, he speaks even bad Greek."

We were shooting for four days when the gods of fate changed our setup. We lost Cary Grant. Betsy Drake, his wife, had taken the *Andrea Doria* ocean liner to return to the States. The boat sank, and miraculously Betsy was among the survivors. Cary flew to America to be with her and passed up his co-starring with Sophia.

"What kind of actor do you need?" Spyros asked me.

"Big, tall, strong—a romantic box-office star if possible. Someone who'll look right opposite the Italian Venus," I answered without hesitation.

"That's all I wanted to know," our president assured me and flew that night to America.

Two days later we got this startling news. Spyros had signed the diminutive-sized Alan Ladd at a fabulous salary. To play opposite Sophia? It sounded then and sounds now pure insanity.

The first meeting between Sophia and Alan confirmed our worst fears. Alan never flew. He came by train from California to New York, by ship to England, and by Blue Train to Athens. He caught a bug, lost twelve pounds, and looked drawn, white, shaky.

"Sophia, this is Alan Ladd," I said. These were the only words exchanged in this encounter. They both mumbled, "How do," and sat there open-mouthed measuring each other. They both lost.

Holes were dug for Sophia to stand in so she could be eye-to-eye and lip-to-lip with Alan. In a walking scene, Sophia had to walk in trenches. How often can a love scene be played with Sophia sitting and Alan standing?

Even the story had to be changed. An SOS cable was sent to Buddy Adler, the new studio head. Ivan Moffat, a brilliant film writer, was rushed from London to change the story from a romantic adventure to a suspense chase melodrama.

We were ready. We sailed to the island of Hydra—the cast, the crew, Dusty, lights, cameras, brutes, generators, sound equipment, jeeps, Ferrari, and Sophia. The whole town was lined up at the harbor watching silently the invasion of their protected island by a horde of noisy voyagers. We had rented an ocean liner from a Greek tycoon at an astronomical price. Its sight was an absurd intrusion in their lives. There was no smile of welcome from the crowd on the quay. Sophia was afraid to get off the ship. The crew started to disembark. The

Hydriots stared impassively. A big crane set down the camera jeep, and the driver got into it.

Suddenly the crowd on the quay started to run as if they were one, animated now as they followed the moving jeep. The village people had never seen a car traveling on its own without being pushed. Our star descended to the quay in peace and quiet. Nobody bothered her for autographs. She was calm but showed a touch of resentment for the mechanical jeep that had taken the limelight away from her.

There were only two houses for rent on the island. Sophia, the costume designer, the hairdresser, and the makeup girl occupied a house on the hill. Dusty, myself, and writer Ivan Moffat got the other one—the house of Catharine Paouris. It had two dozen rooms.

For cooking and for our baths, water was pumped in by a small boy. The tub water was populated by small fish and all kinds of sea algae.

My passion for collecting unusual photographs paid off. Once the shot of a female Japanese pearl diver coming out of the water intrigued me. She wore a yellow old dress, faded and weatherbeaten, a cord tied around the waist, the back of the skirt brought forward between her legs and folded into the belt. It was the model for Sophia's costume as a Greek sponge diver. I insisted on testing the costume in her warm bath. (The film censors were hard on us that year.)

I was right. After the first dunking, an explosive vision appeared, with every detail of her perfect body outlined dangerously. We double-lined the dress. The second dunking gave us a sensual suggestion but not the obvious lusty truth. Satisfied, we sailed to the sea. But I did not anticipate the temperature of the water. The blue-green Aegean Sea was ice cold. When Sophia surfaced, her lovelies were pointing at us with daring accuracy. The still man dropped his camera. The soundman raised his boom. The Greek laborers were thunderstruck.

It was simply too good to record only once. I repeated takes and retakes of the wet dripping yellow dress to my enjoyment and the crew's appreciation.

The "dripping yellow dress" became a sensational poster on every continent and country where the film played.

Our Greek unit manager put under contract a ferocious, impressive young athlete, Oreste, the champion weightlifter of Greece. He drove the Ferrari from location to location, took care of it as if it were a gentle mistress, and was my unofficial bodyguard.

Oreste was a bull, but like most strongmen he was soft and tender. He was in love with a beautiful Greek girl, Melinda, but never gathered enough courage to tell her. He spoke slow, hesitant French, and in our drives he confessed to me his sorrow.

I arranged with Sophia that when Oreste drove her in the Ferrari in any scene she would greet him in Greek and he would answer in his native language. This way I upped his pay to a speaking-part salary. By the end of our location shooting, Oreste was rich. With tears running down his cheeks, he told me that the money he made with us gave him enough courage to ask Melinda to marry him. She accepted, and they were able to buy a small house on the outskirts of Athens.

After the pay raise, he never left my side; and I've never felt better than when I was playing Santa Claus to ferocious Oreste and gentle Melinda.

Sophia—handicapped by Alan's height—was cooperative, pleasant, professional, and ruthless. She avoided rehearsing love scenes with him. Alan assented freely and with no embarrassment to sit behind the camera reading his lines while a better-built double sat with his back to the camera moving his head up and down simulating dialogue. Sophia's English improved by leaps and bounds. By the end of the picture, Sophia had to dub all her earlier scenes. She was quick to catch from the American boys in the crew some fast slang and shocking riddles and deliver them innocently or whisper a four-letter word offhand to the delight of the crew. Somehow, it relieved the tension of the Sophia-Alan relationship.

After two months of work and friendship from the Hydriots, the mayor of the little island bade us a good-humored and ironical farewell: "We went through two wars—the Turks and the First World War. Hydra was unscratched. The wars were soon forgotten and our island stayed free and at peace. Then Hollywood came along with your stars and your machines and we stayed friends. But our poor virgin island is now full of wrinkles, crisscrossed by trenches so that your beautiful Sophia could walk at the same level with her lover. You'll *never* be forgotten."

We moved to Athens and the Acropolis. Phaedra (Sophia), the simple Greek girl, tries to interest the head of a U.S.A. archeological mission (Alan Ladd) in the story of the statue of the "Boy on a Dolphin" she discovered in the bottom of the sea while sponge diving. But Alan, like any red-blooded American, doesn't believe in legends and brushes her off. He is not impressed by the exceptional beauty of this Greek girl. Even though Sophia's figure outlined against the Greek sky has the jealous approval of the caryatid statues in the background supporting the roof of the Temple of Venus. He leaves her standing (the fool!) and hurries to supervise the unloading of a big bas-relief of historical value he uncovered in his last dig.

It was at this precise moment that the chief of the Acropolis Guards advanced and informed us in final terms that "The scene cannot be shot."

"Why?" I asked him.

"It is a fake."

"I know it is a fake." I tried to keep my voice calm. "We copied it from the original in the National Museum. It will look the same."

"No, no, *no.*" The chief became belligerent. "*No permit.*"

"Then you give me a real one. I prefer it," I blasted impatiently.

He rose up in his official dignity: "The Greek Art is not for American cinema. No permit."

Peppi, my assistant, took him aside. We lined up the shot. I whispered to Peppi to hand him some good baksheesh. To my surprise, he refused it. He kept mumbling in fast Greek. I ignored him.

As we started to film the scene, he rushed in front of the camera, gesticulating like a maniac. "*No permit . . . No . . .*"

I got mad and pushed him out of the shot. He collared me and dragged me away (he was strong).

"To police, now," he shouted.

"Oresteee," I yelled. That was all that our Colossus Oreste

wanted. Quick flashes moved rapidly. The police chief was in the air over our heads, his legs and arms gesticulating helplessly like a disjointed marionette. Oreste carried the chief to the outside wall and threw him over it like a toy. We did the scene with the fake sculpture. The Skouras brothers squared the official quarrel. We paid a sizable fine—and lost permission to use the interior of the National Museum, where the original statue of the "Boy Jockey" is located. We had to reproduce the Museum Gallery in Rome with every statue built to scale. It was a costly Balkans encounter—Rumanian temper versus Greek officialism.

In the Gardens of Zappeion, the best and most expensive club-restaurant in Athens, shipping tycoons meet Arab billionaires, showing off the prettiest summer girls, the best of international parasites. Against this background Phaedra was searching for Victor Parmalee (Clifton Webb), the rich collector.

I was watching Sophia—the woman, the actress. So much had happened to her these last three months. I was watching her as she talked to Oreste. It seemed that she was listening only to him, yet she knew that one hundred eyes were watching her: the jealous eyes, the eyes with lust and desire, the critical eyes, the measuring eyes. What made her what she is?

She was rehearsing. She walked unsure on her high-heeled shoes to meet the "man with the money," who wanted the statue for his private collection. She stopped. The high-heeled shoes were uncomfortable; they were her enemy. At the first place she could find she sat and took off her shoes. She was free, secure with the dignity of a proud peasant. She looked radiant and noble. And I had the answer: If she could always remember *to take off her shoes*, to be the free Sophia, with no rules, with no makeup, no acting tricks, she could become a legend.

She had become famous, a star, rich and bankable, but five years later, in *Two Women*, she was the Sophia I saw that day, the Phaedra of *Boy on a Dolphin*, the simple Greek girl who took off her shoes.

*   *   *

Rome. Sophia left for Italy two weeks before us to be close to her Pygmalion, Carlo Ponti. And showered with cables, praise, and applause by the Hollywood executives, she believed too quickly in all these kudos. At times it gave her the false star confidence—the "I-think-I-know-a-better-way-to-read-this-line" attitude. A slight quarrel on the set would be followed by a cold and polite "I appreciate your thinking, Miss Loren, but please do it *my* way." She did it—reluctantly. After the next day's rushes, I received a photo still taken on the set of the two of us with the inscription: "How could you be always so right! S."

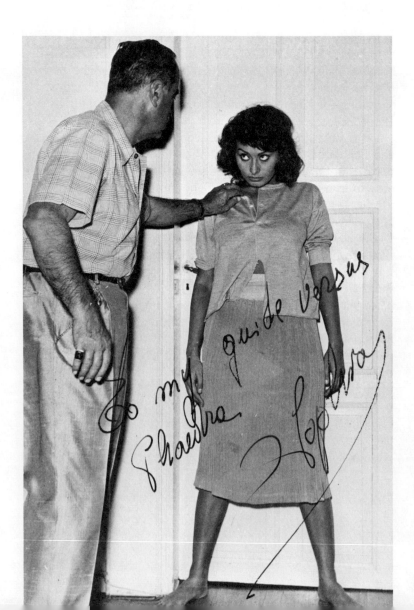

Finally the film was finished, scored, previewed. A solid success:

"Box office of the month."

"Motion picture exhibitors vote *Boy on a Dolphin* one of the best to be currently distributed."

George V. Melas, the Ambassador of Greece in Washington, D.C., informed me that "His Majesty King Paul of the Hellenes has graciously conferred upon you the Knight Cross of the Royal Order of George I in connection with the production of the film *Boy on a Dolphin*."

The critics were praising "Volcanic Sophia," "Gal Grecian glories glow," "Magnetic tempest in film."

Sophia gifted me with a Bulgari watch.

Sophia Loren followed *Boy on a Dolphin* with many films, cleverly cast by Carlo Ponti against big Hollywood stars. Many were good pictures, many were indifferent, but also many were not so good.

She forgot to take off her shoes.

AN EXTRAORDINARY FIND: BERNARD BUFFET

ONE day in Hollywood I woke to the realization that I was making movies, I was part of the industry, and a stream of cash was flowing in. Then I remembered a promise I had made myself thirty years earlier when I was young and hungry in Paris—that if I ever had the opportunity to collect paintings I would buy only young painters.

In 1948 I went to England to film Margery Sharp's book *Britannia Mews*. Paris called. It was Dusty's first trip abroad, her first night in Paris. So the Tour d'Argent was a *must*, the only place to dine. Overlooking Paris and the river Seine, the sight of Notre Dame Cathedral at night is fairylike. Not to forget the three-star cuisine, the restaurant's extraordinary wine cellar, and the fascinating owner, Claude Terrail. He was handsome, elegant, with French energy, and most of all a smooth charmer. When he found out that it was Dusty's first night in Paris he said, "If you could wait until I close the restaurant, let me be her guide to show her Paris at night the way Paris should be seen the first time."

How could we refuse? Besides, a brandy of exceptional vintage was offered by Claude to help with the waiting. We speculated that he intended to show us all the *boites*, the nightclubs famous and infamous, the exclusive and hidden night life of Gay Paree. We were mistaken. Claude drove us through narrow streets, past corners of forgotten Paris. We walked in cobblestoned alleys, climbing long and twisted stairways up in Montmartre, met and talked with workers and street girls. We admired visions of bridges and black trees, spellbinding sights in the moonlight.

To add to this enchantment, a gray dense fog abruptly surrounded us. I drove. Claude mounted the hood and directed us through streets and corners to the last *must* of a first night in Paris: Les Halles. Built of wrought iron and glass, "the belly of Paris," as Emile Zola named it, this much-loved market was the daily supplier of fruits and vegetables and meats and flowers to all Paris. In this rich combination of colors, amid the fast and furious clamor of French calls and the uproar of friendly arguments, our stomachs welcomed the classic hot onion soup, topped with toasted French bread and saturated in stringy Parmesan cheese.

We separated in the early dawn. For a first night in Paris it was a magical night and Claude was responsible.

(How can one reciprocate? Some time later, when Claude came to Hollywood, we gave a dinner for him at our house. And we arranged for him to have what he wanted most in Hollywood—we paired him for the evening with Marilyn Monroe.)

After that night in Paris, at eleven the next day, we were ready for new galleries and young painters. Sidney Sheldon— director, producer, but not yet best-selling author—asked if he could come along. Maybe he too could buy a young painter. (He bought a small Renoir!) The Galerie Drouant-

David was situated at 52 Rue du Faubourg St.-Honoré in a courtyard away from the busy street. The director of the gallery—Emanuel David ("Mano" for his friends)—was everything that is special about a Frenchman: happy, anxious, demonstrative. He was unable and unwilling to utter a word of any language but French, a middle-aged admirer of beauty and with an appreciative eye for curves.

We looked around at the paintings hanging on the walls—big names, already famous, masters.

"Do you have any young exciting painters?" I asked him finally.

"Yes, many." He thought for a moment, looked at me and Sidney, and smiled at Dusty. From behind a curtain he brought out an unframed painting and placed it against the wall.

"Bernard Buffet." That's all he said.

It was a big canvas of an emaciated, angular woman, with enormous black eyes and deep lines crossing her face framed by stringy hair. A blouse stretched over her thin elongated skeleton as she sat at a square table that held a half-empty bottle. Scratches of hard pencil crisscrossed her face and the background. A nervous hard push of the brush palette knife had made a hole in her neck: *The Absinthe Drinker*. It was my first meeting with Bernard Buffet's work. I didn't like it, yet I couldn't take my eyes from it. I criticized it. I fought against it. An enormous signature covered a whole corner of the canvas. It was pretentious and ostentatious. And again, it belonged to the total of the painting. Without it the work was not complete.

"Any other young painters?" I tried to get away from it. Mano lined up against the wall two other painters from his stable: Pierre Bollaert (a pupil of Bonnard's, with pleasant, solid technique to enchant the eyes and satisfy my critical instinct) and Philip Noyer (naive and pleasant). We chose a few of each. Christmas was coming and these paintings would answer most of our needs. Sidney Sheldon bought his Renoir and left to purchase some special scarves at Hermes.

"Do you have any more of him?" I asked Mano.

"Bollaert or Noyer?"

"No. The other one."

"Buffet?"

"Yes. Buffet."

"Upstairs in the attic. Would you like to see them?" Mano asked quietly.

I took one more look at the ugly *Absinthe Drinker*.

"No, thank you. Maybe another time."

I wrote the check for the paintings I purchased, and then Dusty, her intuition always alert: "Why don't you look at them anyway. We have time."

I did.

Upstairs, behind a big dark red door with an ordinary lock, Mano stored thousands of new paintings. We sat on a comfortable sofa. With love and care, Mano started to prop against furniture, boxes, easels, and the wall the latest work of Bernard Buffet: sad landscapes outside Paris, still lifes of a hard and hungry home, a black table with an empty plate and a lonely fork set against the corner of a desolate white wall, angular and triangular gaunt faces lined with black contours, gray tones with chalky splashes, unframed, all witnesses of misery and hopeless despair.

Mano did not receive any comment or encouragement from me. I was bewildered. It was a nightmare, a combination of El Greco distortions against the funeral of a René Clair film.

Dusty felt she should say something. She timidly tried her French. *"Très bon,"* she whispered.

Good was probably the worst polite comment. These paintings were not there to be admired. They shocked and slapped and spat on your face.

"That is all I have." Mano came and sat close to me.

"How many?"

"How many what?"

"How many are there?"

Mano counted the canvases slowly. "Twenty-one."

"How much?"

He took out of his pocket a typed list of prices. "Which one?"

"All twenty-one."

He got up, then sat down, looked at his list, then longer at me.

"All twenty-one?"

"Yes, and all you can get together in the next few days before I return to London."

"I will add the prices."

"You don't have to, Mr. David. There are twenty-one paintings. I'll give you two hundred and ten thousand francs." (In 1948 this was not a big sum but an important one for a young, unknown new painter.) "Two hundred and ten thousand francs and not one cent more."

Mano David had to make a decision. With his French business spirit he added together the prices of the canvases. It probably amounted to much more than I offered him. But he was a good businessman. He accepted. Later he confided to me that he knew he could use me as a public-relations man for Bernard Buffet in Hollywood. He was right.

But why, that day, did I make this impulsive and expensive decision? Because Buffet's paintings shrieked that he painted with hard talent that never fell into facility.

I wanted to meet the painter. Mano arranged a lunch in his Paris apartment. "Bernard, this is Jean Negulesco."

There stood in front of me one of Buffet's characters. He looked as if he stepped down from one of his paintings. He was tall, lean, with a thin nervous face, a long aquiline nose, gaunt cheeks, stooped shoulders. Trying to smile but not knowing how, what he gave us was a forced grimace. He was wearing an American pilot's coat with an imitation-fur collar, splattered with paints. He never took it off. He smoked incessantly.

At the table I sat next to him during an excellent French lunch—nothing like home cooking in France. Bernard gulped it down hungrily and was preoccupied most of the time. I watched his hands, the hands that produced such marvels. He had long, nervous fingers, bony, with nails badly in need of cutting. It seemed as if black paint had been pushed under the nails deliberately with the palette knife. I tried to talk to him about the weather, Paris, sex. We didn't get very far.

"Bernard, why is all your work so tragic? Why so much unhappiness?"

He lit a new cigarette from his old one, inhaled deeply, let his lungs be free again, then, polite but definite: *"La grande peinture n'a jamais faire rire*—Great painting has never produced laughter."

He was wise, but still pompous, an angry young Frenchman. The afternoon ended pleasantly enough, with Mano and

I talking furiously, Dusty looking beautiful, Bernard not listening, absent and chain smoking. We left after we got the promise to have him do our portraits sometime in the near future.

I took with me back to California over sixty new paintings. The Bernard Buffet campaign started. I gave Buffets at Christmas, for birthday gifts, or just gifts. A few Beverly Hills collectors liked him. But fewer of my friends shared my enthusiasm.

How could I live with this kind of painting? was the usual rebuff. Eat in front of it? Kiss or make love in front of it?

"Since when should Bernard Buffet's paintings accommodate your natural joys?" I remarked. One of my friends rejected a painting flatly: "A Bernard Buffet in *my* collection?"

Mano continued to send me all kinds of varied paintings. After another short trip to Paris, my Bernard Buffet collection mounted to over 150.

I began to sell the Buffets. I used a pattern: I charged the price I paid (mostly under one hundred dollars) plus 20 percent for framing, transport, and insurance. If they didn't like it within three months, they could return it and the whole amount would be refunded. Many of my sales were returned.

One point was certain: *like them or not*, Beverly Hills, Hollywood, and as a matter of fact, California became Bernard Buffet conscious.

And then the miracle happened. *Cahiers des Arts* staged its usual every-fifty-years contest. World critics, merchants, and art experts vote for the ten most promising young painters of the generation. Bernard Buffet was voted number *one*, and with this, his prices changed considerably, and I stopped selling.

My telephone rang constantly. Galleries from New York, Chicago, and San Francisco wired offers to buy at any price. I lent to the Los Angeles Museum ten of his canvases for an important exhibition. The very friends of mine who rejected my gifts now paid thousands of dollars for one work.

Bernard Buffet was recognized.

Years passed. A new phase came in Bernard's life. He met and married Annabel, a talented sensitive writer of unusual beauty. She had a great influence on his life. She was the balance, his partner, his mirror and often his inspired model. Bernard is vain, selfish, and proud—overconfident but not arrogant. What counts in his life is the judgment he has of himself.

"Harsh criticism will not stop me from painting. I have the faith of fools and I am proud of it."

Fourteen years after I first met Bernard, in 1962, I was in Sicily making my first independent production, *Jessica*, with Angie Dickinson and Maurice Chevalier.

A poster by Bernard Buffet, I thought. What a send-off for the film! I called him at his new castle, Château de l'Arc, in Aix-en-Provence.

"Yes, why not. Come and spend a week with us," Annabel answered.

A white Rolls-Royce picked us up in Nice. His castle grounds included two picturesque Provence villages and a chapel that he was decorating. He looked at ease, kinder, interested in friends and food. Bernard looked happy, carefully dressed and prosperous. Yet his nails were still saturated with black color.

He invited me one afternoon to see his studio, where he was finishing the panels for the chapel.

It was a big barn, the size of a public garage. The canvases made to fit the chapel walls were all around—on easels, on the floor, on tables, hanging from the ceiling. They were magnificent. Unprepared to be in the middle of this miracle, I was silent and bewildered.

Suddenly Bernard was absent. He had a problem, something he wanted to change on one of the panels. I did not exist. Bernard was alone. He attacked the panel angrily. His movements were sure, definite, the judgment instantaneous and exact. I had time to look around. On a table the length of the studio and the cluttered floor were the proofs of his monumental physical work—no quiet organized labor but the battle of chaos. No colors carefully squeezed on his palette but enormous wrought pots with fresh-dried colors splashed on hard mounds of blue skies, white walls, green leaves, and black lines. A jungle of boxes were filled with new colors and thousands of twisted and discarded tubes—a hodgepodge of empty cigarette packs, hundreds of bottles of oil and turpentine, large plates everywhere covered with all shades of colors, a jam-packed disorder, this was the working room of the *one* the gods had chosen.

Surrounded by the religious panels where every line and every color and every composition listens to his will, I felt that I had trespassed in his special world. I left quietly. Bernard never noticed my leaving.

He made the poster of *Jessica*, now a prized collector's item. As a going-away present, Bernard drew with simple lines a heart pierced by an arrow: "To Jean and Dusty, Bernard and Annabel."

In 1973 in Japan at the foot of Mount Fuji the Musée Bernard Buffet was inaugurated in Boulevard Bernard Buffet. He is, after Picasso and Chagall, the third painter of France to be honored in his lifetime with a personal museum dedicated to his work. Annabel went for the ceremony, Bernard asked forgiveness. He was involved in his work.

In 1974 at the age of forty-six, in Paris, fat, wearing a generous beard, he was nominated Membre de l'Académie des Beaux Arts.

Bernard is rich, yet he has never made concessions to the public taste.

Today, the noisy fame, the world's admiration, and sparkling glory are reserved for the stars of the cinema.

Like Picasso, the magician, the god-monster of art, Bernard Buffet is one painter of our time who has definitely and permanently taken his place among the stars of our century.

DUSTY

PART Cherokee Indian, the rest American mixture, you look directly at me, through me. Then if you don't agree, you do not argue now, but months later you will give the answer, the right one.

You're honest, direct, a natural beauty. You love to flirt, mostly when I'm in the same room, jealous enough to make me proud and feel young. You have a lovely large shoulder on which friends cry out their troubles.

A light beat of sound or primitive music and you'll start a dance of your own, your own interpretation, exclusive, personal, never the same, a happy blend of a carefree race and your sense of ultra-modern style. Your clothes are way ahead of the fashion; you do not ignore it but improve it.

"How did you know I wanted this? How did you know I was going to say this?" We don't finish our sentences—not many words, just being together.

The house is empty, a double vodka on the rocks, a Number 3 Montecristo. How did all this happen? I go back . . .

1944, the Pantages Theater in Hollywood, the opening of *Mask of Dimitrios*. There were no spectacular searchlights for its unveiling, just the first-night showing. The notices were good. I escorted Anita Colby to the premiere. Anita, "the most beautiful face this side of heaven and the sharpest tongue this side of hell," her friend Valdemar Vetlugen, the editor of *Redbook* has said. She was the darling of the photographers. So, later at Ciro's for supper, flashbulbs never stopped popping at us—dining, dancing. Next day a gossip column reported, "Modelovely Anita Colby and Jean Negulesco will announce plans before you can say Adolf Schicklgruber."

"Johnny, did you see the papers?" The "Face" called.

"I like it, I like it."

"But why?"

"Because you're the only woman in the world I'd like to pay alimony to."

"Chances are I'll never be married, Johnny." The "Face" with a brain to match wiped that rumor.

That year, Columbia studios brought fifteen cover girls from New York, the best of the field, for the new Rita Hayworth picture *Cover Girl*. The "Face"—the highest-paid model in America—became a one-woman finishing school for the lovely cover girls: troubleshooter, fixer, fashion expert, and house mother Colby chaperone.

"Any exceptional beauty among them?" I asked Anita over a cocktail.

"All are exceptional," she said.

"Tell me about it," I said.

"Beautiful, clever, good girls." The beauty expert smiled.

"Not one different from others?"

"Of course not. But one is something. I invented her— the *Farm Journal* cover girl: Dusty Anderson."

The name Dusty, D-u-s-t-y, clicked hard in my memory cells.

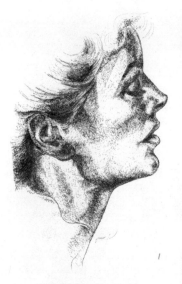

Dusty

The place: Ames Art Galleries auction rooms in Beverly Hills: That night there was no moon, no perfumed breeze among the cherry blossoms, no sound of plaintive violins, but a noisy crowd shouting bets to the auctioneer's hammer. "Come and help me. I want to buy some antique chairs" was Paulette Goddard's invitation for the evening. "You can tell me if they're real and a bargain."

A publicity girl I knew, Dorothy Campbell, was in the crowd. With her was a tall shapely beauty, wearing a black hood, a black turtle-neck sweater, and black leather slacks. A

Vogue, *March 1942*

tasteful Navajo blue turquoise necklace was dangling between her lovelies.

"Jean, meet Dusty Anderson," Dorothy said. I loved Dorothy suddenly with a passion. So this is Dusty, the name I liked, the *Farm Journal* cover girl.

I was ready to start my "foreign-charmer" approach when Miss Anderson's full attention was caught by an exquisite mirror which came up for sale: antique glass and a valuable French frame. She made the first bid. I upped five dollars. She followed with another five. I upped every time until it went well over its right value. The hammer came down: "Sold to the gentleman on the third row. Your name, sir?" I wrote the check, got the mirror, and turned around to offer it to Miss Anderson for a dinner date. Dusty was gone. No dinner date but a mirror I didn't need.

"I'm divorcing my husband. He's away in the Marine Corps." Dusty Anderson answered my call and declined my invitation. I insisted: "Just dinner?" "I'm sorry. My lawyer suggests discretion." A cautious end—short and firm.

And months passed.

I was rehearsing a scene on a stage at Warner Brothers— *Nobody Lives Forever*. I can still see clearly the moment as if it happened yesterday. Geraldine Fitzgerald in a white summer dress was listening to John Garfield, who was giving her one of his famous con-man routines. Wanda, my secretary, underestimated and misunderstood, had just handed me a handful of messages. Listening to John's dialogue, I was glancing with one eye at the messages: "Call your agent." "Mrs. Jaffe wants you for dinner." "Miss Anderson called." "Your business manager wants you—" I stopped reading. Good God, could this Miss Anderson be Miss Dusty Anderson?

I shouted sharply, "Cut," and ran to the telephone.

"Wanda, is this 'Miss Anderson called' Miss *Dusty* Anderson?"

"That's what she said."

"Call her back. Ask her if she can have dinner with me tonight. Or tomorrow night. Or any night."

"O.K., O.K., boss. Don't get excited."

With a triumphant smile, I went back to the set.

*   *   *

Number 517 Camden Drive in Beverly Hills, 1946: A small bungalow I bought with savings from my war bonds.

Dusty, the Screen Tonic from Toledo, was by now my every-day and every-night date. Her boss at Columbia, Harry Cohn, interfered with her private life. "Jean's a playboy," he told her.

"I know, and a good one," she answered.

"He's also homosexual," he snorted.

"I have news for you, Harry." Dusty let him have it.

That same afternoon she was gifted with a three-month layoff. She came home crying. She was low. We quarreled. "I'm going back East." She started to pack.

Stubborn, conceited, I didn't stop her. "Johnny, can you lend me a small suitcase. I collected too many stupid things." She turned her face away. I brought the suitcase and dropped it at her feet. Then I went in the garage to wash the car. But working seemed stupid.

The "Face"

("What's the matter with you? For once in your life you are really loved by the most glorious girl—kind, sexy, clean, fine. You never had such a precious love. And you let her go?")

I went back into her room. She was pushing clothes in the small suitcase and crying.

"Do you have a dollar?" I said from the door.

"A . . . what?"

"A dollar—one dollar. Give it to me."

She opened her purse and handed me the dollar. I took one dollar from my pocket and held them together. "Get in the car. We're going to Santa Monica."

"What for?"

"To buy a license. To get married. It costs two dollars. That's what for."

The *best* investment of one dollar I've ever made.

I come back to "now." The Montecristo cigar is ashes, the vodka glass is empty, and we are together.

You are every miracle which life has offered me.

GABY AND TINA

THIS will be the story of children to love, the two angels we adopted. So many dreams we had for them and so many hopes and so many plans. How many years ago?

Dusty tells the story of the quest.

DUSTY'S QUEST

In this memoir of Jean Negulesco, three fond feminine creatures flit in and out—a wife, Dusty, and daughters Gaby and Tina. To establish who they are, I, Dusty, contribute this tale. Think of me as Dusty—my maiden name was Ruth Anderson—one of those rangy American girls who somehow on the long roads between Toledo, Ohio, and New York and Los Angeles, became a model and a young actress, had the name of Dusty fastened on, and eventually married a flashingly bright, funny Frenchy Rumanian movie director. At that moment, we were so in love, and thirty-eight years later still are.

We had love to spare, love to share with children. We went seriously about the business of having a baby. After five months of pregnancy I was singing every day. Jean was just creating that beautiful movie *Johnny Belinda*, so we decided the baby would be a girl named Belinda. But then something awful happened within me; an ambulance rushed me to a hospital; Jean arrived at the house, trailing in his car; there was struggle and pain and abruptly it was all over. I had lost the baby. Jean put his arms around me—steady, holding, supporting. I had a man who would always be there through life.

With love intensified, we tried again, and once more we were denied a living child. How many couples have been through this delicate imbalance in the procreation process!

What nature couldn't give us, humane society could. We immersed ourselves in the child adoption process.

Jean had to leave the quest to me. He flew to Hong Kong in preparation for a picture, while I, Dusty, talked searchingly with a lawyer. He brought up the case of abandoned children in Germany, a legion of lovely little people who had been born in those poignant days when anguished German girls had found love in the arms of the occupying American military men. In the midst of chaos, the orderly Germans had given the little ones shelter and done their best to keep records of their life lines.

A Stuttgart hospital in Germany . . . In a crib was a pretty baby of perhaps three months, a perfect rosy infant who gurgled contentment. Yes, oh, yes, she would be our Tina. She was there in that hospital only because of the feelings of her religious grandparents. The baby's mother was a girl of

The author and his girls

good family who had loved a young American officer. He wanted to marry her when she got with child, but the grandparents saw the child not as a symbol of love but of a fall from grace, so the little girl went from the bed of her birth to the abandoned children's ward.

Away from the hospital, pondering, the thought of a family Negulesco became clearer to me. Tina must have a sister. There would be more responsibilities, more bills, more everything—*but* more fun for the kids. The good lawyer came up with a piece of information: "Some distance from you, quite a drive over the mountain, there is a little town in which there's a children's shelter, and there is a girl there who could be adopted with almost no complications."

I jumped into my Opel with hardly any preparations and headed up the Autobahn for the mountains. It was late afternoon. The sky darkened. I rounded a bend high in the sky, mixed in with a line of great trucks, and suddenly all stability disappeared. Every vehicle began to slide sideways, and my little car drifted, despite my frantic braking, to the very edge of a deep chasm. I was paralyzed with fright.

A great truck had slid to a stop beside me. As careful as a cat, a large young man padded down from the cab and drew me and my handbag from my car with the grip of a bear.

"*Alles* O.K., *Fräulein*," he said as I faced him, teeth chattering, and he slowly skated me across the road to the mountainside. Out of all those misaligned trucks came men like him, sliding, slapping, and roaring at each other, starting a fire, making coffee, cooking. I became a star, and it wasn't just because there was a bottle of schnapps in my bag. In the morning, four of them picked up my Opel and carried it like a baby carriage over the now dry road to the head of the column. Trucks sped by, sirens blasting, big hands waving. They had done something for womanhood.

At the children's shelter, I was told that I would see the prospective girl in company with other children, so I bought cars for the boys and dolls for the girls, handed my gifts, then made my approach to the designated one. I was turned down. Something, I believe, had happened to that poor girl that made grown-ups her enemies. She just stood there and let me have it with her eyes, her shoulders, her elbows, her feet. I stayed for hours stealing glimpses of her; she faced the world with that attitude she showed to me. I was ready to call the trip a failure, but something happened.

A toddler zigzagged across the floor and touched my hand. She chortled at being so bold and clomped away. She stumbled to the corner of the room, went behind a chair, and undressed her doll. I watched her from the corner of my eye as she returned, handed me the doll, and with big eyes asked me to dress her doll. Again she went away, looked back at me, and smiled. Now in that smile I read the nicest message. She would become our Gaby—the sister of Tina. The night and the mountain had been an augury of wonderful possibilities. A complication emerged. The story of the girl who wanted to be our Gaby was like Tina's—a young American officer and a vivacious German girl. After the birth the mother vanished and the military man went to his destiny. The German authorities with their registration had been able to track her down, a nightclub singer, and in accordance with the law she paid part of the cost to raise her child in the shelter. But for the last eight months she was missing.

"She's a kind of Marlene Dietrich character, even looks on that order," the lawyer said. "However, Mrs. Negulesco, I must warn you there are many Marlene Dietrichs in the nightclubs of Germany. There are many nightclubs, and you cannot obtain custody of that little girl you want unless the mother gives her written consent to the adoption, so it's a case of finding this particular Marlene Dietrich."

For three months, town after town, night after night, the lawyer and I sat in nightclubs, big and small, smart and tawdry, looking through the blue haze at Dietrichs. The lawyer went backstage pursuing every hopeful trail. One night the lawyer bundled me out of a nightclub. "I think the mother is in this place. The police are checking her identity," the lawyer said. "Oh, can I say that you will pay what she owes to the orphanage?" That was the end of the long, nerve-racking process. The final contracts were ready.

So it came about that one day, outside the Stuttgart hospital, I climbed into a taxi, Tina in a basket on one side of me, Gaby clinging to my hand on the other side.

At exactly that moment a blow struck me, utterly unprepared: *I* was a mother.

And one day all of us were in our nice house in Beverly

Hills, the children in glistening white rooms, playing and yelling and growing, splashing in pools, learning to dance, going abroad to a Catholic school, where they accumulated languages and graces and a code of conduct. They are grown now, our Gaby and Tina. We love them and are proud of them. We hope they love us and consider us acceptable. Go to it, girls, it's your world.

*   *   *

"Go to it, girls, it's your world," my Dusty said, and they did—again and again. This year's problem will be solved a year later. The youth belong to each other, and we are left out.

"Why should I belong to somebody? We belong to ourselves, to *our* generation. We must be free. We choose our own friends.

"But, baibee, can I help you?" I said timidly. "Help you to meet people, help you have a good choice of friends? Take advantage of my experience, my connections."

"No way. You just don't know our friends, whom we like."

"Can we meet them?"

"Look, Dad. When I feel that it is right for you to meet him or her, you will meet them. And don't worry. I wouldn't do anything to hurt you or Mom."

And of course she wouldn't hurt us, nor the other one, not deliberately. But they do—every so often, when they decide to justify their existence as people.

And so it starts, and so it ends. And we were like them. And we see ourselves in them. There is no sense in telling them, "When I was your age . . ." We never were their age.

HOLLYWOOD KALEIDOSCOPE

"Spin it, Joe." Joe is my favorite projectionist.
But this is a game. Joe isn't here. I'm at my desk in the long, cool white-bricked living room of our Spanish-style home, underneath the old oak beams, looking past the Paris posters on the walls to the vast fireplace in which dance blue and green spirits, very feminine.

There is no projection machine, only the most marvelous projecting device of all—the mind's eye.

Just imagine that a great camera, a sort of magnified spirit of all the cameras grinding away on the studio lots, is floating in the air like the Goodyear blimp over the Hollywood movie world. It focuses on funny, bizarre, sad, voluptuous, and glorious episodes—and zooms in now and then on the glamorous inhabitants.

I stand beside that camera and over the years, just at the moment things happen, I put them in the film . . . And it is named *Hollywood Kaleidoscope*.

THE TWO CHARLIES

There, we are drawn down to an eavesdropping shot of two men at the Brown Derby on Wilshire Boulevard, two of Hollywood's merry men—Charles Lederer, the nephew of Marion Davies, and Charles MacArthur, the husband of Helen Hayes: brilliant writers both of them, but always ready to explore some madcap notion.

"Charlie, you can't believe how many holes there are in the streets on my route to work," MacArthur says.

"Charlie, they dig these holes in the morning rush and close them when traffic is going home," Lederer says.

"It's irresponsible."

"They should be shown."

Fixed resolve sets their faces as they beckon for drinks.

Early next morning a construction truck drives along Wilshire Boulevard and halts in front of the Brown Derby, snarling traffic. Two men in faded dungaree work clothes jump out. The truck bears the sign LEDART S.A., ROAD IMPROVEMENTS, INC. (Hm—*Led*erer, Mac*Art*hur.) One workman attacks the road with a pneumatic drill. The other drags a wooden barrier marked DETOUR in back of the truck. A helpful cop comes from the corner to direct the crawling traffic. The workmen dig down as if they were going to China.

At noon they pack their machinery, put a sign, MEN AT WORK, beside their crater, wave at the kind cop, say, "Back after lunch," and drive away.

Two weeks later, an official repair crew shows up. The men look puzzled and fill in the ditch.

The two Charlies are watching:

"Charlie, my theory is that the fellow who issues the street permits will dictate a memo about this." MacArthur closes the episode.

The West Side Tennis Club is just that—an afternoon gathering of tennis enthusiasts all year round. There are suntanned beauties watching excellent players, husbands, friends, or lovers on the first court. Then there are the gourmets—the "galoofers"—those who are watching the beauties who are watching the games. And then the bettors—on the game, on the points.

The pro, the tennis teacher at the club, is Siegfried, a Nordic god, a perfect specimen: six feet two, blond, twenty-six, a slave to his body and its rippling muscles, idol of young beauties, and a complete teetotaler. He is also a conceited ass. The two Charlies bet him that they can beat him, with certain conditions.

"No chance," Siegfried brags. "I'll play you two with one

arm tied behind my back, one set, six to nothing."

"One hundred dollars?" Lederer asks.

"One thousand. Any conditions," the pro declaims.

"No, one hundred, and one small condition: Any point you lose, you drink a small liqueur glass of whiskey—straight. Agreed?"

The girls yell. The crowd laughs. The two Charlies are deadly serious. The pro is delighted.

And the match starts. The first three games are murder. The two Charlies run all over the court, trip over each other. The pro is making mincemeat out of their game. The giggles and the applause are mounting. Pressing for a kill, the pro puts the ball into the net. So, the *first* glass of whiskey is swallowed.

Siegfried shakes his beautiful head, breathes deeply, and continues the slaughter. MacArthur returns a ball so softly that it hits the top of the net, slides down on the pro's side, and dies as it touches the ground. A *second* glass. He presses harder to finish the set. The fifth game produces a stupid double fault, and a too-anxious and too-long overhead. So *four* glasses are gulped to put the set out of the way. By now the strong whiskey is doing savage damage on virgin ground. The two Charlies are taking their time. Siegfried wins the fifth game in slow motion. On the sixth game, Lederer serves; by a miracle it goes over on the first ball. And Siegfried does not make any attempt to return it. He is paralyzed. He drops his racquet and runs uncontrolled to the shower room, losing on the way the four small glasses of excellent whiskey.

That evening Siegfried pays the bet ungraciously. "I resent paying you. Clever but not sportsmanship."

"Thank you, Siegfried baibee." Lederer accepts formally. "Revenge?"

"Any time," Siegfried bellows. "Against you two. I'll take any partner—male or female. It won't matter if my partner has never held a racquet. As long as I do the serving for both of us."

The two Charlies go into a quick whispered conference.

"Agreed," Lederer states, "but we pick out your partner. And there will be a rope the length of the court's width that will tie your right ankle to your partner's left ankle. O.K.?"

"No whiskey?" the pro asks suspiciously.

"No whiskey," both Charlies say in unison.

The day of the match the Charlies show up with a small elephant. They link him by a long rope to Siegfried's ankle. Even with this absurd handicap, the pro is murdering the Charlies with smashing serves, slicing returns. The elephant is watching the no-contest match with patient interest. But then, around the middle of the match, the elephant decides that the human exhibition is of no consequence. So it wanders off the court, dragging the hopeless Siegfried along, leaving a free, unoccupied court for the Charlies' soft, looping shots.

Another point for the Charlies.

HARRY KURNITZ

A tall man, stooped shoulders, gentle, mumbling brilliant lines to remember. He is polite not only to ladies, but a joy for a man to spend a lunch hour or an afternoon with; an educated wit, a passionate and knowledgeable musician, a genuine art collector, a valuable addition as a writer on any script.

Harry settles a social problem to the gratitude of successful hostesses. As you entered his party, you were handed a list of names with short descriptive comments:

"DON'T BE A STRANGER.

"At most parties no one knows anyone else. You talk to people all evening, and when you leave they're still strangers. In order to correct this deplorable condition your host has prepared brief biographies of your fellow guests:

"*Armand Deutsch*, Producer, MGM. Is now preparing a story about stewardesses on submarines. Charm, sense of humor, very rich.

"*Charles Feldman*, Agent, Producer. (Will arrive late.) Loaded. Dresses well. Likes to be near telephones. Has formed seven picture companies in the last week. Good businessman.

"*Cary Grant*, Former matinee idol. (Will arrive late.) Real name Archie Leach. Wears collars well. Loves to travel and gives autographs. Difficult type to cast.

"*Tony Martin*, Entertainer. (Will arrive late.) Acts. Tells jokes. Records. Popular with kids at the Roxy. Married to:

"*Cyd Martin,* Housewife-Actress. Very pretty. Appears in pictures under name of Cyd Charisse. Good ballet dancer. Just finished dramatic role. Doesn't have to dance anymore.

"*Jean Negulesco,* Director. Formerly a painter. Hobbies: cooking, painting, and collecting anything movable. Now confines his activities to playing croquet with Zanuck. Married to:

"*Dusty Negulesco,* Younger than Jean. Much prettier. Former top model. Nice girl to have around.

"*Your Host,* Writer, MGM. Young. Bachelor. Good date for tall girls. Collects books and paintings. Broke. Plays piano and sings badly, but without coaxing. Likes his friends. Enjoys being with them. And thanks them most warmly for being here tonight."

One night in Paris, the place Harry liked most, toward the morning hours he and the famous English director Carol Reed and the producer S. P. Eagle (Sam Spiegel) were walking up the Champs-Elyseés looking for one more open late bar. Sam Spiegel, a newly enriched millionaire, is still harassed by unpaid bills. A formidable kick on Spiegel's behind halts their walk. Sam, before turning to face his assailant, lets out a hurried groan: "The check is in the *mail.*"

Harry Kurnitz, a fashionable yet a lonely man. He never short-changed his friends.

THE HOLLYWOOD WOLF

There has always been jealousy between the East Coast of the U.S.A. and the West Coast. The East looks down upon the West Coast progress: "An overgrown village, amateurs, sometimes talented but mostly lucky, definitely amateurs, no sophistication."

The East Coast even insults our glory of being the dangerous "Flickerville Wolves." I take upon myself to define and defend. From an interview I gave to Erskine Johnson in a Los Angeles paper, I quote:

The genuine wolf is a personality of Charm. An ideal companion to a beautiful lady, a master of Continental grace, gourmet extraordinaire and an enemy of the obvious and bad taste. He will never commit the clumsy, unforgivable faux-pas in what so crudely is referred to as "making a pass." Of course he is the "INITIATOR." But once the approach and suggestion has been made, he retreats and waits to be joined by the lovely lady. He dresses well—plain shades of muted colors, a background for the elegance of his companion. He owns a good car which he drives well and carefully. To go somewhere, not to race others. He knows where to go for good food, for atmosphere. He knows how to order—after he has inquired as to the lady's taste and hunger. He transforms a simple dinner into a special feast. He gives a unique importance to this night, an inspired first time. He has an unusually good sense of humor, mostly about himself. He is a superb dancer especially in Rhumba and Tango. He may even be a master of the new-generation gyrations—but on the floor, he will keep tempo in a subdued jitterbug and let all the glory and the show go to his partner. He is well read, talks knowingly about music, collects paintings. He shows genuine interest in the beautiful lady's work and hobbies. He is totally absorbed by her presence to the extent of deliberately ignoring the other beautiful females around. She is the only one in that room. He is observant—and says so—of the dress she wears, the jewelry she wears, or the lack of it. Her perfect make-up or the freshness of her "no make-up." He finds out the flowers she likes and sends them to her the next day. One dozen only.

And if the date and the evening do not turn out to be as promising as he expected—he will take the failure with grace, and will try to make the evening still a delight for the lovely lady.

An ordinary man will offer this beautiful date the temptation of security. The Hollywood Wolf will give her memories. . . .

ROBERTO and INGRID

Sometime in 1949, Arthur Hornblow, an M-G-M producer, calls: "Roberto Rossellini will be at the studio at ten to show a short film with Magnani. He wants to meet you."

"I'll be there."

Roberto Rossellini is a shy man, on the stocky side. Eyes alive, he gives the impression of being always on the move, of doing things. For an Italian, he speaks quietly, with the calm of a man who is at peace with his mark in life.

Lunch at the Beverly Hills Hotel with the Italian consul, Rossano Brazzi, and Ingrid Bergman. (I like to think it is their first meeting.) A one-sided lunch; Roberto and Ingrid stay alone in the crossing of social events, free of any obligation to others. With soft voices and gentle touch they care only about themselves.

I'm listening to the trials and tribulations of the other Latin lover, Rossano, about his first Hollywood film, *Little Women*, and his "Apollo" body insulted by a soft pillow tied to his belly to make him look his part—a middle-aged professor.

"That's Hollywood, Rossano. The suave Charles Boyer's first part was a Gallic chauffeur to Gable and Turner's limousine."

"I know, but a pillow?"

"If ever I have the right part for you, Rossano, it's yours." (I kept my promise. Three years later he played the romantic Italian in *Three Coins in the Fountain*.)

Ingrid leaves with the Italian consul. From the Hotel's flower shop a dozen dark red roses went to Ingrid's home with only one word: "Roberto."

It is now 1954: "The Elopement of the Century." *Stromboli*. The world is shocked . . . two children . . . History is now a bad dream.

In Rome to do *Three Coins* we met Ingrid and Roberto waking in the Via Veneto. "Jean, Dusty, will you dine with us tomorrow night?" "We would love to. We're at the Grand." "I'll call you up for the time and place," Roberto said.

Three days later I sent a telegram: "Dear Ingrid and Roberto, we are hungry. Shall we still wait?"

They were in Paris.

P.G. and ELEONORE

We changed lenses for a closer shot at Beverly Hills, a luxurious home in Rexford Drive. The owner, P. G. Wodehouse, the witty, jolly English humorist, is posing in his tropical garden for a portrait I'm doing.

Creator of the impeccable manservant Jeeves and his thickwitted master, author of ninety-six books, sixteen plays, libretti and lyrics for twenty-eight musical comedies (*Sally, Oh! Kay!, Anything Goes*), light verse, movie scenarios, and criticism, P.G. was an exceptionally happy person and married to the same Eleonore for fifty years. He re-examines "marriage" for my consideration:

"Oh, yes, marriage *is* a prison. I know it. I live through it every day. My room is a cell; they close me in every night. I wake up in the morning tired. I'm afraid to open my eyes. My bones ache—the bed is a wooden plank. Then, I hear the door open. A black shadow crosses in front of me. Slowly I open one eye. The jailer brings in a tray with the same meager slab. A sunny light slaps my face. The monster opens the curtains. *There are no bars on the window* and the jailer has a kind face. Don't trust him, he puts on that face for some new and horrible torture. He pushes a small table near my bed and places the tray on it. I close my eyes. 'Good morning, sir.' The voice is kind, tired. I open my eyes; the jailer walks out in no hurry, and, my God, *he leaves the door open*. I get up. The bed is soft and the pillows softer. There is golden toast and the marmalade I like and a pot of hot tea on the silver tray and the room is flooded with warm California sun. And the door is open. I can walk out and go everywhere I like without being questioned or stopped.

"Is marriage a prison? Is this the prison? Yes to both questions, and . . . I love it."

HITCH, the GOURMET

Chasen's, the Hollywood restaurant for the rich and the famous, the private dining room: The timid Alfred Hitchcock—without doubt the best-known director in the world, a Garbo as a public-eye celebrity, a sadist and immune to any emotional involvement, married for over half a century to the gentle Alma, gourmand and gourmet—welcomes two dozen friends to a dinner in honor of the newly married Eric and Joan Ambler and creates for this happy occasion a perfect menu (a replica of a famous Shakespearean feast):

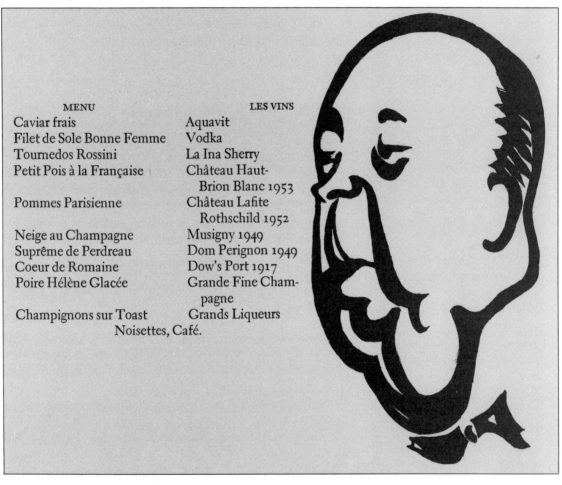

MENU	LES VINS
Caviar frais	Aquavit
Filet de Sole Bonne Femme	Vodka
Tournedos Rossini	La Ina Sherry
Petit Pois à la Française	Château Haut-Brion Blanc 1953
Pommes Parisienne	Château Lafite Rothschild 1952
Neige au Champagne	Musigny 1949
Suprême de Perdreau	Dom Perignon 1949
Coeur de Romaine	Dow's Port 1917
Poire Hélène Glacée	Grande Fine Champagne
Champignons sur Toast	Grands Liqueurs
Noisettes, Café.	

At home you had your usual scotch and soda. Too bad. Now you have to decide between Polish vodka and Aquavit— a *must* for the Russian caviar. And no compromise. The Master is watching.

The dishes, all imports from special countries, follow majestically to the ohs! and ahs! of chosen guests.

My Dusty sits on Hitch's left. With the caviar Dusty has enough, but Hitch sees that she tastes every dish.

After the *sorbet* (Neige au Champagne) he leans over to her and with that slow diabolic smile and even slower voice says, "The peasants didn't observe the menu. Poor miserable gluttons. They doubled on Dover sole and tournedos. They are sure the dinner is concluded. The *sorbet* is only to clear their amateurish palates. Now the dinner starts."

Dusty, ready to collapse, shares with a wry smile his calculated joke.

Hitch, always ready for a little scandal, sits me next to a very beautiful young English blonde. We like each other instantly. Our moods and jokes fit, and our legs are interlocked under the table.

Dave Chasen, the restaurateur and maker of this classic dinner, watches worried as dish after dish is served to the hungry and the famous. Finally he catches my eye, smiles questioningly, and leans to my ear: "How is it, Johnny?"

I turn and face him eye to eye. "Perfect, Dave, perfect."

With this, a relieved and exuberant restaurateur leans further and kisses me smack on the mouth. Proudly he saunters away. (Dave Chasen? That way?) But with this, I suffer serious side effects. The legs of the young English beauty untangle with a snap, and she turns away from me to the anxious young admirer on the other side.

I take a quick look at Hitch. Did he put Dave up to this as a favor to Dusty? Neither he nor she ever confessed.

A CONFRONTATION

The 20th Century–Fox studio, a luncheon: The studio president, Spyros P. Skouras, entertains the powerful leader of U.S.S.R., Nikita Khrushchev. It is an historic encounter for the two aging gladiators, a confrontation of egos—American Democratic System versus the Communist System. I listen:

Skouras (to the interpreter): "Tell our honored guest that

America is a free country with the gift of opportunity to everyone. I was a poor Greek boy born of a poor Greek family. Now I hold in my hand the fate of ten thousand employees."

Khrushchev (through the interpreter): "Tell our humble host and honored brother that in Russia I too was a poor Russian boy born of a poor Russian family. Today I hold in my peasant hand the fate of millions."

ROMANOFF the PRINCE

When our royal restaurateur expands to Palm Springs, he builds on a mountain overlooking the desert and the homes of the rich and calls the place Romanoff's on the Rocks.

Opening night is New Year's Eve, naturally. There is excitement. A full house is expected. Mike Romanoff has the famous and the near-famous of Hollywood in attendance. Among the Palm Springs natives one sedate old couple calls for a reservation. The Prince likes the man's cultured voice on the telephone and appreciates the choice of a perfect dinner with the right wines and a vintage champagne to welcome the midnight spirit. He arranges for a fine table. The old couple live up to his expectations: an old Rolls-Royce driven by an even older uniformed chauffeur, distinguished-looking, white hair and proper dress, good manners, and no obvious jewelry. Everybody's idea of loving grandparents.

The Prince greets them with aristocratic delight, and at midnight he admires the sedate couple waltzing in the good old way and looking with infinite love and gratitude at each other. After a gentle kiss they call for the bill and present the waiter with a hundred-dollar bill to pay the eighty-five-dollar check. The Prince escorts them to the door, bows pleased at the departing Rolls. "An honor, a royal presence from the forgotten past," Mike whispers.

Only Gloria, Mike's wife and tonight's cashier, calls the Prince urgently to the kitchen. Livid with fury, she waves the hundred-dollar bill in his face. "They're crooks. It's a fake bill. Look at it. You can see through."

The Prince's face lights with envious admiration. "You mean, it was an act? They knew all the time they were going to pass a phony bill? What wonderful people. What courage. What finesse. A masterful stroke!"

"You'll end in the poorhouse," Gloria calls after a giggling and happy Mike.

The Prince tells the story again and again with delight and pride. But Gloria is not to be cheated so easily. She sent the phony bill to the Controller of Currency in Washington, D.C. "We're trying to make an honest living, only to be victimized by crooks."

To her surprise and delight a new crisp hundred-dollar bill is enclosed in an official letter: "The old bill is real. No counterfeit. Probably one from a shoebox, long withdrawn from circulation."

"Aren't you a lucky fellow, Mike, to have me around?" Proudly Gloria shows him the official letter and the new hundred-dollar bill.

"You mean they're honest?" A disconsolate Romanoff sighs. "As brazen bill passers they're welcome any time to give that performance. But as real honest people I find them dull."

That's our Mike.

BEN-HUR

It's 1959, and no big box-office star is available to play Ben-Hur.

Charlton Heston's agent is trying to increase Charlton's price per picture from $50,000 to $75,000. He reaches Benny Thau the contract boss at the M-G-M studio:

"Benny, what about Heston for Ben-Hur?"

"You're kidding. Forget it." Benny feels insulted.

England, Italy, and France have no answer to M-G-M's problem. Time passes. Millions are spent. But no Ben-Hur star.

"You can have Heston," the agent insists.

"Get out. I'm busy." Benny Thau closes the argument.

And all stars are busy shooting, tied in hard contracts. M-G-M is frantic. Costly sets have been built, thousands of costumes are ready, a sound unit is shooting in Rome.

Willie Wyler, the director, is impatient. "What about Charlton Heston?" Willie said.

"Heston?" Benny Thau is shocked.

"Yes, Heston, why not? Unless you have a better idea?"

The agent is called in. Benny Thau is condescending: "We're giving a chance to your man Heston for *Ben-Hur*. The chance of his life. One condition—no bargaining, no discussion."

"Anything, Benny. I'll give you Heston for—"

"Two hundred and fifty thousand," Benny interrupts. "*Not one penny more.*"

The deal is closed. Heston plays Ben-Hur. The agent is a hero.

NOEL

Beverly Hills, a few blocks away from my home at the English villa of Merle Oberon, the honey-colored star: We are all there. The best of the social elite of Filmville to welcome the ever-youthful theater man, the brilliant and profuse Noel Coward. His range of abilities—as writer, director, and actor of the roaring twenties, the grim thirties, and the wars of the forties—glorify Sir Noel as the ultimate elegant talent of our period.

"A talent to amuse," as he modestly evaluates himself.

I listen: "In my poverty-stricken youth, I taught myself to write songs. A music publisher guaranteed me fifty pounds a year, which helped my out-of-work father. Bea Lillie took me to meet André Charlot, the London impresario of the 1920s, for fair appraisal." A reflective silence. "I thought I was good. For over an hour I sang several songs with loud liveliness. Only to have Charlot take Lillie aside and whisper, 'Bea,

never do that to me again. This boy has *no* talent whatsoever.' "

To the raucous laughter of his audience, Merle attempts
to sum up his talents: "All of us think of you, Noel, as the
Veritable Prince of Wales of the Music Halls."

"Darling girl, I am no Fred Astaire on my feet. I lack the
rubbery face of a comedian." A reflective pause. "However,
if you are thinking of the Prince of Wales as a character part,
you come close. I am a character to amuse."

"But your musical skits and plays—" objects our hostess.

"My dear Merle, in my plays I would write a song which I
could talk with an air of holding back my great voice. This
gave rise to the legend that I belong to the musical stage."

And the evening continues—noisy, polite, and dull.

Merle had purchased from me some pleasant paintings by
Segovia, the son of the master guitarist. Noel likes them and
says so. He takes Dusty aside and plots in a pleasant whisper:
"Tomorrow is my birthday. Lure me to dinner to see your
young painters. Only me. And talk about paintings and
painters. I have been doing a bit myself, you know." A modest
smile. "I think they are good."

Dusty is enchanted. I find out that Noel was born in 1899.
In my collection of rare wines, seven bottles of 1899 Mouton-
Rothschild are waiting for such an occasion. A bottle of this
gold shall be our present to him.

Next evening I decant the bottle with love and reverence.

I place the empty bottle in front of Noel's chair. He takes
it home with genuine gratitude.

"I'm floating on the ceiling and look down at three people
drinking rare wine and talking. With exaggerated gestures."
Noel sums up our excuse for drinking: "Usually—not the case
this time—I drink so my friends seem more intelligent."

If only I could have a recorder to register his observations
tonight: About Binkie (Hugh Beaumont, a London theatrical
producer) and the Queen and the dinners at Buckingham
Palace and Windsor Castle and the Royal Family and his sadness at not remaining friends with the Prince of Wales, about
plays and actors, but mostly about his work.

We part in the early-morning hours with the promise "I'll
trade you one of my paintings for one of yours." (We never
did.)

Next day we receive a note and a photo of him with his distinguished profile, and signed with his special hieroglyphic:

GREG

Century City, once the back lot of the 20th Century–Fox studio, is now skyscrapers, steel and glass, black and gray and gold.

On the fourteenth floor of one of the skyscrapers, surrounded by powerful partners and capable secretaries, Greg Bautzer works, has fun, and plans. Tall, handsome, with a low booming voice, generous and quarrelsome, ready for a fight at any moment, suntanned in summer and winter, Greg always makes a woman feel that at last he has met the "woman of his life."

A successful lawyer for tycoons and billion-dollar corporations, Greg is the escort chosen by famous beauties of the screen and social set.

During the time when Greg was the favorite lover of Queen Joan Crawford, he considered himself delighted and proud to be selected from among the others to serve as company and pleasure to her whims and rules. He also carried her knitting bag whenever they were out of town. (Joan knits incessantly, everywhere.)

One night at one of the better Hollywood parties, Greg paid more attention than permitted to a newly arrived beauty. Joan noticed and Joan remembered.

On the way to her home in the early hours of dawn she stopped the car in a lonely, deserted stretch of road: "Greg, something is wrong with my back-wheel tire. Be a sweetheart and see if it is flat."

Greg jumped out of the car and went to inspect the tires. *Swish*—Joan and the car zoomed into the night. He had to walk over three miles to call a cab from the Bel Air Hotel.

"And, of course, you told her in no kind terms of her child-ish behavior?" I asked him indignantly.

"Of course. I apologized and sent her flowers. Like always."

A beautiful lover, Greg remembered the Rules.

SWIFTY LAZAR

Irving Lazar is not tall; but give him a problem, an opposi-tion, and he becomes a tower of strength. He reminds me of a captain in a French army who when on the ground is lost among the crowd; but once on horseback, he is splendid, ostentatious, and terrifying.

Irving is among the best-dressed. He is one step ahead of fashion and in strict accord with the country: wearing an artist's beret in Paris, a striped jersey in Pamplona, rainbow colors and cowboy hat in horse country—all in good taste. A man of our time, he can afford and will settle for no less than a private flat in New York, Claridge's in London at Ascot time, a tycoon yacht in the Greek Islands, the Cannes Film Festival, and the luxury of music in Salzburg. He collects beautiful friends, distinguished wives, and painters in vogue (Dubuffet, not Bernard Buffet), classics and wild ones. He pops anywhere discoveries and history are made and sells the literary rights for astronomical prices.

A many-times millionaire, he lives like one. A lucky and wise investor, he has to have the latest invention and be the first to use it. Oversensitive about cleanliness and hygiene, he travels with seven toothbrushes—one for every day of the week—and asks in a new luxury hotel for an extra dozen bath towels to line up for his walk between bed and shower (and be the first to catch athlete's foot).

Among international literary agents, Irving Lazar is the Rolls-Royce with a touch of Lamborghini. Presidents of coun-tries let him handle their memoirs, and so will the Mafia and geniuses—and whatever deal he makes for them, he comes out fine.

Antony has his Cleopatra, Romeo his Juliet, Swifty his Mary.

GUARDIAN of DESTINY:
CHARLES KENNETH FELDMAN

He is the best agent of our time, without a doubt, a free-wheeling gambler who plays his cards well but takes the risks of free enterprise, a polished, handsome man who is the most amusing companion and beloved playboy around town, a Casanova, a man of action, a business genius. He sinks millions into properties that Hollywood considers sure box-office poison (Tennessee Williams' *The Glass Menagerie* and *Streetcar Named Desire*). "If it's a Pulitzer Prize play, it should be a success—or at least it should be given a chance," he says while seemingly preoccupied only with the question of a new date every night. And he makes his gamble pay off in one way or another—not least in his reputation for being a man of discrimination and courage.

Soft-spoken, self-effacing when he has made a spectacular success, and unbowed by a failure, Charlie is the intimate friend of all tycoons, the rival of the heads of all the studios. He never disappoints his clients. What is his secret? A smile: "Never talk bad of anybody." And he simplifies the problem of his life. He orders blue suits, white shirts, black or light gray ties, black shoes, by the dozen. "The hours I save not having the problem of selecting the color of my suit and combining a shirt and tie every day!" ("How right he is," I mumble, trying to quiet down my rainbow waistcoat.)

The moment when Charlie rises to great heights, when his intuition about the thinking of the tycoons comes into play, is when a client feels the ship is sinking.

I put my worries bluntly to Charlie: "My last two pictures are failures. My option is coming up three weeks from now. I want a straight seven-year contract, no option, no lay-offs, three thousand dollars a week."

Charlie looks straight at me, calm, thinking. He calls his secretary. "Miss Dobish, please get me Mr. Schreiber [D.F.Z.'s right hand] and put the call on speaker." We wait. A buzzer.

"Lew, I'm thinking of buying from you—at your price— the story on prostitution that nobody at the studio can lick."

"Thank you, Charlie. You'll never regret it."

"I know, Lew. . . . Oh, by the way, Negulesco's option is coming up. We want straight seven years, no option, no lay-off, only three thousand a week. O.K.?"

"You know, Charlie, his last two pictures are fiascos."

"I like 'em and so does L.B.," Charlie says straight.

"We may not exercise the option."

"Can I have this in writing?" Charlie asks anxiously. I collapse.

"Why?" Lew's question is cautious.

"Jean is the hottest client I have. I'll come by in the morning. Have ready his release in writing."

"Wait a minute, Charlie. Let me have a word with Darryl."

We wait. I sweat. Miss Dobish opens Charlie's appointment book.

"O.K., Charlie. Come by to sign Jean's new contract."

"Our way?"

"What else?" The package is wrapped up.

"O.K.?" That's all Charlie says to me. We start talking about Modigliani and girls, pre-Columbian art and girls, Cap d'Antibes and girls . . .

Only once his manipulations turned against him: in Paris, 1948, the year I discovered Bernard Buffet. The lobby of Hotel George V: "Have you discovered any new painters, Johnny?"

"Three: Bollaert, Noyer, and Buffet." Carefully I wrote their names in his notebook and the address of the Galerie Drouant-David. That evening we had dinner with Mano David. He was excited. Charlie Feldman visited the gallery that afternoon.

"How many Bollaerts did Mr. Negulesco buy?" Charlie was reading from his notebook.

"Eight." Mano was reading from his notes.

"Give me nine."

"Which ones?"

"Any ones. How many Noyers?"

"Eleven."

"Give me twelve. How many Buffets?"

"Twenty-one."

Now Charlie thought for a while. He couldn't have twenty-two, so he lowered his aim. "Give me ten."

"When I have them, would you like to see them?"

"It isn't necessary. Just air-freight everything to this address, my office in Beverly Hills. Half paid now, the balance on delivery."

And the deal was closed on the spot, to the delirious joy of a French merchant.

The Bollaerts and Noyers Charlie disposed of easily—gifts to his office staff, his girls, his clients. But when he saw the Buffets—very large sizes—the gallery had sent him, he was appalled. Enraged, he hid them in his cellar.

A new joke was told at his dinners and cocktail parties: "My friend Jean! A connoisseur, an expert! So in Paris he made me buy portraits of a starving Howard Hughes, of prison camps."

One night he took us all down to the cellar. Each guest could have any one, just to get them out of his house. I took the two biggest ones—nine feet by three—self-portraits.

Within ten years Bernard Buffet became the most promising young painter of the generation. And with this, his prices went sky high.

I was in Greece doing *Boy on a Dolphin*. I received this telex from Charlie Feldman: "Dear Johnny, Remember the two self-portraits of Bernard Buffet I loaned you? . . ."

This shrewd bargainer, charming playboy, and valued friend of many people always wants to be in the minds of his friends. He loves his friends—the people of Hollywood, his clients, and the cinema. He leaves to The Old Actors' Home more millions than any tycoon, any star. He cannot accept that one of his friends had left us. Back from the funeral, he is physically sick for days. So when he enters the hospital for minor surgery, the doctors send him home as a "terminal" case. Within a week he marries his girlfriend of a year. He remembers what each of his friends liked or disliked out of his valuable collection. Methodically, a dozen of us share his paintings, his sculptures, his African and pre-Columbian art. His helpers are taken care of for life. For Charlie, existence is to be in the minds and hearts of friends. So when we see him in the week in which he dies, what he is thinking is the same old Charlie philosophy. Leaving for Iran and a new picture, I come to say goodbye.

"Talk about me" are his last words in a farewell embrace.

AMERICAN BASICS

Three blocks away from the Beverly Hills Hotel is a small bungalow in Camden Drive with a white fence and olive trees.

Dusty sends a telegram to her parents in Toledo, Ohio: "I'm marrying Jean Negulesco." Back comes a puzzled reply: "What's that?" Dusty answers, "That is a Rumanian film director." "Be careful," Mom warns her. "Good luck, daughter," from Pop. They are the original Grant Wood Americans—tall, skinny, erect, and careful—part Cherokee Indian, part Swedish.

On their first visit to California I try to impress them: exclusive dinners in gourmet restaurants, carefully arranged glamorous parties at home. Stars, Hollywood, glorious beauties, and famous people don't impress them. And a joke from Bogart to Mom—"So this is how Cherokee Indian broads look like"—doesn't help.

Tyrone Power and Lana Turner—one of the loveliest sights—are coldly judged: "How long have they been married?"

"Why, Mom?" I ask.

"To act like they do in front of everybody."

"They're happy. They're beautiful. And they're not married yet." I feel guilty.

Mom grows taller as she swallows the American dignity cane.

"Disgusting, if you ask me," she snaps back at me.

Mom as a young girl had a phenomenal voice and had a chance to sing at the New York Metropolitan Opera, but gave up the chance to marry Pop. She never lets him forget. Pop likes to play around the yard at home and dreams impossible inventions. So there is no surprise that Hollywood glamour has no message for them.

But I don't give up: "Dusty, *who* do they believe is the

greatest person alive today—the most important man in America?" I ask her one sleepless night.

"The President of the United States," Dusty answers without hesitation. (So, how do I compare myself favorably to the President of the U.S.A.?)

Sunday breakfast: orange waffles, maple syrup, crisp bacon, and strong coffee. Dusty is still asleep. Mom and Pop, dressed for Sunday—hard collar and tie—enjoy their breakfast in silence, glancing disapprovingly at my outfit: striped jersey, light blue jeans, and barefoot.

"You know, Mom, Hollywood is a wonderful generous place. Dreams come true and miracles happen. A pretty girl stands behind a soda fountain counter serving ice cream and Cokes. A producer sees her, and a few weeks later a new star is born. Bel Air home, swimming pool, two Cadillacs, and a fortune in the bank—and this miracle only Hollywood can provide." Mom doesn't look up, but she listens.

This gives me courage. "Look at *me*, Mom." Pop looks up. "I'm a Rumanian refugee, an enemy alien. Yet Hollywood accepts me because I have something to offer. And you know, Mom"—and the rest I say slowly, deliberately—"that my salary is *twice* the salary of the President of America?"

Mom stops eating, takes off her glasses, turns to Pop, and says with finality, "Dad, I tell you, the President is *not* paid enough." And she goes back to her waffles.

I still don't give up. We meet in the bar before dinner for tasty hors d'oeuvres that Dusty prepares and a double vodka martini for Dusty and me. Mom and Pop never touch alcohol. At home in Toledo they keep a bottle of brandy. One gets a spoonful only when dangerously sick. My plan: Over crushed ice in a shaker I combine one measure of white Bacardi rum, half a measure of dark Rum Negrita, a measure of lime juice, the white of one egg, three dashes of Pernod and half a measure of grenadine. I shake vigorously, and a smooth, sweet pink drink fills the shaker. A turn of lemon on the rims of two champagne glasses. Deep rims of sugar and orange slices decorate the glasses.

"Try this, Mom. It's a pink angel fruit cocktail," I say, serving the concoction.

She tastes and smacks her lips: "It's like ice cream. Try it, Dad."

They do, and they have another. They are safe as long as they sit. When they get up, things seem to come toward them—floors, walls, doors, chairs. The food helps, and Mom never stops talking.

"Would you like a drink?" Dusty asks them the next day as they meet at the bar.

"No, thank you, daughter." Mom smiles at her. "We better wait for Johnny. He'll make us that lovely pink fruit cocktail."

The problem is resolved. Mom ends by adoring me. "Best move my daughter ever made!" I came quite close to Dad. He is a gentle soul and a happy dreamer. We part friends.

THE UNOFFICIAL CLOWN
of GANGLAND CHIEFTAINS

One day as Darryl Zanuck leads me into Romanoff's for lunch we pause slightly for a greeting to George Raft, note the distinguished white-bearded man who appears to be lecturing him, and pass to our table. Well-fed, I ask Darryl about Raft and his companion. He looks mysterious. "That is the famous inventor of heavy water. George Raft, as you may not know, is an educated scientist who follows the latest developments in every field. I'll take you over."

Darryl introduces me, explains to Raft and the companion that he has revealed the identity of the inventor of heavy water, that component of atomic weapons, and he seats me next to the oracle.

"Ah, yes, heavy water." Old white-beard lectures for some time with Latin words and baffling lingo on "the mathematical equations that demonstrate the impermeability of the neutronic atom."

Respectfully, I wait to ask a question: "Sir, for an uninitiated person, can you define just how heavy water differs from ordinary water?"

"Of course," says the savant. "The basic ingredient of heavy water is kangaroo pee."

I couldn't laugh. After all, penicillin is found in strange garbage. The science man draws a colored handkerchief from his pocket, unfolds it, and brings into sight an array of sparkling jewelry.

"Sir, would you care to buy a watch?" old white-beard asks formally. Darryl and George Raft laugh uproariously.

This turns out to be the famed Swifty Morgan. The only con man alive who threw a plate of spaghetti into Al Capone's face and got away with it.

It happens during a dinner in a small Italian restaurant in Chicago. Al Capone offers an insultingly low price for one of Swifty's ties. S-l-o-p goes the plate of spaghetti. Capone jumps up from the table and slowly wipes his face of spaghetti al' vongole. He reaches into his pocket and pulls out a roll of hundred-dollar bills and buys ties for everybody at the table at Swifty's asking price. The gangland chief realizes the little thief's impulse was right.

Darryl tells me afterward of the romantic star who waits at this very table for the famous actress who will be his date. It's his birthday, and when Swifty joins him he tells how his girl always arrives late, claiming she has looked for a birthday present for him but has not found the right thing. Swifty acts as if the story has no interest for him. His real interest is having possession ever so briefly of the actor's cuff links. "Truly beautiful. I want to show them to a friend. You'll get them right back."

Dubious, but yielding to Swifty's strange persuasive power, the actor parts with his cuff links. A few minutes later, the lovely date sweeps in, all smiles. The actor tries to hide his cuffs.

"This time," the great lady of the screen says triumphantly, "I did not forget your present." With her eyes sparkling, she hands over the actor's cuff links. "Happy birthday, darling. I just bought them, a bargain, from Swifty Morgan—the right gift for you."

TOBY

The mind's eye camera in a rotating mood of nostalgia and humor can focus from the present to the past—1934.

Toby Wing is a starlet at Paramount studios. Her acting career is short—four pictures from 1934 to 1934. Toby is not a beauty. She is more than that—fresh, pink, almost ripe and tempting. When she passes by, no matter how serious your conversation, you will falter in your speech and feel guilty with shades of forbidden fruit. Toby is bursting with delicious youth.

Every man in the studio, no matter what age or position, will smile at her, then start a conversation and try to date her for lunch, or better still, for dinner, and hopefully for break-fast. Toby does not have a brilliant conversation, but you feel good and naughty when she leaves you abruptly with half a sentence, not accepting but with no refusal.

I am new in the studio—assistant to an important producer, and temporarily a bachelor. So I join the Toby Wing crowd and ask for a date—for dinner at my small home in Brent-wood. And I am ready to insist and argue. She gives me no chance: "Yes, I would like to."

The dinner is right—gourmet food and a special bottle of iced Traminer. But then the evening suddenly takes on a different aspect than my anticipated follow-through. It becomes physical, but not the right kind. In my living room I have a game, a table game with sticks and paddles and a plastic Ping-Pong ball that one has to try to push into one of the openings located at each end—a miniature football contraption. And what Toby lacks in fascinating conversation, she makes up in accuracy at the stupid game—with delighted and healthy screams. I can't concentrate. Toby's curves are undulating. Her boobs are bouncing, and the moisture of her neck shines and dares. I miss the silly ball regularly.

It is past midnight when she has enough. I am a wreck, a wet rag.

"Johnny, what do you call it?" Toby is putting on her cardigan.

"Well, I call it . . . 'Push-Push.'" I had just baptized it.

"Push-Push—terrific."

And she leaves without even a peck on the cheek. I go to sleep that night with serious doubts about my Balkan charm.

Next day at lunchtime I am walking toward the studio's cafe with my boss Barney when we join a group of executives standing around the studio's head, Manny Cohn. They're discussing a serious problem, an expensive production that was mutilated by the censors. I try to listen with exaggerated concentration, hoping for a chance to say something of value. The president is in the middle of significant decisions when his tirade fluctuates visibly. All heads turn to the left. Toby saunters by. Aware of her message, she slows her step, gives a sidelong glance and a setup smile: "Gentlemen . . ." a velvety voice. Then she sees me. She stops for a second:

"Johnny, when are you going to invite me again for another game of Push-Push?"

I cough, clear my throat, and manage to answer in a high voice to the departing vision, "Soon, Toby, soon."

They all turn to look at me. I fix my tie and shrug my shoulders with Rumanian indifference.

Manny Cohn tries to return to the censorship problem: "Any idea what we should eliminate in the future?"

Suggestions pour from everybody. Only, I think, they have the answer right there—Toby Wing.

BY ANY OTHER NAME

Of course, when we gather into a glittering assemblage we realize that our dinner companions are not only glamorous. They are downright fictional. They have names they weren't born with and, naturally, personalities they assume with the new names. After all, our Queen and King are Gladys Smith, who became Mary Pickford, and Douglas Ullman, who got to be Douglas Fairbanks. How far would this fabled couple have gone as Gladys Smith and Doug Ullman? And would Marion Douras have been the charmer at William Randolph Hearst's side if she had not decided to be Marion Davies? We might all say, How did you ever think of such a name? But we all knew something had to happen to change a Wampas Baby of 1922 from Kathleen Morrison into that strange, lovely tomboy and tragedienne, Colleen Moore.

Here, meet some others:

	Real Name
Binnie Barnes	Gittel Enoyce
John Barrymore	John Blythe
Ricardo Cortez	Jacob Krantz
Joan Crawford	Billie Cassin
Bette Davis	Ruth Elisabeth Davis
Marie Dressler	Leila Koerber
Greta Garbo	Greta Gustafsson
John Gilbert	John Pringle
Al Jolson	Asa Yoelson
Stan Laurel	Arthur Stanley Jefferson
Carole Lombard	Carole June Peters
Fredric March	Frederick McIntire Bickel
Paul Muni	Muni Weisenfreund
Ramon Novarro	Ramon Samaniegoes
Merle Oberon	Estelle Thompson
Mickey Rooney	Joe Yule, Jr.
Barbara Stanwyck	Ruby Stevens
Anna Sten	Anjuschka Stenski
Erich Von Stroheim	Erich Oswald Hans Karl Marie Stroheim Von Nordenwald

And how far can a lady go with Rudolph Valentino if she has to whisper, "I love you, Rudolph Alfonso Raffaele Pierre Filiberti Guiglielmi di Valetino d'Antogueila"?

THE HOLLYWOOD HUMOR

The humorist is that special person who says whatever comes to his or her mind—with a difference: He says it better than you. Their wit will be delivered in the most unexpected manner, immediate and surprising.

The gift of a humorist presents to our everyday life the change in the drudgery of our happenings, makes him a precious friend.

Sam Hoffenstein, the sensitive comic verse writer, put into words for all time, for all the writers of the world brought to Hollywood, the *great* complaint: "The movies. They bring you from your faraway home, they use your dreams and cheapen your thoughts, they change your way of living and buy your dignity, your integrity, tear all the heart, hope and ambition out of you and all for what? *A lousy fortune!*"

———

Billy and Audrey Wilder, a plus to any party, be it an intimate dinner or an official banquet. Billy is brilliant. His films are classics. His caustic *esprit* is concise, sharp as a knife, delivered with bullet precision. Billy reduces exasperating trivia to a moment of delight. Friends will say that Billy is mean. Of course he is. And how right he is to enrich our day with words to repeat and remember. Why should we expect a brilliant mind to be kind? Witty, inspired, sometimes demoniac, Billy Wilder observes sardonically, "Just as the whole world hates America, America hates Hollywood. There is that deep-seated notion that we are all phonies. Making ten thousand dollars a week and no taxes. Banging all those tall dames. Indoor and outdoor swimming pools. Sixteen in help. All driving Jensen Interceptors. Well . . . It's all true. Eat your heart out."

Audrey too gifts your day with a chuckle, a laugh. A pure joy, she sees in the course of a normal day a thousand pleasant shadings. Blessed with stylish beauty, she delights her friends with her ability to create instant limericks with any given word or impossible name.

"Try one with Jean Negulesco," a jealous girlfriend dares her. Audrey brings out that year's Christmas card:

> There was a lewd man from Unesco
> Who was humping a lady al fresco.
> From the gathering crowd,
> A voice clear and loud:
> "Why, it's Jean Negulesco."

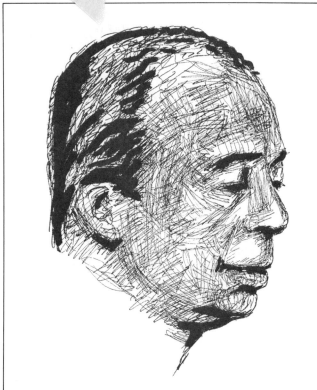

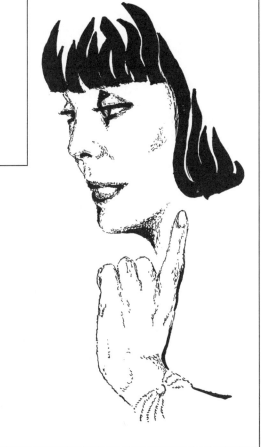

Billy and Audrey Wilder

Oscar Levant slicing down to the right size a pretentious bore: "Ordinarily, I never forget a face. But in your case, I'm more than willing to make an exception."

IT ISN'T ENOUGH TO BE HUNGARIAN; YOU HAVE TO HAVE TALENT is the slogan pasted over the writers' table at the M-G-M studio commissary.

Someone poses the question to the witty Herman Mankiewicz as to the mystery job a relative of L. B. Mayer has at M-G-M: "What does Abe really do for his fifteen hundred dollars a week?"

"Abe has a very important job—important for L.B.," says Herman. "From his window in his office on the second floor he is watching from nine in the morning till nighttime. And if he sees an iceberg coming, he rushes into L.B.'s office to warn him of the danger."

Armand Deutsch—neighbor and understanding friend. "Just because we're neighbors—Johnny—is no reason to invite me every time you have a party. Don't feel embarrassed. I'll understand." So next time I have a party I don't invite my neighbor Ardie Deutsch. So . . . When he returns from the studio and sees a dozen cars parked in front of my house he knocks at my door long, loud and furious: "What do you mean having a *big* party and not inviting me?"

"Debonair Jean Negulesco owns 69 pairs of sports trousers, 53 waistcoats, 500 ties, 3 dozen hats, dozens of silk and sports shirts and 50 pairs of shoes, which help to make him Hollywood's Best Dressed Director," writes the *Chicago Tribune* magazine on September 26, 1954.

Peacock flattered, I read further: "And after all this, one expects J.N. to be a tall, lanky guy like Gary Cooper. Wrong—he is a middle-aged pudgy fellow."

Clifton Webb is completely devoted to his mother, Mabel. When the dear old lady dies in her late nineties, Noel Coward calls Hollywood from London. Clifton is so moved, his voice keeps breaking and he sobs out his loneliness.

After fifteen minutes Noel interrupts: "Clifton, I didn't call a seventy-four-year-old orphan to listen to his endless song of grief. If you don't stop it immediately, I'll reverse the charges!"

———

A misprint in *Louella Parsons'* column in the *Hawaiian Post*: "Jean Negulesco is as good a cock as he is a director, and that's high praise."

All I ever cooked for her was stuffed cabbage.

———

Don Rickles: "Hi dummy . . . I've never met a man I didn't dislike."

———

Gene Fowler: "Old age has many advantages? . . . Name one!"

———

Dean Martin: "I only drink when I'm alone or with somebody."

———

Bob Hope: "I lost my best friend today. I broke my mirror."

———

Jack Benny: No words . . . just his tormented stares—his offended dignity.

And the kaleidoscope images of Hollywood follow in slower motion, one after another. . . .

A Hollywood that exists in a flimsy embroidery of playful letters, astounding pranks, sardonic evaluations of the human condition—the product of inventive minds on the loose. There is the Hollywood *humor*, humor of . . . in . . . and by . . . Hollywood.

SUMMING UP

IT takes a great deal of living to be young again. I am young again—and happy. And I am in love with Spain.

A tasty paella and eight rusty screws were the decisive reasons for me to move and live in Spain for a while.

It started sometime in the summer of 1963 in Los Angeles. Cyd Charisse and Tony Martin, Cyd's husband, were flying to Monte Carlo as guest performers for a benefit gala sponsored by the original and ruthless social dictator Elsa Maxwell for Princess Grace of Monaco. "There's an extra first-class ticket, all expenses paid," said Tony. "Tempted, Johnny?"

Monte Carlo. Elsa Maxwell, the cumbersome butterfly, staged her night parties with unbelievable mixtures of the great and near great: two weeks of nights without sleep, gourmet food with old friends and new friends from Spain. "Come and see us, and Madrid. You will love it" was their goodbye.

A week later I was in Madrid and I had my first paella. Into a paellera (a metal casserole with two handles) goes saffron-flavored rice, the base. Then garlic, paprika, and oregano to your liking. Then shrimps, clams, lobster, chicken, ham, pork, and chorizo sausages, along with personal variations of selected vegetables cooked in chicken broth. Is it a savory dish? Always. But the first time is an *experience*.

That afternoon I spent two hours in the Prado Museum, and I was spoiled for life.

I rented an apartment—sunny, spacious, and richly furnished; only old-fashioned paintings covered the white walls. That Sunday I decided to hang some of my modern lithos in the flat. I had the frames. I called a friend: Where could I find some hanging screws for my frames?

"Today is Sunday," he told me, "and on Sunday the only open place in Madrid is the Rastro. Look on the Poor Side of the Rastro—the *ferretería*, the secondhand iron place. You may find what you need."

The Rastro (thieves' market) is the Sunday place all over Spain, where one can find all kinds of native knickknacks, stolen art, wobbly primitive furniture, and once in a while some valuable pieces.

I found my screws. A skinny old Spaniard, ageless and barefooted, had picked up rusty nails and screws, locks and chains, and rusty metal buttons—anything he could scavenge around the streets. He placed them methodically in small piles in front of him and spread them all on an old *A.B.C.* newspaper (the morning Bible of every Spaniard). I picked up the eight screws I needed and showed them to him.

"*¿Cuanto?*—How much?" I asked him in my one-week-old Spanish.

He counted them with his bony fingers in my hand: "*Uno, dos, tres, cuatro*—" Then he stopped, narrowed his eyes, watched me for a few seconds, then asked, "*¿Francés?*"

I shook my head. "No."

"*¿Inglés?*"

"No."

"*¿Alemán?*"

"No." I slapped my chest and said, "Rumanian—*Rumano*."

"*¡Ah, Rumano—lo mismo que los Españoles!*—The same as the Spanish."

"Yes . . . Si . . . *¡Latinos!*"

I was quite pleased to hold a conversation in Spanish. I came back to my screws problem. Pointing at them, I repeated, "*¿Cuanto?*"

He dismissed our financial haggling with a dramatic wave of his right arm and his head high: "¡Amigo, nada!—Friend, nothing!" He was proud and enjoying his generosity. I put the screws in my pocket and took out my gold cigarette case and offered him a cigarette.

"Cigarettos?" (I add "os" to everything and think it is Spanish. *Cigarrillo* is correct.)

"¡Ah, amigo, muchísimas gracias!" And with the dignity of a nobleman he took a cigarette and offered me a light. Smiling at each other, we smoked, shook hands and parted friends.

This could never have happened in any other place in the world. That a poor man refused to sell his wares for money—which probably meant his lunch—and made a present of them because you were a guest in his country. At that moment Spain became the country where I wanted to spend my days.

I bought an apartment furnished with Spanish antiques, and called Dusty: "Rent the house, pack the kids, and sail to Spain—our new place of work and fun and holiday."

And this is how a perfect paella and eight rusty screws, a gift from a noble friend, changed my American habits to Spanish hours: my vodka at nine in the evening, start dinner at eleven, finish at 2 A.M. And the afternoon siesta. And *mañana*—Spain's greatest contribution to civilization.

Spain has been my country for twenty years. For twenty years I made friends and tried not to have enemies. For twenty years I have adapted myself to the Spanish way of thinking. For twenty years I have known Paco and Enrique and Amparo and have loved them and listened to them. For twenty years I crossed this wonderful country and led a film festival in San Sebastian. And I have been close to God in Toledo and to El Greco, and I sat in his chair in his studio in front of an unfinished canvas. And got drunk with Orson Welles at the *feria* in Sevilla. And filmed in the Prado—the Palace of Gods—where 114 Goyas, 50 Velasquezes, 32 El Grecos, and 49 Riberas were the background for my American actors. And built a house on the Costa del Sol in the shade of five fig trees. And listened to names like Ceuta, San Pedro de Alcantara, Sotogrande, Ronda. I watched and shared evenings with some of the *greats* of Spain: El Cordobes, the spectacular star of the *corrida*; the elegant Dominguin, who dominated the bulls; the grandees of the flamenco: Lola Flores, Antonio Gades, José Greco; the genius of high style, the grace of haute couture, Balenciaga . . . and others—an expression of today with total respect for *tradition*.

Three years ago on a rainy day on a Spanish road on my way to Madrid there was a light, a shining light after a quick rain—like nothing else anywhere. The hills of Venice red with their rows of precisely spaced silver-gray patches—the olive trees—took on brighter colors from the wetness. An El Greco sky with black clouds opened enough to let the sun explode on white villages cradled in the hills. The car hummed smoothly. The miles rushed by.

I felt lucky. I felt safe. I grew excited with the anticipation of a new commitment I was formulating. My life has been a succession of changes of hobbies—from girls to croquet, to films, and so on—and of vocations, avocations, adventures, and commitments. And from this I have learned that one never suffers in taking on a new commitment if every duty, job, accomplishment and failure is absorbed as an experience. I felt blessed by fortune. And loved. Dusty was with me and playful. I felt rich, because at that moment, on a rainy Spanish road, I decided to write this book.

I lived three golden periods of my time: Paris in 1920; the Riviera in 1927; and Hollywood from 1930 to 1970.

The trouble with turning memories into memoirs is that when one is finished a sneaky feeling comes along: "Things never were that way, anyway." Nevertheless, I have settled my commitment to tell about these golden periods and the great people I had the luck to meet and what they meant to me.

And then comes the realization that there were little people who rounded out the canvas. They too are legends to me. They come more often to my mind because they have been closer to me. They have accepted easier the blunders of my youth and the foolishness of my maturity, the zig-zag pattern of my doings.

A navy captain once told me that when he assumed command of a new ship he told his crew: "I have orders to be the commanding officer of this ship. That puts me up front, but let everyone bear in mind—I'm first *among equals*." He realized that the captain can't sail the ship alone, unless he was very fast running back and forth between the wheelhouse and the engine room.

Now, in the bonus of my life, I find that age doesn't answer anything:

"You're over eighty? You don't look it."

"Look closer . . ."

I always have been, am, and always will be in love. With life. And people. And the mornings and the nights. And I earned the right to say no when I should and want to say no. I can afford to choose. That's the privilege I exercised on that Spanish road I mentioned. I chose to go to work on this storytelling when it was such a tempting time to play.

Now, let's have that glass of vodka. . . .

FILMOGRAPHY

SHORTS

All were made for Warner Brothers as part of the following series: *Melody Masters* (MM), *Technicolor* (T), *Technicolor Specials* (TS), *Brevities* (B), *Broadway Brevities* (BB), and *Featurettes* (F).

1940: "Flag of Humanity" (T); "Joe Reichman and Orchestra" (MM); "Alice in Movieland" (F, with Joan Leslie); "Henry Busse and Orchestra" (MM).

1941: "USC Band and Glee Club" (MM); "Carioca Serenaders" (MM); "Jan Garber and Orchestra" (MM); "Cliff Edwards and His Buckaroos" (MM); "Freddy Martin and Orchestra" (MM); "Skinnay Ennis and Orchestra" (MM); "Marie Green and Her Merrie Men" (MM); "Hal Kemp and Orchestra" (MM); "Those Good Old Days" (MM); "At the Stroke of Twelve" (BB); "Dog in the Orchard" (BB).

1942: "Gay Parisian" ("Gaite Parisienne," Ballet Russe de Monte Carlo) (TS); "Spanish Fiesta" ("Capriccio Español," Ballet Russe) (TS); "California Junior Symphony" (B); "A Ship Is Born" (TS); "Daughter of Rosie O'Grady" (B); "The Spirit of Annapolis" (B); "The Spirit of West Point" (B); "Carl Hoff and Band" (MM); "The Playgirls" (MM); "Leo Reisman and Orchestra" (MM); "Richard Himber and Orchestra" (MM); "Don Cossack Chorus" (MM); "Emil Coleman and Orchestra" (MM); "Glen Gray and Band" (MM); "Army Air Force Band" (MM); "Six Hits and a Miss" (MM); "U.S. Marine Band" (MM); "Borrah Minnevitch and His Harmonica School" (MM).

1943: "Women at War" (TS); "Army Show" (B); "The Voice That Thrilled the World" (F); "Over the Wall" (F); "U.S. Navy Band" (MM); "Ozzie Nelson and His Orchestra" (MM); "U.S. Army Band" (MM); "Childhood Days" (MM); "All American Band" (MM); "U.S. Services Band" (MM); "Hit Parade of the Gay Nineties" (MM); "Sweetheart Serenade" (MM); "Cavalcade of the Dance" (MM).

1944: "Grandfather's Follies" (MM); "Roaring Guns" (F); "South American Sway" (MM); "All-Star Melody Masters" (MM); "Listen to the Bands" (MM).

AS SECOND UNIT DIRECTOR

This Is the Night, Paramount, 1932 (Lilly Damita, Cary Grant, Roland Young).
The Big Broadcast, Paramount, 1932 (Bing Crosby, Burns and Allen).
Bed Time Story, Paramount, 1933 (Maurice Chevalier).
Way to Love, Paramount, 1933 (Maurice Chevalier).
Story of Temple Drake (*Sanctuary*), Paramount, 1933 (Miriam Hopkins, Jack LaRue).
Farewell to Arms, Paramount, 1934 (Gary Cooper, Helen Hayes, Adolphe Menjou).
Captain Blood, Warner Bros., 1935 (Errol Flynn, Olivia de Havilland).
Crash Donovan, Universal, 1936 (Jack Holt).

ORIGINAL STORY WRITER

New Orleans, Universal.
Fight for Your Lady, RKO.
Beloved Brat, Warner Bros.
Swiss Miss, Hal Roach.
Rio, Universal.

SPECIAL DOCUMENTARY FEATURE

The Dark Wave, 20th Century–Fox, 1956 (produced by 20th Century–Fox for the Variety Clubs Foundation to Combat Epilepsy). Writer, Eugene Vale; producer, Spyros Skouras. CAST: Cornell Borchers, Charles Bickford, Nancy Reagan, Russ Conway.

FEATURE FILMS

Three and a Day, 1931, no release. Producer, writer, and director, Jean Negulesco. CAST: Mischa Auer, Katya Sergava, John Rox.

Kiss and Make Up, Paramount, 1934. Co-director with Harlan Thompson. CAST: Cary Grant, Genevieve Tobin, Helen Mack.

Singapore Woman, Warner Bros., 1941. Producer, Bryan Foy; scenario, M. Coates Webster and Allen Rivkin, from a story by Laird Doyle. CAST: Brenda Marshall, David Bruce, Virginia Field, Rose Hobart, Jerome Cowan.

Mask of Dimitrios, Warner Bros., 1944. Script by Frank Gruber, from the novel *Coffin for Dimitrios*, by Eric Ambler. CAST: Sydney Greenstreet, Peter Lorre, Zachary Scott, Victor Francen, Faye Emerson, Monte Blue, Steven Geray, John Abbott, Eduardo Ciannelli.

The Conspirators, Warner Bros., 1944. Script by Vladimir Pozner and Leo Rosten, from a novel by Frederic Prokosch. CAST: Hedy Lamarr, Paul Henried, Sydney Greenstreet, Peter Lorre, Victor Francen, Joseph Calleia.

Nobody Lives Forever, Warner Bros., 1945. Book and screenplay by W. R. Burnett; producer-writer, Robert Buckner. CAST: John Garfield, Geraldine Fitzgerald, Walter Brennan, George Tobias, George Coulouris, Faye Emerson.

Three Strangers, Warner Bros., 1946. Screenplay by John Huston and Howard Koch, from an original story by John Huston. CAST: Geraldine Fitzgerald, Sydney Greenstreet, Peter Lorre, Joan Loring, Robert Shayne, Alan Napier, Rosalind Ivan.

Humoresque, Warner Bros., 1946. Producer, Jerry Wald; screenplay, Clifford Odets and Zachary Gold, adapted from Fannie Hurst's original story. CAST: John Garfield, Joan Crawford, Oscar Levant, Tom d'Andrea, Joan Chandler, J. Carroll Naish, Ruth Nelson, Craig Stevens, Peggy Knudsen.

Deep Valley, Warner Bros., 1946. Screenplay by Jack Moffat, additional dialogue by William Faulkner, from a book by Don Toteroh. CAST: Ida Lupino, Dane Clark, Henry Hull, Wayne Morris, Fay Bainter.

Johnny Belinda, Warner Bros., 1948. Scenario by Irmgard von Cube and Allen Vincent, from a play by Elmer Harris; producer, Jerry Wald. CAST: Jane Wyman, Lew Ayres, Agnes Moorehead, Charles Bickford, Steve McNally, Jan Sterling, and people from the small fishing village of Fort Bragg in Northern California.

Road House, 20th Century–Fox, 1948. Producer and script, Edward Chodorov, from a story by Margaret Gruen and Oscar Saul. CAST: Ida Lupino, Richard Widmark, Cornel Wilde, Celeste Holm.

The Forbidden Street, 20th Century–Fox, 1949. Producer, William Perlberg; scenario, Ring Lardner, Jr., from the novel *Britannia Mews* by Margery Sharp. CAST: Dana Andrews, Maureen O'Hara, Dame Sybil Thorndike, Wilfrid Hyde White, Diane Heart, Fay Compton, Anne Burchart.

Under My Skin, 20th Century–Fox, 1950. Producer and scenario, Casey Robinson, from a short story, "My Old Man," by Ernest Hemingway. CAST: John Garfield, Micheline Presle, Luther Adler, Orley Lindgreen, Ann Codee.

Three Came Home, 20th Century–Fox, 1950. Producer and screenplay, Nunnally Johnson, based on the book by Agnes Newton Keith. CAST: Claudette Colbert, Patrick Knowles, Florence Desmond, Sessue Hayakawa, Sylvia Andrew, Mark Kewning, an outstanding supporting cast and Oscar performance extras.

The Mudlark, 20th Century–Fox, 1950. Producer and scenario, Nunnally Johnson, from a book by Theodore Bonnet. CAST: Irene Dunne, Alec Guinness, Andrew Ray, Finlay Currie, Beatrice Campbell, Anthony Steel, Constance Smith.

Take Care of My Little Girl, 20th Century–Fox, 1951. Producer, Julian Blaustein; scenario, Julius J. and Philip G. Epstein. CAST: Jeanne Crain, Dale Robertson, Jean Peters, Jeffrey Hunter, Mitzi Gaynor, and 65 young student girls.

Phone Call from a Stranger, 20th Century–Fox, 1952. Producer and scenario, Nunnally Johnson, from a story by Ida Alexa Ross Wylie. CAST: Bette Davis, Gary Merrill, Shelley Winters, Michael Rennie, Keenan Wynn, Beatrice Straight, Evelyn Varden, Craig Stevens, Warren Stevens.

Lydia Bailey, 20th Century–Fox, 1952. Producer, Jules Schermer; scenario, Michael Blankfort and Philip Dunne, from a novel by Kenneth Roberts. CAST: Dale Robertson, Anne Francis, William Marshall, Charles Korvin, Louis van Rooten.

Lure of the Wilderness, 20th Century–Fox, 1952. Producer, Robert Jacks; script, Louis Lantz, from a story by Vereen Bell. CAST: Jean Peters, Jeffrey Hunter, Walter Brennan, Constance Smith, Tom Tully.

"The Last Leaf," episode from *O. Henry's Full House*, 20th Century–Fox, 1952. Producer, André Hakim; scenario, Ivan Goff and Ben Roberts, from O'Henry's short story. CAST: Anne Baxter, Jean Peters, Gregory Ratoff.

Titanic, 20th Century–Fox, 1953. Producer, Charles Brackett; scenario, Charles Brackett, Walter Reisch, and Richard Breen. CAST: Clifton Webb, Barbara Stanwyck, Brian Aherne, Thelma Ritter, Robert Wagner, Audrey Dalton, Richard Basehart, Allyn Joslin.

Scandal at Scourie, M-G-M, 1953. Producer, Edwin J. Knopf; screenplay, Norman Corwin, Leonard Spiegelglass, Karl Tunberg, based on a story by Mary McSherry. CAST: Greer Garson, Walter Pidgeon, Agnes Moorehead, Donna Corcoran, Arthur Shields, Rhys Williams.

How to Marry a Millionaire, 20th Century–Fox, 1953. Screenplay by Nunnally Johnson, based on plays by Zoë Akins, Dale Eunson, and Katherine Albert; producer, Nunnally Johnson. CAST: Marilyn Monroe, Lauren Bacall, Betty Grable, William Powell, Rory Calhoun, David Wayne, Cameron Mitchell, Fred Clark, Alex D'Arcy.

Three Coins in the Fountain, 20th Century–Fox, 1954. Producer, Sol C. Siegel; screenplay, John Patrick, from a novel by John H. Secondari; the title song, Sammy Cahn and Jule Styne. CAST: Clifton Webb, Dorothy McGuire, Jean Peters, Louis Jourdan, Maggie McNamara, Rossano Brazzi, Cathleen Nesbitt, Howard St. John, Kathryn Givney, Modugno.

Woman's World, 20th Century–Fox, 1954. Producer, Charles Brackett; scenario, Claude Binyon, Mary Loos, and Richard Sale, from a story by Mona Williams. CAST: Clifton Webb, June Allyson, Lauren Bacall, Fred MacMurray, Arlene Dahl, Cornel Wilde, Van Heflin.

Daddy Long Legs, 20th Century–Fox, 1955. Producer, Samuel G. Engel; screenplay by Phoebe and Henry Ephron, from the novel by Jean Webster; words and music by Johnny Mercer; ballets by Roland Petit; ballet music, Alex North. CAST: Fred Astaire, Leslie Caron, Thelma Ritter, Fred Clark, Terry Moore, Charlotte Austin, Sara Shane, Ray Anthony.

Rains of Ranchipur, 20th Century–Fox, 1955. Producer, Frank Ross; screenplay by Merle Miller, from the novel *The Rains Came,* by Louis Bromfield. CAST: Lana Turner, Richard Burton, Fred MacMurray, Joan Caulfield, Michael Rennie, Eugenie Leontovich.

Boy on a Dolphin, 20th Century–Fox, 1957. Producer, Samuel G. Engel; scenario, Ivan Moffat and Dwight Taylor, from the novel by David Divine. CAST: Alan Ladd, Sophia Loren, Clifton Webb, Alexis Minotis, Jorge Mistral, Laurence Naismith, Charles Fawcet, Orestes Rallis, Piero Giagnoni, Greece and Panegyris, the Society of Greek Folk Dancers and Music.

The Gift of Love, 20th Century–Fox, 1958. Producer, Charles Brackett; scenario, Luther Davis, from a story by Nelia Gardner White. CAST: Robert Stack, Lauren Bacall, Anne Seymour, Lorne Greene, Evelyn Rudie, Edward Platt.

A Certain Smile, 20th Century–Fox, 1958. Producer, Henry Ephron; scenario by Frances Goodrich and Albert Hackett, from a novel by Françoise Sagan. CAST: Joan Fontaine, Christine Carere, Rossano Brazzi, Bradford Dillman, Eduard Franz, Kathryn Givney, Steven Geray and Trudy Wyler.

Count Your Blessings, M-G-M, 1959. Producer and scenario, Karl Tunberg, from the novel *The Blessing,* by Nancy Mitford. CAST: Deborah Kerr, Rossano Brazzi, Maurice Chevalier, Martin Stephens, Patricia Medina, Tom Helmore.

The Best of Everything, 20th Century–Fox, 1959. Producer, Jerry Wald; scenario, Edith Sommer and Mann Rubin, from the novel by Rona Jaffe. CAST: Hope Lange, Joan Crawford, Stephen Boyd, Suzy Parker, Diane Baker, Brian Aherne, Martha Hyer, Louis Jourdan, Robert Evans, Brett Halsey, Sue Carson.

Jessica, United Artists–Dear Films, 1962. Producer-director, Jean Negulesco; scenario, Edith Sommer, from the novel *Midwife of Pont Clery*, by Flora Sandstrom; music, Marguerite Monnot; lyrics, Dusty Negulesco. CAST: Angie Dickinson, Maurice Chevalier, Noël-Noël, Gabrielle Ferzetti, Agnes Moorehead, Marcel Dalio, Sylva Koscina, Danielle de Metz, Marina Berti, Kerima, Georgette Anys—and Italian children and peasants of Forza d'Agro and Taormina.

The Pleasure Seekers, 20th Century–Fox, 1964. Producer, David Weisbart; scenario, Edith Sommer, based on the novel *Three Coins in the Fountain*, by John Secondari; music, Sammy Cahn and James Van Heusen; flamenco, Antonio Gades. CAST: Ann-Margret, Carol Lynley, Tony Franciosa, Pamela Tiffin, Brian Keith, Gene Tierney, Gardner McKay, André Lawrence, Antonio Gades.

The Heroes, United Artists, 1969. Producers, Mostafa and Morteza Akhavan (Moulin Rouge Co., Iran); scenario, Chester Erskine and Guy Elmes, from the novel *The Heroes of Yuca*, by Michael Barrett. CAST: Stuart Whitman, Elke Sommer, Curt Jurgens, Ian Ogilvy, Behroz Vossogy, Poozan Banaai, Lon Satton, Jim Mitchum.

Hello-Goodbye, 20th Century–Fox, 1970. Producer, Darryl F. Zanuck and André Hakim; screenplay, Roger Marshall; music, Francis Lai; lyrics, Dusty Negulesco. CAST: Michael Crawford, Curt Jurgens, Genevieve Gilles, Ira Furstenberg.